THE RIVER

THE RIVER

A Cherokee Principal Chief's Fight for Family, Truth, and Vindication

Patrick H. Lambert

On the Boundary Press
Cherokee, North Carolina

Published in the United States of America

First Edition: April 2026

Hardcover ISBN (KDP): 979-8-9950293-5-9 | Hardcover ISBN (IngramSpark): 979-8-9950293-1-1 | Paperback ISBN: 979-8-9950293-0-4 | eBook ISBN: 979-8-9950293-2-8 | Premium Edition ISBN: 979-8-9950293-3-5

Library of Congress Control Number: 2026905168

Cover design by Andy Meaden

Interior design and typesetting by On the Boundary Press

For information about special discounts for bulk purchases or author appearances, please contact: Patrick@PatrickLambert.com or patricklambert@hotmail.com

www.PatrickLambert.com

This is a work of nonfiction. The events and experiences detailed herein are recounted to the best of the author's recollection. All individuals are identified by their real names. Where possible, accounts are supported by contemporaneous documents, court

Printed in the United States of America

For Cyndi—my constant through every chapter, every season, every storm.

and

For my mother, Patsy—the quiet strength behind everything I became, and the first person who believed I could.

PREFACE

This is a work of memory.

I have done my best to tell the truth as I lived it, to reconstruct events, conversations, and moments from more than six decades of life with as much accuracy as memory allows. Where documentation existed—letters, court records, audit reports, official correspondence, news coverage—I have relied on it. Where it did not, I have relied on my recollection and, in some cases, the recollections of others who were present.

The dialogue in this book is not presented as verbatim transcription. No one carries a tape recorder through their life. The conversations I recount reflect my best memory of what was said, the substance and spirit of exchanges as I experienced them. In some cases, I have condensed or clarified dialogue for readability while preserving its essential meaning.

When I describe the actions, motives, or intentions of others, I am offering my perception—what I observed, what I believed at the time, and what I have come to understand in the years since. I cannot know what was in another person's heart or mind. Where I speculate about motive, I have tried to make clear that I am doing so. Readers are entitled to reach their own conclusions.

Readers who wish to examine the primary documents referenced in this book, including court filings, audit reports, official correspondence, and the Cherokee Supreme Court decision, may access them in the Evidence Vault at PatrickLambert.com.

A word about Cherokee gaming: The success of our Tribe's gaming enterprise was never the work of one person. Countless Tribal members, elected leaders, commissioners, employees, attorneys, and partners contributed their vision, labor, and sacrifice over many years to build what exists today. I do not claim sole credit for any of it. This book tells my story, my experiences, my contributions, my perspective on events I witnessed and decisions I helped shape. Others who were there may remember things differently or emphasize different contributions. Their stories are theirs to tell. This one is mine.

To my family, my mother, my father, my sisters, who shaped the early chapters of this story: Memory is an imperfect instrument. The childhood events I recount here are filtered through my own eyes, my own understanding, my own sense of what mattered. Your memories may differ. You may remember details I forgot or forgot details I remember. I have written what I recall as honestly as I can, with the utmost respect and love for each of you. Nothing in these pages is intended to diminish anyone or claim that my version is the only truth. You gave me my foundation. I am grateful beyond words. My father and two of my sisters have passed on since the events in this book. I honor their memory and wish they could have seen these words. I hope I have done right by them.

I have made every effort to be fair, even to those who opposed me. I hold no bitterness. But I also owe it to myself, my family, and the Cherokee people to tell the story as I experienced it—not as others might wish it to be remembered.

This is my story. These are my memories. And I stand behind every word.

Patrick H. Lambert Qualla Boundary, North Carolina 2026

CONTENTS

FOREWORD

"Does another do me wrong? Let him look to it. The disposition was his and the activity was his. I have what universal nature wills me to have; and I do what my own nature wills me to do."

— Marcus Aurelius, Meditations V:25

"There are two kinds of people—victims and volunteers; neither should claim to be the other, and self-awareness is the goal."

— Lydia Buffalo

The River is Patrick Lambert's story. This story, like the river, traces its course from its source, quiet and uncertain, slowly finding its way, moving and being moved along, unsteady and uncertain of its nature or whether it would sustain or destroy those along its banks.

Without sentimentality and with a clear self-awareness of how his own nature impacted each step, Patrick leads the reader through the course of his life so far and the people and events which, at times, lifted him and, at others, challenged his view of the world and the place he sought to make for himself and his Tribe in it. In a world of either victims or volunteers, Patrick understands that difference and does not claim to be one when he is the other. That alone makes the book worth reading, and his style of telling it will keep you turning the page.

This well-told mosaic of time and events takes the reader on a captivating journey of a man finding, making, and remaking himself again — sometimes of his own choice and sometimes driven by the confluence of times and events — but each iteration having, as a constant, the drive to serve his people.

Patrick is my friend; one born from brutal honesty and each striving to serve our respective clients. He was a regulator and I represented the regulated. The key difference between regulating commercial gaming and Tribal Nations gaming is that with the former, the regulator is watching the company watch its own money, save the tax, and in the latter, the regulator is watching an outside company watch the Tribe's money. It is all theirs and many times, it is the primary source of the funds that secures a Tribe's right of self-determination and its capacity to serve the many needs of its people. The perspective and consequences of a regulatory failure are very different between the two. Understanding this is essential to understanding Patrick as a Cherokee and a regulator.

I hope you find your experience along The River worth the trip and can take something away from it.

William L. Buffalo

PROLOGUE

The Day the Walls Closed In

"The truth is like a lion; you don't have to defend it. Let it loose; it will defend itself."

— St. Augustine

I walked into that chamber carrying nothing but the truth and knowing the charges were baseless. The lion was already loose.

◆ ◆ ◆

O N THE MORNING OF May 25, 2017, I stood alone in my office behind the Council Chambers, my hands resting on a wooden table polished smooth by decades of political battles. The surface was cool beneath my palms, worn by the weight of countless documents signed and arguments waged in this room over the years.

The air conditioning hummed its steady mechanical rhythm, but sweat gathered at the small of my back anyway. Not from the heat. From the weight of what was coming.

I had been Principal Chief of the Eastern Band of Cherokee Indians (EBCI) for just twenty months. Twenty months to eliminate $120 million in Tribal debt and pay off all outstanding loans that had accumulated under previous administrations. Twenty months to stabilize programs, strengthen families, order forensic audits that would expose years of financial mismanagement, and chart a future our people deserved. Twenty months of insisting on transparency in a system where some people had grown very comfortable in the shadows.

And now, after twenty months, I would face something no Chief had faced in over two decades: impeachment.

Inside my office, the silence was so tight it felt like it had weight. Like I was breathing it in and couldn't quite get enough air. The fluorescent lights buzzed overhead with a faint electrical hum that seemed unnaturally loud in the quiet.

I looked down at the stack of papers in front of me—the accusations, the statements, the political fabrications dressed up as formal "findings." Twelve articles of impeachment, each one crafted to sound damning, each one designed to create the impression of serious wrongdoing where none existed. I had already read them a hundred times, marked them with notes my attorney and I had prepared, identified the weaknesses and contradictions and outright falsehoods. Yet they felt foreign, like I was holding someone else's life in my hands rather than defending my own.

The charges were baseless. Procedural disagreements inflated into misconduct. Routine administrative decisions reframed as abuses of power. Actions that previous Chiefs had taken without question suddenly declared illegal when I was the one taking them.

I remember thinking, as I stood alone in that room: So this is how they intend to do it. Not with evidence that could withstand scrutiny. Not with justice applied evenly and fairly. But with politics, fear, and one of the oldest weapons in Cherokee government—power wielded by the few against the will of the many.

A knock sounded at the door—three sharp raps that echoed in the small space.

"Chief, they're ready for you."

The voice belonged to one of the security officers, a man I had known since childhood, whose family had lived on the Boundary as long as mine. I heard the discomfort in his tone, the reluctance of someone who did not want to be the one to summon me to my own execution. He was doing his job. None of this was his doing.

I straightened my tie—navy blue, conservative, the kind you wear when you want to project calm authority even as everything around you threatens to come apart. I picked up my folder of carefully organized documents and exhibits, took one full breath, and opened the door.

The hallway stretched before me like a tunnel. As I walked toward the chamber, the crowd that had been milling about fell into a sudden hush. Faces turned. Eyes followed. Some held worry—supporters who had stood with me through months of attacks and manufactured controversies. Some carried anger—citizens who saw through the theater and resented what was being done to their elected Chief. A few looked satisfied, their expressions marked by the quiet confidence of people who believed the outcome had already been decided.

I held my head high. Shoulders back. Steps steady.

Because I knew the truth: I had done nothing wrong. Nothing illegal. Nothing unethical. Nothing that justified the spectacle waiting behind those heavy wooden doors.

When I stepped into the Council Chambers, every seat was filled. Elders sat in the back rows, their faces weathered by decades of watching our government at its best and its worst. Veterans wore Tribal caps, arms crossed. Young families sat with children on their laps, some too young to grasp the moment but old enough to sense its gravity.

Television lights burned hot and unforgiving. Camera lenses recorded every movement for posterity.

Council members sat elevated at the front, arranged like a tribunal. Some avoided my eyes. Others met my gaze with a determination shaped by whispers and agendas that had little to do with the truth and everything to do with what the audits threatened to reveal.

I took my seat at the table facing them. My attorney sat beside me, legal pad already filled with notes and citations. He leaned over and whispered, "Let me handle the procedure. You handle the truth."

I nodded.

The chairman lifted the gavel. He was a man I had worked with for years, broken bread with at community events, disagreed with and agreed with over time. That morning his face was unreadable. The irony was not lost on me: He was the son of the Chief who had been impeached over two decades earlier.

"Principal Chief Patrick Lambert," he said, his voice formal and measured, "this hearing will now come to order."

The gavel struck the block with a crack that seemed to echo longer than it should have.

As the chairman began reading the formal charges, I caught sight of something that would carry me through the weeks ahead.

In the back rows, the elders sat calm and unmoving amid the tension. One white-haired woman met my eyes. She placed her hand over her heart and nodded once.

Stay strong.

And in that moment—standing before a political firing squad, cameras rolling, my reputation being dismantled by those who feared transparency more than they valued truth—I felt something rise that was stronger than fear.

Resolve.

This was not the end of my story.

And I would make damn sure of it.

PART I

ORIGINS

CHAPTER 1

BORN ON THE BOUNDARY

"The soul would have no rainbow had the eyes no tears."

— Cherokee Proverb

Dirt roads, cold floors, a father fighting his demons, and a mother holding everything together. The struggles of the Boundary are what forged the man.

◆ ◆ ◆

I **WAS BORN ON THE** Qualla Boundary, the homeland of the Eastern Band of Cherokee Indians, where the mountains roll like ocean swells frozen in time and the fog settles into the valleys most mornings like it belongs there. Most people drive through Cherokee on their way to somewhere else, and think this is a tourist town tucked into the edge of the Great Smoky Mountains—a place of roadside shops selling moccasins, tomahawks, and souvenir T-shirts.

But to me, the Boundary was never a tourist destination. It was the center of the universe. It was home in the deepest sense—the place that lived in me and shaped who I would become.

The House Where the Creeks Meet

Our house is in the Birdtown community on one piece of flat ground where Fisher Branch meets Goose Creek, a modest block structure that always held more love than square footage. From the outside, it wasn't much to look at back then—painted cinder blocks, a roof that leaked in heavy rains until Dad climbed up to patch it, windows that rattled when the winter wind came howling down from the high ridges.

Winters on the Boundary were cold enough that frost painted the inside of the windows each morning, delicate patterns of ice crystals that caught the early light and sparkled like something magical before the warmth of the woodstove melted them away. I could see my breath when

I woke, the quilts piled heavy on the bed, my nose cold above the covers.

The floors were cold on bare feet—that's something you never forget, the shock of stepping onto wooden boards that had been chilling all night, the way it made you move fast toward the living room where the woodstove was already crackling with the fire Dad had started before any of us were awake.

Our world was simple but full. Firewood stacked in neat rows outside the back door. Garden rows in the side yard turning the soil dark and rich in spring, my mother's hands working the earth like she was having a conversation with something ancient and alive. And always, always, the sound of family—six kids and two parents somehow fitting into that small house, making room for each other even when space was tight and tempers were tighter after long days and short money.

We didn't have much by any measure. But I never knew we were poor. We always had food from the garden. We had clean clothes, even if they came from the Sears catalog layaway plan. We had warmth in the winter, shade in the summer, and a roof that mostly kept the rain out.

Life Before Pavement

Goose Creek had no pavement then—none anywhere near our house. You drove toward pavement, not on it. Our world was dirt. Dirt roads, dirt yards, dirt footpaths carved by generations of kids running barefoot in summer. When a car went by, dust rolled behind it in long brown clouds. When it rained, the roads turned to thick, sucking mud that could swallow a shoe whole.

Dad's solution was a "sidewalk" made of old lumber boards laid end to end like a balancing beam. We walked them like tightrope artists, arms out for balance, determined not to slip off into the muck.

One night after days of steady rain, the car couldn't make it up the slick incline to our driveway. Dad stopped, sighed, and said, "We'll have to walk it." Six kids and two adults stepped out and immediately sank nearly to our knees in cold, sticky mud—the kind that holds you a second longer than it should, like it's deciding whether to let go. Dad muttered some choice words under his breath as he hauled us through it. By the time we reached the house, we were soaked, filthy, half-laughing, half-complaining. Hard sometimes. But it was ours.

Water from the Mountain

Clean drinking water wasn't something you turned on with a faucet. It was something you worked for. Back then, no one had drilled wells in our part of the Boundary—that took machinery no one around us owned. So Dad did what people had done for generations. He went up the mountain behind our house, located a clear spring bubbling from the rocks, and built a water system from scratch. He hauled two concrete reservoir tanks up that hill and connected them with whatever pipe he could get his hands on. The water trickled down by gravity, giving us all the pressure you'd expect from a homemade springline—which is to say, not much.

Dad always said, "If you see a salamander in the branch, you know the water's clean. They're sensitive little things. If they can live in it, we can drink it." And sure enough, our spring was full of them—small orange salamanders with black speckles, slipping through the water like tiny flickers of fire.

The only problem was that every so often, one of them would slip into the pipe and ride the water all the way down to the house. Mom would turn on the kitchen faucet and out would plop a salamander into the sink. She'd let out a shriek loud enough to shake the windows and go streaking out of the kitchen like the house was on fire. I'd fall over laughing every time.

Other times a salamander would get stuck somewhere along the line and block the flow entirely. Dad and I would have to climb the hill, dig up sections of pipe, cut out the clog, and clamp it back together. That old line had so many patched spots it looked like a snake that had shed its skin in squares.

Even today, I can walk behind my home and see pieces of that old pipe poking out of the dirt, and those two concrete tanks still resting quietly in the tree line—monuments to how hard my parents worked so we could have something as simple as clean water.

Chief Henry—The World's Most Photographed Indian

My father was known to the outside world as Chief Henry—The World's Most Photographed Indian. That title wasn't official, of course. Nobody certified it or gave him a plaque. But it was probably true. For decades, every summer when the tourist season roared into full swing, he'd stand along Highway 441 in his full regalia, and the visitors would come.

The regalia was impressive—feathered headdress that swept back from his forehead in a cascade of eagle feathers, beaded vest covered in intricate patterns, leather leggings, and moccasins. It was hot as hell to wear in July, sweat running down his back beneath the beaded vest. But he never complained where the tourists could hear. To them, he was the image of an Indian Chief, stoic, dignified, timeless.

They'd pull over in their station wagons and sedans, cameras clutched in eager hands, children bouncing with excitement about meeting a "real Indian." They'd pose beside my father, then pay their money and drive away with a photograph to show the neighbors back home.

To them, my father was a spectacle. A souvenir.

To me, he was a father doing whatever it took to feed his family.

He used Polaroid cameras—the old kind that required pulling both a white tab and a black tab in sequence, then waiting sixty seconds for the image to develop. "Sixty seconds, folks," he'd say, holding the photo facedown. "Let it develop in the shade." Then he'd flip it over to reveal their faces beside his, hand it over with a smile, and collect his payment.

Twenty-five cents per photo in the early days. More later as prices rose. Two dollars per pack of film. The math was simple: sell enough photos, buy enough film, and what remained was what fed us.

When I was old enough, maybe eight or nine, I started working beside him. My job was to load the fresh film into the cameras, pull the tabs after each shot, and collect the money while he was already positioning the next group. I'd earn a quarter for each photo I helped with. On a good day, I'd go home with ten dollars folded carefully in my pocket, feeling like the richest kid on the Boundary.

The Man behind the Headdress

But my father was so much more than the image he sold to strangers. Behind the stoic pose was a complicated man carrying burdens I didn't fully understand until I was much older.

His hands told part of the story—thick and calloused, mapped with scars from a lifetime of hard work. Those hands had built our house, board by board and nail by nail. They had stacked the firewood that kept us warm each winter. They had held fishing rods on cold mountain streams, patient and still. They had held me when I was small.

He carried pride in those hands. But he also carried pain. My father fought a long battle with alcohol that was part of our family for as long as I can remember. The drinking would take him away from us sometimes—not in anger, but in absence. He was never mean to any of us kids. It was more like the alcohol just took him somewhere else, somewhere we couldn't reach him.

But I never doubted his love for us. Even in the hardest times, I knew that the man underneath loved his children fiercely.

When he was sober—truly sober, clearheaded, and present—he was the father I wished he could be all the time. He'd laugh from somewhere deep in his chest. He'd take us to the river and teach us to fish with a patience he didn't always show in other parts of life. He'd tell stories about the old days, about what the Boundary was like before the tourists came, about what it meant to be Cherokee in a world that had tried so hard to erase us.

My Mother—The Foundation

If my father was the fire in our house—unpredictable, passionate, sometimes warming—my mother was the foundation. Solid. Unshakable.

She was thin, of medium height, and unbreakable in spirit. She ran our household with a quiet strength that didn't need volume to make itself felt. Her Bible stayed open on the kitchen table, its pages soft and worn from years of daily turning. Her faith wasn't something she talked about constantly—it was something she lived.

One conversation shaped my entire life.

I was thirteen, wrestling with a decision I can't even remember now—something that felt earth-shattering at the time. I came to her in the kitchen, where she was peeling potatoes at the sink.

"Mama," I said, "what do you think I should do?"

She kept peeling for a moment. Then she set down the potato, wiped her hands on her apron, and turned to face me.

"Son," she said, "I can't make that decision for you. You must choose to do that yourself."

I was frustrated. That wasn't the answer I wanted. I wanted her to tell me what to do.

"But what do you think?" I pressed.

She just smiled—that knowing smile mothers have when they're teaching you something you don't yet understand.

"I think you'll make the right choice. You just have to trust yourself."

Years later, when I stood at crossroads that mattered—joining the military, applying to law school, deciding to run for Chief—I heard her voice: You must choose to do that yourself.

And I did. Every time.

Learning to Hustle

Working the roadsides with my father was my first education in business. I learned that tourists wanted more than a photograph—they wanted a story, something authentic. My father would tell them about the Boundary, about Cherokee history. He'd make them feel like participants in something meaningful rather than just customers.

And they were getting something real. My father was a real Cherokee. The stories were true. But he was also working. Every smile was genuine and strategic at the same time. I learned from watching him that there's no contradiction in that—you can be completely honest and still be smart about business.

On the side, I ran my own operation. I'd walk the streets and roadsides, filling a burlap sack with the glass bottles people tossed from their windows. Each bottle was worth a nickel at Jenkins Grocery. Five cents didn't sound like much. But fifty bottles was two dollars and fifty cents. A hundred bottles was five dollars.

My mom would sit for weeks before school started, looking through the Sears and Roebuck catalog to buy us school clothes. She would dog-ear the pages with pictures of boys my age wearing polyester shirts and bell-bottom jeans so wide you could lose your shoes inside them.

When those catalog orders finally arrived, six weeks later, in brown paper packages, I wore those clothes like they were custom tailored by the finest designers in the world.

Because I had earned them. Every photograph. Every bottle. Every nickel. That made them mine in a way that nothing handed to me could ever be.

CHAPTER 2

SISTERS AND DIRT BIKES

"In every conceivable manner, the family is link to our past, bridge to our future."

— Alex Haley

Five sisters, dirt empires in the backyard, and a household that was loud, chaotic, and full of love. The Lambert family wasn't just my childhood—it was my foundation.

◆ ◆ ◆

GROWING UP AS THE only boy among five sisters meant I was outnumbered—six to one if you counted Mom, which you absolutely had to because she ran everything. It meant the bathroom was always occupied when I needed it. It meant the house was never quiet, filled with a constant soundtrack of laughter and arguments and music playing and sisters calling to each other across rooms. It meant I learned early how to navigate emotions, negotiations, and the complex social dynamics that most boys don't encounter until they're married and suddenly realize they have no training for it.

But back then, I never really wished for a brother because the truth is, I had something better. I had Dee-Dee.

The Lambert Girls—A Force of Nature

Our house where the creeks meet wasn't large, but it held five distinct personalities. Henrietta was the oldest, and she carried that position with the gravity it deserved—the second mother when Mom was overwhelmed, the one who kept things running. She didn't need to yell or threaten. She'd just stand there, arms crossed, waiting, until you did what you were supposed to do. Disappointing her felt worse than any punishment.

Pat came next—the quiet one who simply handled things without fuss or need for recognition. She remembered birthdays, kept track of everyone, and just did what was right because it was right. That was enough for her.

Dee-Dee was my partner in crime, my co-conspirator, my best friend throughout early childhood. Close enough in age that we operated as a unit, our names spoken together like a single word: Patrick-and-Dee-Dee. Where you found one of us, you'd usually find the other, covered in the same mud, guilty of the same mischief, sharing the same adventures.

Before we ever rode dirt bikes together, we built empires in the dirt beside our house. The old garden spot that wasn't being used that year became our construction site, our kingdom, our world. We'd spend entire Saturday mornings on our knees in the dark, rich dirt, carving roads with sticks and flattened tin cans, smoothing the dirt with our hands until it was packed hard enough to support our Tonka trucks. We created elaborate highway systems with names for every section—the Big Curve that wound around a protruding root, the Mountain Pass where we'd built up ridges of packed earth, the Downtown that was just a flat area near the fence but felt urban and important to us.

One summer afternoon when the heat was heavy and the cicadas and katydids were screaming in the trees, we decided our highway system needed a river. We hauled water in buckets from Fisher Branch, dug channels through our carefully constructed roads, and created what we were certain was an engineering masterpiece. Within an hour, our roads had dissolved into muddy trenches and our trucks were stuck axle-deep in mud sludge that sucked at the wheels like quicksand.

Dee-Dee just laughed, her hands and knees caked with dirt, her curly hair sticking to her sweaty face. "Well, now it's a flood zone. We'll have to rebuild the whole thing."

And we did. That was what made her such a perfect companion—nothing stopped her. Every setback was just another chapter in the story we were creating together.

Angie was the determined shadow who followed us everywhere. Most of the time we let her tag along. Sometimes we didn't, and she'd run crying to Mom, and we'd get in trouble. One time we were building a fort and told her she was too little. She marched back to the house, returned with a hammer and a handful of bent nails she'd straightened as best she could, walked past us without a word, and started hammering with fierce determination. Dee-Dee and I looked at each other, quietly laughed, and shrugged. Angie had earned her place.

Edwina was the baby, and she carried all the privilege that position implies. She could get away with anything just by deploying that smile at the right moment. Dad was especially soft with her—he'd come home exhausted from a long day taking photos with tourists, and Edwina would throw her little arms around his legs, and his whole expression would transform. He'd scoop her up, spin her around, and the weight he'd been carrying seemed to lift, at least for those few moments.

The Dirt Bike Days—Freedom on Two Wheels

The day Dad brought home that first small dirt bike, my entire world exploded with possibility.

It was a beat-up little Honda, maybe 50cc, with faded red paint and a dented gas tank that looked like someone had dropped it on rocks. The seat was torn in places, patched with tape that was peeling at the edges. To anyone else, it probably looked like junk. To me, it looked like freedom.

Dad rolled it off the truck bed, kicked the starter a few times until the engine sputtered and caught with a buzzing roar, and looked at me.

"Don't kill yourself," he said.

That was the full extent of my safety training.

I spent the rest of that afternoon tearing around the yard, learning how the throttle responded to my grip, how to lean into turns without losing balance. By evening, I had mud splattered across my face like war paint, my jeans torn at both knees, scratches on my arms from a close encounter with a torn bush, and a grin so wide my cheeks ached.

A few weeks later, Dad came home with a second bike—smaller, older, more battered, but functional. He nodded toward Dee-Dee. "Your turn." Her face lit up like Christmas morning, Thanksgiving dinner, and birthday presents all combined into one moment of pure joy.

From that day forward, we rode together. Through the woods behind the house where the trails wound between oak and hickory and pine. Down along the creek where the ground was sometimes soft and treacherous. Up into the hollows where the air turned cool even in summer and the light filtered green through the dense canopy overhead.

One afternoon, we decided to see how far we could go before we ran out of gas. We packed peanut butter sandwiches, filled up both tanks, and headed up into the mountains with no particular destination in mind. We rode for hours, farther than we'd ever gone before, past the landmarks we recognized and into territory that felt wild and unexplored.

At one point, Dee-Dee's front wheel caught a root at a bad angle. The bike stopped but she didn't—she went flying over the handlebars, disappearing into a patch of ferns with a crash of breaking stems.

I skidded to a stop, my heart pounding with sudden fear. I dropped my bike and ran toward where she'd landed.

But she was already sitting up, leaves tangled in her hair, dirt streaked across her face, laughing so hard she could barely breathe.

"Did you see that?" she gasped. "I flew! I actually flew!"

We turned back when the sun started dropping toward the ridgeline, racing the fading light, arriving home exhausted and filthy and happier than we had any right to be. Mom took one look at us and pointed silently toward the garden hose.

Those are the days I think about when people ask what my childhood was like. Not the struggles with money or my father's drinking or the complexity of family dynamics. Just two kids on dirt bikes, exploring a world that felt infinite and entirely their own.

Mischief and Memory—The Cigarette Load Incident

My father smoked heavily—Marlboro Reds, easily two packs a day. He'd sit on the porch after work, light up, and just exhale the tensions of the day along with the smoke.

One afternoon, I found an old novelty pack of "cigarette loads." They were tiny prank explosives you could hide inside a cigarette. I snuck one into Dad's cigarette and climbed up into the maple tree outside. Then I settled in to wait.

That evening, Dad settled into his usual chair with a tired sigh, pulled out the pack, and lit up. I watched from my perch, heart pounding with guilty anticipation.

He took a few drags, relaxing into the evening quiet. Then—Pow!

The cigarette exploded in a shower of sparks and shredded tobacco. Dad jumped out of his chair, cursed with impressive creativity, threw what was left of the cigarette off the porch, and stared at the smoldering remains like they had personally betrayed him.

I laughed so hard I nearly fell out of the tree. He shouted, looked up, saw me in the branches practically crying with laughter, and for one moment I thought I was in serious trouble.

Then his face cracked into a grin. He shook his head slowly, the way you do when you've been gotten good and can't even be mad about it.

"You little shit," he said, but he was laughing too.

Moments like that were the threads that wove our family together—humor, mischief, and love.

Lessons in Responsibility

Responsibilities in our house were assigned along old-fashioned lines that nobody questioned because that's just how things were done. The girls handled inside work: washing dishes, doing laundry, sweeping floors, helping Mom with cooking. I had the outdoor chores: stacking firewood in cords that would see us through winter, hauling trash out, mowing the yard. Was it fair by modern standards? Probably not. Did anyone complain? Not really. Everyone worked. Everyone contributed. That's just what families did.

Mom insisted I work every summer without exception. If I wasn't helping Dad on the roadside taking photos, I was traveling with Mom on her postcard route. She had a business supplying postcards to tourist shops throughout Cherokee, and summers meant restocking runs that could last all day. She'd load up the van with boxes of glossy cards—images of the Smokies in their autumn colors, Cherokee dancers in traditional regalia, Kuwohi (formerly Clingman's Dome) jutting above the clouds—and we'd drive from shop to shop on a route she'd refined over the years.

My job was carrying the heavy boxes while she handled the business end. Watching her work taught me professionalism long before I knew there was a word for it. She kept meticulous records in a small notebook, every sale tracked, every payment noted. She treated every shop owner with respect regardless of how they treated her.

"Your word is your bond," she'd tell me as we drove between stops. "If you say you'll do something, you do it. Period. People remember when you keep your promises, and they remember even longer when you don't."

That lesson embedded itself so deeply that breaking a commitment still feels physically wrong to me, decades later.

A House Full of Chaos, Faith, and Love

Our house was always loud—sisters talking, singing, fussing, laughing. Mom humming hymns while folding laundry. Dad coming home tired from the roadside, dropping his regalia in the chair, sitting beneath the maple tree with a cigarette and a cup of coffee. Neighbors would stop by, and I'd climb the tree overhead and eavesdrop as Dad talked about the weather, local gossip, or the tourist season. My world was small, but it felt full.

CHAPTER 3

THE LAND THAT RAISED ME

"The land knows you, even when you are lost."

— Robin Wall Kimmerer

My father taught without lectures—he taught by walking the mountains and letting the land speak. The Boundary was never scenery. It was teacher, witness, and anchor.

◆ ◆ ◆

I GREW UP IN A place where the mountains themselves seem to breathe.

On cold fall mornings, when the world is still and the sun hasn't yet climbed above the eastern ridges, the fog curls through the valleys like something alive, rising off the Oconaluftee River in soft layers that feel older than human memory. There's something about watching it that makes you feel connected to every generation that has watched the same fog rise from the same valleys for thousands of years.

To most people passing through, the Qualla Boundary is just a small dot on a map. To me, the Boundary has never been just a location. It is an inheritance passed down through generations who fought and sacrificed to remain here when removal would have been easier. It is an identity woven into the landscape itself. It is the land that remembers us even when the outside world forgets.

And I learned to see all of this walking beside my father.

The First Lessons—Taught without Words

My father was not a man who delivered lectures or sat you down for formal instruction. He taught by doing—by taking me to places, by showing me things, by creating space for the land itself to speak in its own voice while I learned to listen.

Some of my earliest and most vivid memories are of hiking with him into the backcountry, just the two of us, leaving the house before sunrise with a canteen of water and whatever simple food Mom had packed. We'd follow trails he'd known since his own boyhood, paths that didn't appear on any map because they existed only in the memory of people who had walked them generation after generation.

One fall morning when I was maybe nine or ten, we climbed the ridge above our home. My father moved with an easy confidence I tried to imitate, never rushing, placing his feet with a precision that suggested the mountain itself was guiding him. We'd hiked the Thomas Divide, all the way over through Deeplow Gap into Deep Creek. This is where legend says Tsali hid from the soldiers who hunted him and his sons during the Trail of Tears.

At the top, we stopped on an outcropping of granite that jutted from the ridge like the prow of a ship. The world opened up below us—a sea of treetops painted in fall colors, the mountains rolling away toward the horizon in ridge after ridge of blue haze that seemed to go on forever.

My father didn't say anything at first. He just stood there looking out across the land like he was reading something written there that I didn't yet have the language to understand. Finally, he knelt down beside a boulder covered in thick green moss and pressed his palm flat against the cool stone.

"Patrick," he said, his voice quiet in that way it got when something important was coming, "put your hand here. Feel this stone."

I knelt beside him. The rock was cool, rougher than it looked, solid in a way that went deeper than just physical hardness.

"This stone has been here longer than any of us can imagine," he said. "Longer than your grandparents. Longer than their grandparents. Longer than the Cherokee have been a people. And it'll be here long after we're gone too." He was quiet for a moment. "When things get hard, and they will get hard, son, you remember this. Whatever trouble you're facing, it's small compared to this. The stone doesn't care about any of that. It just holds. It just endures. And you can too."

I didn't fully grasp what he meant. I was nine years old, more interested in exploring the ridge top than contemplating geological time. But the moment planted itself somewhere deep, like a seed that wouldn't sprout for years.

Years later, when the life I'd built was under attack and people I'd trusted turned against me, I thought of that stone. Still there. Still holding. Unchanged by the small dramas of human politics. And I understood finally what my father had been teaching me: That perspective rooted in something permanent carries you through any season.

Learning to Read the Land

My father knew the Boundary the way some people know Scripture—chapter and verse, every hollow and ridge, every creek and trail. He carried a map in his memory that no cartographer had ever drawn, accumulated over a lifetime of walking these mountains and passed down from his own father and grandfather before that.

He taught me how to move through the woods quietly, placing my feet deliberately, avoiding the dry branches that would crack and announce my presence. He showed me how to read animal tracks in soft mud—the delicate pointed prints of deer, the handlike marks of raccoons, the larger, more ominous impressions left by bears. He taught me that the forest was always communicating if you knew how to listen.

Fishing Hazel Creek—The Place We Returned To

Some places become sacred not because of what they are but because of what happens there. For my father and me, that place was Hazel Creek.

We'd make the trip several times each year, packing light because we had to carry everything on our backs: sleeping bags, a cast-iron skillet blackened by years of use, a small coffee pot, fishing rods broken down to fit in our packs, hooks and line, a little cornmeal for breading the fish. We'd hike in for hours, and by the time we reached our camping spot, the outside world felt impossibly far away.

Out there, my father was different. The weight he carried in regular life—whatever battles he fought with alcohol, whatever pressures he felt from work and family, seemed to lift. He laughed more easily. He talked more openly. He was present in a way that felt rare and precious.

One evening, we'd caught enough trout for dinner and cooked them in the skillet over our fire. The sun had dropped below the ridgeline, the first stars appearing. Fireflies blinked along the creek bank, and somewhere in the distance an owl called.

My father poured himself a cup of coffee, wrapped his hands around its warmth, and stared into the dying flames.

"You know, son," he said, "this is what life's supposed to be. Sitting by a fire. Catching your own supper. Having all you need right here. Not worrying about money. Not worrying about what people think. Just you, the land, and what you can carry."

Now I understand. He was describing the clarity that comes when you strip away everything unnecessary and encounter life directly. The rest was noise.

The Land Provides

One summer afternoon when I was perhaps twelve, we were deep in the backcountry, miles from the nearest road. The day was hot, the air thick with humidity, and my canteen had been empty for over an hour. My mouth felt like cotton, my head was starting to ache, and I was trying not to complain because complaining to my father about discomfort never accomplished anything except make him less sympathetic.

He stopped suddenly on the trail, held up a hand for me to be still, and tilted his head as if listening to something I couldn't hear.

"What is it?" I whispered.

"Hush. Listen."

I closed my eyes and focused. At first there was nothing but the usual forest sounds—birds calling, insects buzzing, the rustle of leaves. Then, faint and almost imaginary, I heard it: a soft sound, like a whisper, coming from somewhere to our left.

"Water," my father said. "Come on."

We pushed off the trail, through thick laurel that grabbed at our clothes and scratched our arms, down a small slope I hadn't noticed. And there, bubbling up from between two moss-covered rocks, was a spring—cold, clear water emerging from the earth like a gift.

My father knelt, cupped his hands, and drank deeply. Then he motioned for me to do the same.

That water was the sweetest thing I've ever tasted, before or since. Cold enough to make my teeth ache, clean enough to see through to the rocks below.

"The land provides," my father said, wiping his mouth with the back of his hand. "You just have to know how to listen. How to pay attention. How to receive what it's offering."

He refilled my canteen from the spring, and we continued on our way. But that lesson stayed with me: The land will sustain you if you learn its language. It will give you what you need if you approach it with respect and attention.

CHAPTER 4

THE PATH TO CYNDI

"A smooth sea never made a skilled sailor."

— Franklin D. Roosevelt

I dropped out at fifteen, worked underground in mines, joined the Army, and eventually graduated law school with two kids and a new wife. Every detour built the navigator.

◆ ◆ ◆

THE PATH THAT EVENTUALLY led me to a law degree from the University of North Carolina, one of the most respected law schools in America, began in a place that would have made most people believe I'd never set foot in any university, let alone graduate from one. It began with failure. With closed doors. But it also began with a choice. And choices, I learned, matter more than circumstances.

The Day I Quit—Or Was Pushed

As a young child, I did well in school. The work came easily enough, I was curious about the world, and I had parents who expected effort even if they couldn't help much with homework. I graduated at the top of my eighth-grade class at Whittier Elementary and was chosen to deliver the Graduation Key Note address—a significant honor that felt enormous at the time.

The title I chose felt very sophisticated to my fourteen-year-old mind: "College: Pros and Cons."

Standing at that podium, I carefully listed all the sensible reasons a person might pursue higher education—and all the reasons they might reasonably choose not to. I leaned heavily toward the latter, which in hindsight feels like prophecy, though not the kind I recognized at the time.

By the time I entered high school, I had lost interest in almost everything about it. School felt pointless, the structure arbitrary, the lessons disconnected from anything that mattered. Halfway through ninth grade, I transferred from Swain County High School to Cherokee High. The stated reasons were various, but the real reason was simpler and today more embarrassing: I was chasing an older girl I'd started dating.

Teenage logic at its finest.

At a fall dance that year, a group of guys decided to jump me. I fought back—what else was I going to do?—and the next morning, I was summoned to the principal's office.

"You were involved in a fight last night," he said. Not a question.

"I was jumped. I was defending myself. I didn't start anything."

"Doesn't matter. You participated in a fight on school property."

He wasn't interested in that distinction. To him, I was the problem that needed removing. I was suspended. They let me come back twice a week for an hour—just long enough to finish Driver's Ed. Once that class was done, I walked off campus for the last time.

I was fifteen years old. A high school dropout. No diploma, no plan, no clear path forward.

That moment could have defined me. For a lot of young people, it does. But that wasn't what happened. That moment didn't define me.

It pushed me.

Work Becomes My Classroom

Like most Cherokee teenagers without diplomas, I went to work. My first real job was with the Tribal Fish and Game program, stocking rainbow trout in the streams that tourists would later pay to fish. The work was cold, wet, and physical—early mornings driving along mountain roads with tanks of fingerlings sloshing in the truck bed, wading into frigid creeks to release them.

It was honest work. Hard work. But after a few months, a truth I'd been avoiding became impossible to ignore: Without a diploma, the future I wanted simply wasn't possible. Every door I might want to walk through later would be locked.

So I did what would become a pattern throughout my life when faced with obstacles: I found another way.

I enrolled at Southwestern Community College and registered for the GED exam. I passed easily. By sixteen, I was technically a dropout who held a diploma-equivalent credential—a contradiction that would have confused anyone trying to fit me into neat categories.

Not long after, a friend mentioned he was applying to a program in Washington State that involved fisheries work. I applied, was accepted, and within months found myself in Bellingham, Washington, living where the mountains met the ocean in ways I'd never imagined. It was my first major leap away from home. I discovered that the world was far larger than Cherokee, that I could function in it, that the skills I'd learned—hard work, reliability, figuring things out— translated across geography.

I stayed there for a year and a half. But home had gravity. The mountains called in ways that the Pacific Coast couldn't match. I'd learned something important, though: I could leave, survive, even thrive. Using the college credits that I earned in the program, I applied to a few universities and was accepted into Tennessee Technological University in Cookeville. I started into a university before my high school classmates had graduated from high school.

In 1982, while attending TTU, I married a girl from Tulsa, Oklahoma. We had my first daughter, Tiffany. That marriage didn't last, but Tiffany has always been and will always be my daughter and a part of my life.

Spain and the Education of Distance

In 1984, while attending TTU, I was accepted into a study-abroad program and moved to Seville, Spain, for a year. Living with a host family who spoke no English, I had no choice but to learn Spanish—not textbook Spanish, but living Spanish, the kind you absorb through daily necessity and inevitable embarrassment. I got lost in narrow streets that are older than the United States. I ate food I'd never heard of. I attended a university where the lecture halls had educated students since before Columbus sailed.

When I returned to Cherokee in May 1985, I was twenty-one years old. I'd been a dropout, received a GED, got college credits from a fisheries program in Washington State, got accepted into a university, and became an international student.

And then I met Cyndi.

The Woman Who Changed Everything

She was nineteen years old—intelligent, grounded, and strikingly beautiful in a way that had nothing to do with cosmetics and the person looking out through her eyes. We met at a friend's house. I'll never forget when I first saw her. She came out of a bathroom and had a towel wrapped around her head. She saw me and ducked away into a side bedroom.

I waited, and when she came back out, I introduced myself, I'm sure somewhat awkwardly. I said something I'm sure was less smooth than it sounded in my head. She smiled—not a polite smile, but an actual one that reached her eyes—and we started talking. I was instantly taken. There was something in the way she held herself—calm, confident, completely comfortable in her own skin.

Although she'd grown up in San Jose, California, Cyndi's Cherokee identity was strong. She was one-quarter Eastern Cherokee from her father's side. On her mother's side, she was one-quarter Pima—desert people from Arizona whose relationship with the land was as deep as any Cherokee's. Altogether, she carried well over one-half Native blood degree from three different tribes. I've joked throughout our marriage that this explains why she's so strong—a line that always earns me one of her looks, the kind that proves my point while making me glad I said it.

We connected fast and deep, the way you sometimes do when you meet someone and recognize them even though you've never seen them before. She didn't need me to be perfect or to have my life figured out. She just needed me to be real.

Tiffany, my daughter from my first marriage, became part of the family Cyndi and I would build together.

We married on April 30, 1986.

That decision, choosing her, being chosen by her, was the most important one I ever made. Nearly forty years later, I can say without hesitation that the life we built together has been more than I could have imagined at twenty-one, standing there in my friend's house hoping a beautiful woman might want to talk to me.

Becoming a Father, a Soldier, a Man with Purpose

By the time we married, I knew I needed a clear path forward. The drifting years were over. I had responsibilities now, and those responsibilities demanded a plan.

So I enlisted in the United States Army.

Basic Training at Fort Dix, New Jersey, was cold in every sense—the winter extreme of January against exposed skin and the drill sergeants, bitter in their assessment of every mistake. The army taught me to follow orders I didn't always understand, push through exhaustion, and trust the people beside me with my life.

Advanced Individual Training at Fort Lee, Virginia, taught me to be a 76V10—a material storage and handling specialist. The skills involved organization, logistics, attention to detail, and systems management that I'd use throughout my career. Because I'd already accumulated two years of college credit, I entered as PFC E-3 and was promoted to Specialist E-4 within six months.

Our daughter Gina was born in January 1987 at Fort Richardson in Anchorage, Alaska. I remember the first time I held her—impossibly tiny, her face red and scrunched, her fists curled tight—and feeling the world shift on its axis. Our son Nelson arrived in 1988, and the shift deepened. I was no longer the restless boy who'd dropped out of high school. I was a husband, a father, a soldier, a man with purpose and people depending on him.

From the Mine Shaft to the Law Library

After my army service, I took a job deep underground in Bad Creek, South Carolina, helping construct a massive hydroelectric pumped-storage facility. The work was hard in ways that made the work before seem gentle—blasting through solid rock, pouring concrete in tunnels where the air was thick with dust and the darkness pressed in from every direction.

The money was good. But something in me knew this wasn't my destination. Working underground, I felt a growing certainty that I wanted more—not more money or more prestige, but more scope. More ability to shape outcomes.

So I went back to school, this time with the GI Bill covering the costs and a family providing motivation. I reenrolled at Tennessee Technological University and threw myself into academics with an intensity that would have shocked my fifteen-year-old self. In December 1989, I graduated with a double major in Criminal Justice and Sociology, near the top of my class.

I returned home and took a job as a drug and alcohol counselor at the Cherokee Indian Hospital's Chemical Dependency Unit. That work gave me an unvarnished education in the struggles our people faced—addiction, trauma, generational pain passed down like inheritance. It sparked something in me—a desire to change not just individual outcomes but the systems that shaped those outcomes. Counseling helped people one at a time. But policy, law, governance—those tools could help entire communities.

So I did something that would have seemed impossible to the boy who'd given that speech about the pros and cons of college:

I applied to the University of North Carolina School of Law.

Surprise! I got in.

UNC Law—Books, Babies, and Sheer Determination

Walking into UNC Law in the fall of 1990 felt like stepping into a different universe. Many of my classmates came from Ivy League programs, from families where law was a tradition spanning generations. I came with a wife working full-time, two small children who needed care, and a mortgage-sized sense of responsibility.

Daycare was expensive and often unavailable. Gina could attend Head Start, but Nelson was too young, which meant I frequently brought our children with me to class. Nelson became a fixture in the law school during his toddler years, sitting beside me with a coloring book and crayons, staying remarkably quiet for a three-year-old.

The Socratic method—that brutal teaching style where professors call on students at random and interrogate them about the day's reading—was terrifying in ways that never fully went away. At any moment, without warning, you might hear your name, and you'd better be ready. It doesn't reward good effort or partial understanding. It exposes exactly how much you know and exactly where your preparation fell short, in front of the entire class.

One morning in Real Property class, my professor's voice cut through the quiet room:

"Mr. Lambert . . . explain the Rule Against Perpetuities."

Every lawyer reading this just winced in sympathy.

The Rule Against Perpetuities is one of the most notoriously confusing concepts in American property law—a centuries-old doctrine about the validity of future interests in land. There's a famous quote often attributed to a California Supreme Court justice: "Determining whether or not the Rule Against Perpetuities has been violated is a task which ought properly to be undertaken only by the combined faculties of Harvard and Yale."

But I'd studied it. Hours upon hours. Nelson sat beside me, focused on his coloring book, unaware of the academic drama unfolding inches away.

I stood up, straightened my shoulders, and began: "The Rule Against Perpetuities provides that no interest in property is valid unless it must vest, if at all, not later than twenty-one years after some life in being at the creation of the interest . . ."

I walked through the entire doctrine. When I finished, for a couple of seconds, the silence in the room felt quieter than before I had started.

He nodded once, the closest thing to a compliment his teaching style allowed.

"Correct. You may sit down."

I sat down. Nelson looked up from his coloring and whispered, barely audible:

"Did you do good, Daddy?"

I smiled and whispered back: "Yeah, buddy. I did good."

Years later, that same little boy, now a grown man with his own law degree, would work in Tribal Realty, dealing with land and allotment issues rooted in the very property doctrines he'd witnessed me explain while he colored pictures. And my daughter Gina, who also attended class with me, would also go on to graduate law school and get her JD degree.

Life has a way of circling back to where it started, connecting moments you didn't know were connected.

Graduation—A Moment That Meant More than a Degree

May 1993. Chapel Hill, North Carolina. Clear skies and warm spring air.

My parents had made the trip from Cherokee—my father in his best shirt, my mother with tears welling up before the ceremony even started. Cyndi stood with me, holding Gina's hand on one side and Nelson's on the other, both children dressed up and confused about why all the adults were so emotional about people wearing funny hats.

After the formal proceedings, the dean approached our small group to offer her personal congratulations. She made polite conversation, radiated warm professionalism.

My father, never one to miss an opportunity for a memorable line, grinned at her and said:

"Not bad for a boy who quit high school, huh?"

The dean appeared to freeze. Her professional smile flickered as she processed what she'd just heard, trying to reconcile the successful graduate standing before her with the dropout history she'd been completely unaware of.

That moment—her shock, my father's pride, the distance between who I'd been and who I'd become—said more about my path than any diploma ever could.

The boy who quit high school was now Patrick Lambert, Esquire.

And he was just getting started.

CHAPTER 5

SNOW-CONES AND FIRE

"I have not failed. I've just found 10,000 ways that won't work."

— Thomas Edison

A snow-cone stand, a hotel bought at a bankruptcy auction, a fire that burned it all down, and the rebuild that followed. Every setback was just research for the next attempt.

◆ ◆ ◆

WHEN I GRADUATED FROM UNC Law School in May 1993 and moved back home to Cherokee, I thought the hard part was over. I had a law degree, a wife, two kids, and ambition to match. The path forward seemed clear: practice law, build a career, provide for my family.

What I couldn't have known then was that the real education was just beginning. And it would come not from courtrooms or legal briefs, but from snow cone machines, cash registers, insurance claims, bankruptcy auctions, and eighteen-hour days that stretched into years.

The Beginning

I got a job immediately with Ben Bridgers, the attorney I'd clerked with during my summers in law school. Cyndi got a job with the Tribal Finance Office. Together, we were earning two professional salaries. By Cherokee standards in 1993, we were doing well.

But "doing well" and "getting ahead" are two different things.

By 1995, Cyndi and I started having conversations that would change our lives.

"We can't just work for other people forever," she said one evening, looking at our budget spread across the kitchen table. "We need to build something of our own."

She was right. We'd seen it growing up—the families who worked for wages their whole lives and never got ahead, and the families who took risks, built businesses, and created something lasting. We knew which path we wanted.

Snow Cones: The First Hustle

In 1995, we took our first step into entrepreneurship. It wasn't glamorous. It wasn't even a real business, technically.

It was a snow cone stand.

I set up a small folding table on the front porch of a craft shop in downtown Cherokee—one of those tourist spots where my father sometimes worked as "Chief Henry," posing for photos in traditional regalia. The shop owner let me use his porch in exchange for 25 percent of whatever I made.

Every morning, I drove to the local ice plant and bought fifteen or twenty bags of ice. I loaded them into a cooler, hauled them up to the craft shop, and set up my little operation: a hand-cranked ice crushing machine, a row of flavored syrups, some paper cones, and a handwritten sign.

Then we stood there in the summer heat and hollered.

"Snow cone! Get your snow cone!"

Hour after hour. Day after day.

On a good day, we made $100 to $150. My kids thought it was the greatest thing in the world—Gina and Nelson would help scoop the ice and take the money, learning their first lessons about work and earning.

It wasn't much. But it was ours.

The Craft Shops: Learning to Run a Real Business

That snow cone summer taught us something important: The real money wasn't in selling snow- cones on someone else's porch. The real money was in owning the porch.

In 1996, there had been a fire at a row of shops near where we'd been selling snow cones. The buildings were being rebuilt, and I knew the owner—the same man whose porch we'd been using, the same man my father had worked for as "Chief Henry."

I talked to him about leasing some of the new spaces. We reached an agreement, and suddenly Cyndi and I were in the retail business.

We didn't start with one shop. We started with three. "Kid's World" sold candy and toys. "God's World" sold religious items and inspirational gifts. "Chief Henry's Gifts"—named after my father—sold traditional Cherokee crafts and souvenirs.

We had never run a business before. We didn't know how to order supplies, make payroll, operate a cash register, or balance the books. So we learned. We learned by doing, by making mistakes, by staying up late going over receipts and getting up early to open the doors.

Within a year, we consolidated. Our neighbor went out of business, so I took over his lease and combined operations into one larger location. Chief Henry's Gifts and More became our flagship.

Fire: When Everything Burns

And then, one night, it all burned down.

I got the call in the middle of the night. Fire at the shop. By the time I got there, flames were tearing through the building, firefighters were hosing down what was left, and all we'd built was turning to ash.

The investigation determined it was arson—someone had deliberately set the fire. They never caught whoever did it.

But here's what I learned that night, standing in the glow of the flames: A building is just a building. What we'd really built—the knowledge, the relationships, the will to keep going—none of that burned.

We had insurance. We filed the claim. We got the payout. And then we rebuilt.

We found a new location—actually, we got an even better spot, closer to the main tourist traffic. Chief Henry's Gifts and More came back stronger than before.

Expanding: The Laundromat, the Car Wash, and the Putt-Putt Course

Once you learn you can survive that kind of loss, you start thinking bigger.

We added a laundromat near the four lanes. Then I noticed something: Cherokee didn't have a car wash. So I bought a piece of land and built one—four self-serve bays and one automatic bay. We even added a small putt-putt golf course near the downtown area.

By the early 2000s, we had a portfolio: the craft shop, the

laundromat, the car wash, and the putt-putt course. We were no longer just surviving. We were building something real.

I'd wake up before dawn and start at the Gaming Commission, where I was now working as executive director. I'd handle Tribal business all day. Then, after a full day at the Commission, I'd head to the businesses. Check on the car wash. Stop by the laundromat. Walk through the gift shop. Cyndi would be there, too, often with the kids in tow, all of us working together. We'd get home late, fall into bed exhausted, and do it all again the next day.

Neither one of us had anything in our lives except family and work. No hobbies. No social life. No vacations. That's how we balanced it. We just worked harder than seemed humanly possible.

The Loss That Changed Everything

In November 2007, my father passed away from lung cancer. We buried him on Thanksgiving Day.

By then, the craft shop business was already declining. Cyndi and I decided to close the shops and focus on the car wash and the laundromat.

It was the right call.

The Bankruptcy Auction: "You Did WHAT?"

In August 2012, I saw an advertisement in the local paper: Inn of the Seven Clans—Bankruptcy Sale. A local hotel being sold at auction on the steps of the Bureau of Indian Affairs building.

I didn't even mention it to Cyndi.

I just went to watch. That's what I told myself. But when the bidding started, something came over me.

I raised my hand.

And I kept raising it.

And when the auctioneer's gavel came down, I'd won.

Purchase price: $950,000. Down payment required immediately: $50,000.

I stood there in shock, realizing what I'd just done.

I called Cyndi.

"Hey . . . so . . . I bought a hotel."

There was a long silence on the other end.

"You did WHAT?"

"I bought a hotel. At the bankruptcy auction. I need to come up with $50,000 right now."

Another silence. Longer this time.

"Are you crazy?"

Maybe I was. We didn't have hotel experience. And $950,000—plus the debts owed to the Tribe that brought the total to $1.2 million—was more money than we'd ever dealt with in our lives.

But I'd made the bid. The gavel had fallen. The deal was done.

So we figured it out.

We scraped together the $50,000 for the down payment. We went to the banks and negotiated financing. Cyndi was reluctant, understandably so. She didn't want to figure out how to operate another business we knew nothing about.

But that move, that crazy, impulsive, terrifying move, was perhaps our best move ever.

Turning It Around

The first few years were rocky. We had to learn the hotel business from scratch, just like we'd learned the rest. We worked at it. We studied. We made mistakes and fixed them.

And slowly, we turned that bankrupt property into a thriving hotel in Cherokee. We remodeled the entire building. We changed the name to the Cherokee Grand Hotel. We provided jobs to enrolled Tribal members. We operated openly, transparently, honestly—the same way we'd run every business we'd ever owned.

The Education of an Entrepreneur

When people ask me how I went from law school to Principal Chief, I tell them the story isn't just about politics or law or tribal governance.

It's about snow cones.

It's about learning to operate a cash register when you've never touched one before. It's about figuring out how to make payroll when you're not sure there's enough money in the account. It's about rebuilding after a fire destroys what you've built. What I learned in business—resilience, adaptability, financial discipline, risk management—prepared me for leadership in ways law school never could.

And execution is what you learn when you're standing on a porch in 95-degree heat, hollering "Snow cone! Snow cone!" to tourists who might not even look your way.

PART II

THE RISE

CHAPTER 6

THE DISCOVERY

— Aristotle

In a dusty law library during a summer clerkship, I found the statutory change that made Cherokee gaming possible. Not luck, not politics—just a law student reading statutes line by line.

◆　◆　◆

THE SUMMER OF 1992 smelled like hot asphalt and fresh-cut grass, and the mountains around Cherokee held the heat like a blanket that wouldn't lift until well after dark.

I was twenty-eight years old, between my second and third years at UNC Law, and I had come home to work for Ben Bridgers, the Tribal attorney for the Eastern Band. This was my second summer clerking for Ben. The previous summer, I had begun organizing the Tribe's laws, compiling ordinances, helping build something that looked like a modern legal code. Now I was back to continue that work and see it through.

But that summer turned into something else entirely.

Building the Code

Ben Bridgers was a steady, principled man with warm eyes and a deliberate way of speaking. He didn't waste words, and he always showed great respect for everyone's opinion. He was steeped in the Tribe's legal history and did extensive writings on it. And he also wrote poetry. He was brilliant and a true friend to the Cherokee. And if you earned his respect, you had it for life.

The task he had handed me seemed simple at first: organize the Tribe's laws.

What I found wasn't a code. It was sediment—layers of old ordinances, resolutions, carbon copies, committee notes, and legal scraps stored in filing cabinets and cardboard boxes scattered across multiple offices. Our government had grown faster than its paperwork. What we needed wasn't filing. What we needed was a foundation.

Over two summers, I pieced together every law I could find. Old Council resolutions from the 1970s. Archived ordinance packets with faded typewriter ink. Handwritten edits scrawled in margins. Committee notes from meetings no one remembered. Stacks of legal opinions that referenced statutes I had to hunt down one by one. And all the files with resolutions at our TOP (Tribal Operations office) were the original and produced by a real typewriter with keys. The digital age was just beginning.

Some days I felt less like a law clerk and more like an archaeologist, reconstructing a government layer by layer.

My office was in Ben Bridgers's law firm's library, a two-story building in Sylva with fluorescent lights that buzzed overhead and an old electric typewriter that clacked with every keystroke. This was before the internet. Before you could pull up a statute with a single search. Research meant books, heavy statute volumes that lined the walls, yellow legal pads covered in handwritten notes, carbon paper for copies that smudged if you weren't careful.

I worked at a wooden table near a window that looked out into the parking area. And I made a deliberate decision during that work, one that would shape Cherokee law for decades.

I would model the structure of the Cherokee Code on the North Carolina General Statutes.

Not to copy them. To signal legitimacy.

A code that looked familiar to courts, agencies, and regulators would elevate our sovereignty, not diminish it. When state officials or federal judges opened our code, they would see a structure they recognized, chapters, articles, sections, all organized in a way that said: We are serious. We are professional. We know what we're doing.

But there was something else I was studying that summer, something that consumed my thoughts even more than organizing ordinances.

I had come across Ben's earlier legal opinion, issued to the Tribe in 1990, analyzing whether the Eastern Band could lawfully enter casino gaming under the newly passed Indian Gaming Regulatory Act.

His legal answer had been no.

And at the time, he was right.

The Legal Landscape in 1990

Congress had passed the Indian Gaming Regulatory Act, IGRA, in 1988, following the Supreme Court's decision in *California v. Cabazon Band of Mission Indians*. The law was groundbreaking: It affirmed that federally recognized tribes had the inherent sovereign right to conduct gaming on Indian lands.

But there was a catch.

For what the law called "Class III gaming"—slot machines, blackjack, and other casino-style games—a tribe had to negotiate a compact with its home state. And under IGRA's framework, if a state prohibited a form of gaming, the tribe could not operate it. But if a state regulated it, even minimally, the tribe had the right to negotiate.

That distinction, prohibitory versus regulatory, was the key.

In 1990, North Carolina law was prohibitory. The statute banned video gaming outright. There was no regulatory framework, no exceptions, no lawful avenue forward.

Ben's opinion was clear, correct, and final: The Eastern Band could not pursue Class III gaming under IGRA.

The door was closed.

That summer, I read Ben's opinion over and over, tracing the legal citations, studying the cases—*Seminole Tribe v. Butterworth*, *Cabazon*, the text of IGRA itself. I wasn't looking for a loophole. I was trying to understand the framework, to know whether the door might ever open.

And then one afternoon, after working through lunch, I walked across the street to get a snack.

Everything changed in that moment.

The Mountain Breeze—2:00 p.m.

The law office is located in Sylva, a small mountain town just outside the Boundary. Directly across the street, at the corner of Savannah Drive and West Main Street, was a Texaco gas station called the Mountain Breeze.

It was the kind of place you'd stop for gas, a Coke, a pack of cigarettes, or—in my case—a midafternoon snack when the work got long and my stomach reminded me I'd skipped lunch.

Around two o'clock that day, after hours of sorting through ordinances and statute books, I needed a break. I stood up from my table, stretched my back, and walked across the street to the Mountain Breeze.

The afternoon sun was bright, almost harsh. Someone was close by the store cutting grass. A few cars sat at the pumps, engines ticking in the heat. Inside, the store was quiet—just the hum of coolers and the faint jingle of the bell above the door as I walked in.

I grabbed a pack of peanut butter crackers from the shelf and a Coke from the cooler. I was thinking about the statute books waiting for me back at the office, about the ordinances I still needed to organize, about Ben's 1990 opinion and the door that seemed permanently closed.

And then I saw them.

Two machines. Sitting against the wall near the back of the store.

They looked like slot machines: spinning reels, bells, cherries, the whole visual setup. Bright lights. Digital displays. The kind of thing you'd see in a casino.

But they were right there. In a gas station. In North Carolina.

I walked over, curious. Someone was playing one of them, feeding bills into the slot, pressing buttons, watching the reels spin. I stood there for a moment, staring.

And then I noticed something on the side of one of the machines.

A small sticker. Maybe three by four inches. White background. Black text.

I leaned in closer and read it.

"In conformance with North Carolina General Statute § 14-306(b)(2), games involving the use of skill or dexterity may be operated. Any prizes over $10 is a criminal offense."

I read it again.

Games involving the use of skill or dexterity.

Not based on skill or dexterity.

Involving.

My heart started racing.

I had just read that statute, or at least the old version of it, a few days earlier while reviewing Ben's 1990 opinion. The old statute prohibited video games based on skill or dexterity. But this sticker said involving the use of skill or dexterity.

That wasn't the same language. That was a change.

And if the statute had changed from prohibitory to regulatory—if the state was now allowing games that involved skill or dexterity instead of prohibiting them outright—then everything Ben had written in 1990 was no longer true.

The door wasn't closed anymore.

It was open.

I stood there in the Mountain Breeze Texaco, holding a pack of peanut butter crackers, staring at a three-inch sticker on the side of a slot machine, and I realized the implications were enormous.

The Research

I didn't finish my snack.

I walked straight out of the gas station, back across the street, and into the office. I sat down at my table, opened the North Carolina General Statutes volume, and started searching.

No internet. No quick search. Just books.

I flipped through pages, tracing legislative history, comparing versions of the statute, looking for amendments, looking for the exact language change.

And I found it.

The old statute, the one Ben had relied on in 1990, described a legal video gaming machine as one where "the operation of which depends upon the skill or dexterity of the player."

The new statute, by Session Law 1991-1011, was amended to now define a legal machine as "video games . . . that involve the use of skill or dexterity to make varying scores or tallies."

It was a subtle change. Most people wouldn't notice it. Most people wouldn't care.

But to a lawyer studying the intersection of federal Indian law and state criminal law, it was monumental.

Under IGRA's framework, the question wasn't whether North Carolina liked gaming. The question was whether North Carolina prohibited it or regulated it.

If the state banned gaming outright, prohibitory, then tribes couldn't operate it.

But if the state allowed certain forms of gaming under specific conditions, regulatory, then tribes had the right to negotiate a compact.

The old statute was prohibitory: Video games based on skill or dexterity were not allowed.

The new statute was regulatory: Video games involving the use of skill or dexterity to make varying scores or tallies were allowed.

That shift, from "based on" to "involving," transformed the entire legal landscape.

North Carolina was no longer prohibiting gaming. It was regulating it.

And that meant the Eastern Band of Cherokee Indians now had a legal right to pursue Class III gaming under IGRA.

I sat at that table the rest of the afternoon, tracing every citation, pulling case law, building the argument line by line. *Seminole Tribe v. Butterworth*, regulatory versus prohibitory. *California v. Cabazon*, tribal sovereignty over gaming. IGRA itself, the compact negotiation framework. North Carolina General Statute § 14-306(b)(2)—the amended language.

By evening, I had the skeleton of a legal memo.

By the next morning, I had a full draft.

And that afternoon, I walked into Ben Bridgers's office and handed it to him.

"Let's Get to Work"

Ben's office was just down the hall—small, neat, with a wooden desk covered in files and a window that looked out toward the mountains.

I knocked on the doorframe. He looked up from his desk.

"I need you to read something," I said.

He took the memo without a word and started reading.

I stood there, watching him. He read slowly, carefully, the way he read anything. His face didn't change. He didn't nod. He didn't react.

He just read.

When he finished, he set the memo down on his desk, leaned back in his chair, and looked at me for a long moment.

Then he said four words I'll never forget:

"You might be right."

Coming from Ben Bridgers, a man who measured every word, who didn't give praise lightly, who had spent decades practicing law with precision and caution, that was the highest compliment he could give.

He stood up.

"Let's go," he said.

"Where?"

"Across the street."

We walked out of the office together, crossed Savannah Drive in the afternoon sun, and entered the Mountain Breeze Texaco. The same two machines were still there. Someone was still playing one of them, feeding dollar bills into the slot, pressing buttons, watching the reels spin.

Ben walked over to the machine, leaned down, and read the sticker—the same three-by-four-inch sticker I had read the day before.

He stood there for a moment, hands in his pockets, staring at it.

Then he looked at me, smiled, and nodded.

"Let's get to work," he said.

Taking It to the Council

Over the next several days, Ben and I worked together to refine the legal argument, anticipate objections, and prepare a presentation for Principal Chief Jonathan L. "Ed" Taylor and the Tribal Council.

This wasn't just a legal opinion. This was a proposal to fundamentally change the economic future of the Eastern Band of Cherokee Indians.

If we were right, if North Carolina's statute had shifted from prohibitory to regulatory, then the Tribe had the legal right to demand that the state negotiate a Class III gaming compact.

If we were wrong, if the state or the federal government disagreed with our interpretation, we could waste years in litigation and end up with nothing.

The stakes were enormous.

When we finally presented the memo to Chief Taylor and the Council, the room was full of debate. Some Council members were hopeful, eager to pursue anything that might bring economic opportunity to the Tribe. Others were skeptical, worried about litigation, worried about the state's reaction, worried about whether gaming was even the right path forward.

But the legal argument was airtight.

North Carolina had changed its statute. The state was now regulating video gaming, not prohibiting it. And under IGRA, that meant the Tribe had standing to negotiate.

Chief Taylor and the Tribal Council listened carefully, asked questions, and then made a decision.

The Tribe would move forward. We would draft a new Tribal Gaming Ordinance. We would establish a formal Tribal Gaming Commission. And we would demand that the State of North Carolina come to the table and negotiate in good faith.

Building the Foundation

By late 1992, the Cherokee Code was complete. The first published copies came out in early 1993, paperback for the public, hardback for the government, modern order for a modern Tribe.

It was more than a book. It was a declaration.

At the same time, the Tribal Council enacted a new Gaming Ordinance designed to meet IGRA's standards and establish the Tribe's regulatory authority. The ordinance created the Cherokee Tribal Gaming Commission—a three-member independent body tasked with regulating all gaming activity on Cherokee lands.

The first commissioners were appointed: J.L. Burgess as chairman, a respected businessman who owned several properties in downtown Cherokee; Tom Haigler, owner of local motels, known for his steady judgment and military discipline; and Robert "Birdie" Saunooke as vice chairman—owner of a shopping mall and craft shops in the Saunooke Village business area.

These men would serve in those roles for twenty years, from 1992 to 2012, providing stability and consistency as Cherokee gaming grew from nothing into one of the most successful tribal gaming operations in the United States.

With the ordinance in place and the Commission established, I was appointed to serve as legal counsel to the Commission. My job was to draft regulations, build compliance systems, and make sure that all our work met the standards of both IGRA and the newly formed National

Indian Gaming Commission in Washington.

It was cutting-edge work—the kind of work that was happening in only a handful of places across Indian Country.

And I threw myself into it completely.

The Lawsuit Against Governor Jim Martin

But there was a problem.

The Tribe had made a formal request to the State of North Carolina to begin compact negotiations under IGRA.

Governor Jim Martin refused.

He didn't respond. He didn't negotiate. He didn't even acknowledge the request.

Under IGRA, a state's failure to negotiate in good faith gave a tribe the right to bring the matter to federal court and compel the state to the table.

So in the fall of 1992, the Eastern Band of Cherokee Indians filed suit against the State of North Carolina for violating its obligation to negotiate.

It was a bold move. It was also the only move we had.

This very provision of IGRA, forcing a state to negotiate, would later be ruled unconstitutional under the Eleventh Amendment. But in 1992, it was our only recourse.

And we used it.

All of it traced back to that summer afternoon in 1992 when I walked into a gas station to buy peanut butter crackers and noticed a sticker I wasn't supposed to see.

And today, more than thirty years later, the Mountain Breeze Texaco is still there. Still at the corner of Savannah Drive and West Main Street. Still operating machines. In fact, they've built a little side room where five or six of those machines run day and night.

Every time I drive past that gas station, I think about that afternoon. I think about how small moments can carry the weight of history. I think about how one observation, one question, one stubborn refusal to accept that the door was closed can change the trajectory of an entire Nation.

CHAPTER 7

TIME TO CLEAN UP

"Well done is better than well said."

— Benjamin Franklin

Plenty of people talked about what Cherokee gaming could be. A small team of us shut down the illegal operations and actually built it.

◆ ◆ ◆

THE PHONE RANG IN Principal Chief Ed Taylor's office on a gray January morning in 1993, just weeks after Jim Hunt was sworn in as Governor of North Carolina for his third term.

We had been waiting for this call. State attorneys had been talking to Tribal attorneys for days, setting up a time, making sure both sides were ready for a conversation that could change the Tribe's future.

The lawsuit we had filed against Governor Jim Martin in the fall of 1992—the suit demanding that the State of North Carolina negotiate a gaming compact in good faith under the Indian Gaming Regulatory Act, was still pending in federal court. Governor Martin had refused to negotiate. He hadn't responded, hadn't acknowledged our request, hadn't even pretended to consider it.

Governor Hunt made a different choice.

The Call from Raleigh

Chief Taylor took the call in his office. I wasn't in the room for those first few minutes, but I know what he told us afterward.

Governor Hunt was direct. He acknowledged the lawsuit. He acknowledged the Tribe's legal standing under IGRA. And he made an offer: If you dismiss the lawsuit, I give you my word that my administration will sit down and negotiate with you in good faith.

Chief Taylor didn't agree immediately. He told the governor that if the Tribe was going to dismiss the case, it would be done without prejudice—meaning that if the state failed to negotiate in good faith, we could refile the lawsuit and pick up right where we left off.

Governor Hunt agreed.

The deal was made.

Within days, our attorneys filed a voluntary dismissal of the case. The lawsuit was gone. But the door to negotiations was open.

For the first time in the Tribe's history, the State of North Carolina had agreed to come to the table and talk about casino gaming on Cherokee land.

The Chaos Before the Calm

But before Governor Hunt's call, before the compact negotiations, before any of the structure we were trying to build could take hold, there was chaos.

It started in the summer of 1992.

Word had spread across Cherokee that gaming was coming. The Tribe had passed a new Gaming Ordinance. The Cherokee Tribal Gaming Commission had been established. People knew something big was coming.

And some local business owners decided they weren't going to wait.

Machines started appearing in shops and businesses around town. Not just one or two, dozens. Business owners bought what they called "gaming permits" from the Tribal Finance Office for ten dollars apiece, stuck the permits in their windows, and filled their stores with video poker machines, pull-tab machines, waterfall machines, anything they could get their hands on.

Most of the machines came from a South Carolina company called Pot-O-Gold. They were brightly colored, loud, and completely unregulated. No background checks on operators. No cash-handling procedures. No licensing beyond that ten-dollar permit. No oversight of any kind.

It was the Wild West, gambling up front, and since alcohol was still illegal on the Boundary, bootleg liquor in the back.

The first time I truly saw the scale of the chaos was when the United States Attorney and the North Carolina Attorney General came to Cherokee to inspect the machines. Federal and state officials showing up in town wasn't common, and when it happened, people noticed.

They came to look at two specific types of machines that were spreading across Cherokee. The first were waterfall machines, quarters stacked on a moving platform, players pushing a bar to try to knock them off the edge. The officials ruled those illegal immediately. Pure games of chance, no skill involved, prohibited under federal and state law.

The second were pull-tab machines—video versions of the paper pull-tab games you'd see at a church bingo hall. The officials withheld judgment on those. They needed more time, more research, more legal analysis.

But the message was clear: The federal government was watching. The state government was watching. And if the Tribe couldn't prove it could regulate its own gaming operations, someone else would step in and regulate them for us—or shut us down entirely.

Kenny Cuthbertson and TeePee Village

One of the biggest operations, and one of the biggest problems, was a place called TeePee Village.

It sat in the heart of Cherokee, right across from Saunooke Village, in a strip of businesses catering to tourists. Souvenir shops, craft stores, T-shirts, moccasins, dream catchers—the kind of places that made their money in the summer and barely survived the winter.

The owner was a man named Kenny Cuthbertson.

Kenny was hard to miss. He was flamboyant, flashy, fast-talking. He wore slick, shiny suits and jackets—the kind of clothes that stood out in a small mountain town where most people dressed in jeans and work boots. His hair was slicked back. His voice was high-pitched and distinctive, the kind of voice that carried across a room whether you wanted to hear it or not. His laugh could fill a building.

And he drove a Jaguar.

In a place where most families were scraping by, where poverty was still the norm, where people drove pickup trucks with rust on the fenders and hope in short supply, Kenny Cuthbertson drove a Jaguar.

He was personable, easy to talk to, easy to like if you didn't look too closely. But he was also shrewd. He knew how to use money to get influence. He knew how to work the system. And he knew that if gaming was coming to Cherokee, he wanted to be the one controlling it.

By 1993, TeePee Village was packed with machines. Seventy-eight of them, running day and night. People lined up to play. Cash flowed in faster than anyone could count it.

And Kenny operated as if the rules didn't apply to him.

Larry Callicutt Falls

Not everyone believed the legal argument we were building.

Not everyone believed that North Carolina's statute change from "based on" to "involving" skill or dexterity was enough to support a compact.

One of the skeptics was Larry Callicutt, the Tribe's finance director. Larry was sharp, practical, and brutally honest. He didn't buy into hype, and he didn't trust legal arguments that sounded too good to be true.

One afternoon, we were at Cherokee Bingo, a gaming operation owned by Tomahawk Gaming. We were there to discuss cash-handling procedures, internal controls, and compliance standards for the machines they were operating. The three gaming commissioners were there, J.L. Burgess, Tom Haigler, and Robert "Birdie" Saunooke, along with Bill Beck, the general manager of Tomahawk Gaming, several bingo staff members, and Larry.

We were standing in the main area, going over procedures, when Larry interrupted.

"There's no such thing as skill and dexterity in a machine," he said, shaking his head. "You can't put skill and dexterity in a slot box. This whole compact idea is built on a fantasy."

I started to respond, but Larry wasn't done.

"You want to know what skill and dexterity looks like?" he said, grinning.

Then he did something I'll never forget.

Larry tilted his head back, raised one leg off the ground, extended one arm, and tried to touch his nose with his finger while balancing on one foot.

"This is skill and dexterity!" he announced.

And then his foot slipped.

He went down hard, flat on his back, arms and legs splayed out, hitting the concrete floor with a sound that made everyone in the room gasp. For a split second, nobody moved. We all thought the same thing: *Oh my God, Larry's hurt.*

But then, like a bouncing ball, Larry popped right back up to his feet, brushing himself off, face red with embarrassment.

I couldn't help it. I turned to him and said, "Yeah, Larry. That's skill and dexterity."

The room exploded in laughter. Even Larry laughed, though I could tell his pride was bruised more than his back.

It became one of those moments you never forget. In the middle of all the tension, all the pressure, all the regulatory chaos swirling around us, it reminded us that we were still human. And sometimes, the best way to prove a point is to fall flat on your back and get up laughing.

Cash on the Tables

But not all the moments were funny. Some were terrifying.

One evening, around six or seven o'clock, I stopped by TeePee Village to meet with the general manager, Denny Rochester. He had some questions about procedures, and I wanted to keep the lines of communication open even as tensions were building between the Gaming Commission and Kenny's operation.

When I walked into the building, I noticed immediately that the door to the counting room was ajar. Not wide open. Just cracked. Enough that I could see inside.

The tables were loaded with cash.

Stacks of bills. Piles of money. Ones, fives, tens, twenties, fresh from the drop, spread across the tables like someone had just dumped it there and walked away.

And there was nobody around.

No staff. No manager. No security. Just cash. Sitting there. Unguarded.

Anyone could have walked in off the street, the same path I had just taken, and walked out with thousands of dollars.

I stood there for a moment, stunned. Then I quietly pulled the door closed, turned around, and left the building.

I got in my car and immediately called J.L. Burgess, the chairman of the Gaming Commission.

"We have a problem," I said.

I told him what I'd seen.

The next day, we called an emergency meeting of the full commission. This wasn't just about compliance anymore. This wasn't just about regulations or procedures or federal oversight.

This was about the survival of Cherokee gaming.

If state officials saw this—if federal regulators walked into a building and found cash sitting unguarded on tables—the compact negotiations would be over before they started. The state would argue that the Tribe couldn't be trusted to regulate itself. The federal government would step in. And all we had worked for would collapse.

We had to act. And we had to act fast.

Ben Falls Ill

By late 1994, the compact negotiations were moving forward. Slowly. Carefully. With constant tension.

I was working twelve to fifteen-hour days, every day. Drafting regulations. Reviewing contracts. Preparing briefing materials. Building the legal framework that would support what the Tribe was trying to do.

And through all of it, I leaned on Ben Bridgers.

Ben was still serving as Tribal attorney, still guiding the legal strategy, still providing the steady, experienced hand that kept us grounded. But in late 1994, his health started to decline.

He didn't talk about it much. He kept working. He stayed involved in the compact negotiations, in the discussions with gaming companies, in the daily legal work that kept the Tribe moving forward.

But by early 1995—after the compact was signed in August 1994 and as we entered the even more complex management agreement negotiations—Ben had to step back.

In March 1995, he left his position as Tribal attorney to focus on his health.

And just like that, I was alone.

I was thirty-one years old. I had been practicing law for less than two years. I was working on the most complex, high-stakes legal negotiations in the history of the Eastern Band of Cherokee Indians.

And my mentor was gone.

The work didn't scare me. I was used to long hours. I was used to pressure. I was used to diving into complex legal problems and working until I found solutions.

But the judgment calls scared me.

In a courtroom, you have rules. You have precedent. You have a judge who makes the final call. But in negotiations, in politics, in the messy, unpredictable world of tribal governance, there are no clear answers. Every decision is a gamble. Every move has consequences you can't always see.

And I was making those decisions alone.

I thought about my mother in those moments. I thought about all the times growing up when I had come to her with a problem, something I didn't know how to handle, something I wasn't sure about, something that required a choice I was afraid to make.

And almost every time, she would listen carefully, look me in the eye, and say the same thing: "You have to decide that for yourself."

Ben was gone. I couldn't lean on him anymore. I had to decide for myself.

I still called him at home a few times, asked his advice on specific issues. But I knew I couldn't keep bothering him while he was recovering.

The First Shutdown

By the summer of 1994, the compact negotiations were nearing completion. But there was still a problem.

Tomahawk Gaming and TeePee Village were still operating, still running machines, still taking in money, still operating outside the regulatory framework we were trying to build.

We had given them repeated notices. Repeated warnings. Repeated opportunities to come into compliance.

They couldn't. Or wouldn't.

The machines they were running simply weren't capable of meeting the standards we needed. The cash-handling was a disaster. The recordkeeping was nonexistent. The whole operation was a liability.

And the State of North Carolina was watching.

If we wanted the state to sign the compact—if we wanted them to believe that the Tribe could regulate its own gaming operations with integrity, we had to prove it. We had to show that we would enforce our own laws, even when it was hard. Even when it was unpopular. Even when it meant shutting down sources of gaming revenue.

In July 1994, the Cherokee Tribal Gaming Commission made its first decision.

We were shutting down Tomahawk Gaming.

It was just the four of us that day: me and the three commissioners—J.L. Burgess, Tom Haigler, and Robert "Birdie" Saunooke. No police. No security. No fanfare. Just us.

We arrived at Cherokee Bingo, the location where Tomahawk Gaming operated, around five o'clock in the afternoon. The building wasn't open yet. We had timed it that way.

We walked in, posted closure notices on the doors, cut the power to the machines, and locked the building.

Then we left.

I felt a knot in my stomach as we walked away. We had just shut down a major gaming operation.

But we weren't done yet.

The Final Showdown

A few weeks later, it was time to finish what we had started.

TeePee Village, Kenny Cuthbertson's operation, was still running. Still packed with machines. Still operating outside the regulatory framework.

We had given Kenny every opportunity. Every warning. Every chance to comply.

And we couldn't wait any longer.

On August 5, 1994, we made the final move.

Kenny knew we were coming. We had given him notice. We had told him exactly what would happen if he didn't come into compliance. When we arrived, again, just the four of us, his people were out of the way. He wasn't there. The building was quiet.

We walked in with chains and padlocks. We posted the closure notices. We cut the power. We wrapped the chains around the door handles and snapped the locks shut.

And then we stood there for a moment, looking at each other.

J.L. spoke first.

"Well," he said quietly, "hope this works."

I nodded. Because we had just shut down the Tribe's last source of gaming revenue. First Tomahawk Gaming in July. Now TeePee Village in August. The machines were silent. The buildings were locked. And we had no idea if the state would actually sign the compact.

We had just eliminated every dollar of gaming revenue the Tribe had, and we didn't have a signed compact yet. But we knew we were close. We knew the state was watching. And we knew this was the last test.

We locked the doors. We posted the signs. We walked back to our cars.

And we went home.

Six Days Later

On August 11, 1994, six days after we padlocked TeePee Village, and a few weeks after we had shut down Tomahawk Gaming—the Eastern Band of Cherokee Indians and the State of North Carolina signed the Tribe's first Class III Gaming Compact.

I don't think that timing was a coincidence.

I think the state was watching. I think they were waiting to see if we had the courage to enforce our own laws. I think they needed proof that the Tribe could regulate itself, in practice.

And when we shut down those operations, when we locked those doors, when we chose the long-term future of the Tribe over short-term revenue, we gave them that proof.

The compact authorized one casino with up to sixty thousand square feet of gaming space, games involving skill or dexterity, regulatory oversight by the Cherokee Tribal Gaming Commission, and a framework for revenue sharing, dispute resolution, and enforcement.

It wasn't perfect. But it was ours.

And it opened the door to what came after.

CHAPTER 8

THE COMPACT

"In the middle of difficulty lies opportunity."

— Albert Einstein

North Carolina in 1993 had no casinos, no lottery, and deep skepticism about gambling. But the law was clear, and the state had to come to the table.

◆ ◆ ◆

ON AUGUST 11, 1994, six days after we padlocked TeePee Village, the Eastern Band of Cherokee Indians and the State of North Carolina signed our first Class III Gaming Compact.

This is the story of what happened in those negotiating rooms leading up to the signing of the compact.

The Table

The conference room was on the third floor of a state office building in Raleigh. Fluorescent lights hummed overhead. A long rectangular table dominated the space. Windows looked out over a parking lot where winter rain streaked the glass.

It was late 1993. I would help negotiate the document that would determine the economic future of the Eastern Band for generations.

On one side sat representatives of the state, attorneys from the attorney general's office, staff from the governor's office. They had come to protect the state's interests, to limit what we could do.

On our side sat Principal Chief Ed Taylor, Ben Bridgers, several Council members, and me, thirty years old, just months out of law school, carrying the weight of knowing that every word we agreed to would echo for decades.

Why This Mattered

The Indian Gaming Regulatory Act required tribes to negotiate compacts with their home states for Class III gaming. IGRA was a compromise: Tribes gained federal recognition of their gaming rights; states gained a seat at the table.

But North Carolina in 1993 had no commercial casinos, no state lottery, and deep-rooted cultural skepticism about gambling. To many officials in Raleigh, a full-scale casino in the mountains felt foreign, even threatening.

We had to work through all of that. But we also had something working in our favor: The law was on our side.

Under IGRA, if a state allowed any form of gaming a tribe wanted to conduct, even in a limited, regulated way, the state had to negotiate. The statute change I had discovered in 1991, the shift from "based on" to "involving" skill or dexterity, meant that North Carolina was now regulating video gaming rather than prohibiting it.

That gave us standing. That gave us leverage.

But leverage alone doesn't build a partnership. And a compact, if it was going to work, had to be something both sides could live with.

The Sticking Points

The first few sessions went smoothly enough. We agreed on basic frameworks, established ground rules, found common language on issues that seemed contentious but turned out to have obvious solutions.

But then we hit the hard stuff.

The state wanted significant regulatory oversight of Cherokee gaming. They wanted their officials to have access to the casino floor, to audit our books, to investigate complaints.

We understood the concern. But we also had to protect our sovereignty. If state regulators could walk onto Cherokee land anytime they wanted and dictate how we ran our business, were we really exercising sovereign authority? Or were we just operating under state supervision?

We went back and forth on regulatory language for days.

The Battle Over Games

One of the most difficult battles was over something that might seem simple: what games could be played.

The state wanted a large role in deciding which games the casino could offer. If they had unilateral authority to approve or reject games, they could strangle our operation before it even started, dragging their feet on approvals, rejecting games for political reasons. We would be at their mercy.

I insisted that game classification decisions had to be made by an independent body, not the state, not the Tribe, but a neutral commission.

After days of back and forth, we found the solution: a three-member Certification Commission. The Tribe would appoint one member, the State would appoint one member, and the chairman would be mutually agreed upon from a list of candidates acceptable to both sides.

Neither sovereign controlled the Commission. The chairman, chosen by consensus, would be the tiebreaker.

It was a genuine compromise. And it set a precedent for how the Tribe and the state would work together in the years to come.

The Dispute Resolution Battle

But the real battle, the one that nearly broke the negotiation, was over dispute resolution.

The state wanted any disputes arising under the compact to be resolved in state court. We couldn't accept it. State courts had no experience with federal Indian law, no history of respecting tribal sovereignty. We insisted on arbitration or federal court.

We argued about it for hours.

At one point, the lead attorney for the state, Andy Venore, leaned back and said, "Patrick, you're asking us to give up our home court advantage."

"This isn't a game," I said. "It's a partnership. And partnerships don't work when one side holds all the cards."

The room went quiet. Then Andy said, "Let's take a break."

The Breakthrough

We broke for lunch. I walked outside into the cold and found a bench near the parking lot.

I didn't eat. My stomach was in knots. Did I push too hard?

We had been working toward this moment since that afternoon at the Mountain Breeze. The discovery. The lawsuit against Governor Martin. Governor Hunt's phone call. Everything had led to this negotiation.

When we reconvened, Andy was different. Andy was more relaxed.

"You made a fair point this morning," he said, and slid a piece of paper across the table. "Binding arbitration. Neutral arbitrator selected by mutual agreement. Neither side gets home court advantage."

I read it carefully. It wasn't perfect; there were details to work through. But the core principle was there.

I looked at Ben. He gave me a small nod. I looked at Chief Taylor.

"This works," I said. "Let's keep going."

Over the next several hours, we worked through the remaining issues with a momentum that had been missing all morning. By the end of the day, we had the framework of an agreement.

As we packed up and shook hands, one of the governor's aides said, "We all knew this was going to happen eventually. The question was whether we did it together, or spent years fighting in court."

He was right. And that day, we chose to do it together.

The Long Road to August

The negotiations continued through the winter of 1993 and into 1994. More meetings, more drafts, more compromises.

By the summer of 1994, we were close. But we still had a problem—the Wild West operations still running on the Boundary, still making us look like we couldn't regulate ourselves.

That's when we made the decision to shut them down. Tomahawk Gaming in July. TeePee Village on August 5.

Six days later, the compact was signed.

I've always believed those shutdowns were the final proof the state needed. We had shown them that the Eastern Band was serious about integrity, serious about regulation, serious about building something that would last.

There was no signing ceremony. The governor signed the compact in Raleigh on August 10 and overnighted it to Cherokee. The Tribe's signatures went on the following day, August 11. The most consequential economic agreement in our Tribe's modern history arrived in an overnight envelope.

What the Compact Meant

The compact gave the Eastern Band the legal authority to operate

Class III gaming on our trust lands. It established a regulatory framework that protected both Tribal sovereignty and state interests. It created the Certification Commission for fair decisions on game classifications. And it created a foundation of trust between the Tribe and the state, one we'd rely on for decades.

Within a few years, Harrah's Cherokee Casino would open. Within a decade, it would become a powerhouse—the premier tribal gaming destination in the eastern United States. Within a generation, it would transform the Eastern Band from a community struggling with poverty into a community with resources to invest in education, health care, infrastructure, and the future of every enrolled member.

None of that would have been possible without the compact.

CHAPTER 9

THE COMMISSION

"The strength of a nation lies not in the height of its buildings, but in the character of its people."

— Cherokee Teaching

Three businessmen from the Boundary—not lawyers, not professional regulators—became our first Gaming Commissioners and built something that lasted decades. They brought character, not credentials.

◆ ◆ ◆

WHILE WE WERE NEGOTIATING the compact and shutting down rogue operations, we were also building something else—the regulatory structure that would make Cherokee gaming work for decades.

The first time I sat down with all three members of the new Tribal Gaming Commission in the same room, I knew we had something.

It was the fall of 1993, and we were crowded into Tom Haigler's small apartment above the Drama Motel office, directly across the street from the Tribal Council House complex. The apartment was modest, a living room with a worn couch, a kitchen barely big enough to turn around in, windows that looked out toward the flowing, full banks of the Oconaluftee River.

We didn't have office space yet. We didn't have staff. We didn't have infrastructure or budget or any of the things a regulatory body is supposed to have.

What we had was four people sitting in a living room, trying to figure out how to build something that had never existed before.

J.L. Burgess sat in an armchair near the window, his reading glasses pushed up on his forehead. Tom Haigler was in a straight-backed chair he'd pulled from the kitchen, sitting the way he always sat, upright, shoulders square, like he was still in the military. Robert "Birdie" Saunooke had taken the couch, leaning forward with his elbows on his knees, listening more than talking.

And I was there with a legal pad full of notes and a head full of questions about how we were going to pull this off.

J.L. was also a farmer—a man who raised cattle and maintained a beautiful stretch of land with the kind of care that told you everything about how he approached life. Nothing sloppy. Nothing half-done. Everything deliberate. When J.L. made a decision, it stayed made.

Tom didn't talk much, but when he did, people listened. His words carried weight because he never wasted them.

Birdie was still a fairly young man, same age as me, but he carried a sense that time was precious and yet was always so generous.

They were not lawyers. They were not professional regulators. They were businessmen—local entrepreneurs who had built successful operations in a place where success was hard to come by.

And from the very beginning, they worked as a team. Not just three individuals appointed to a board. A team. They had a strong work ethic, were flexible on meeting times, and took the job seriously. I cannot remember a single argument between them. Not one. Every decision I can recall was made by unanimous agreement.

The First Conversation

That evening in Tom's apartment, the conversation centered on one question: How do we organize this commission so it actually works?

I was focused on three things.

First, independence. The commission had to be independent from political pressure. If the Tribal Council could override our decisions, fire us when they didn't like what we did, or control our funding, we would never be able to regulate effectively. We would just be a rubber stamp for whoever held power at any given moment.

Second, funding. The commission needed its own funding source—not dependent on annual appropriations that could be cut when enforcement got too aggressive.

Third, staffing. Eventually, we would need investigators, compliance officers, licensing specialists.

But in 1993 and 1994, there was no staff. It was just me serving as legal counsel to the Commission, and the three commissioners, doing everything ourselves: the enforcement actions, the compliance orders, the closures of Tomahawk Gaming and TeePee Village, the preparation for compact negotiations. All of it done by four people, meeting in living rooms and makeshift offices, building something from nothing.

J.L. looked at me that night and said, "Patrick, you tell us what we need to do to make this work. We'll do the work. But you have to show us the path."

"The path," I said, "is independence. Everything else flows from that."

The Failed Model We Replaced

Cherokee's first attempt at a Gaming Commission didn't work.

In 1989, the Tribe had established a Gaming Commission consisting of Ed Taylor, the Principal Chief; Dan McCoy, the Chairman of the Tribal Council; and Wilbur Paul, the BIA Superintendent.

Two politicians. One federal employee. It was a disaster waiting to happen.

The Principal Chief and the Chairman of Council were the two most powerful political figures in tribal government. They couldn't regulate independently—every decision would be filtered through political calculations, constituent pressures, and the demands of the next election. And the BIA Superintendent was a federal employee whose loyalty was to the Bureau of Indian Affairs, not the Tribe.

So in 1991, the first major amendment to the Tribal Gaming Ordinance dissolved the old commission. We created a new model with independent commissioners who weren't politicians, weren't federal employees, weren't beholden to anyone except the law and the Cherokee people.

We appointed J.L. Burgess, Tom Haigler, and Robert "Birdie" Saunooke.

Becoming Executive Director

In the fall of 1995, the Tribe's world turned upside down.

Principal Chief Ed Taylor had been impeached earlier that year. Joyce Dugan had been elected as the new Principal Chief. And the Tribe was entering a new phase—moving from compact negotiations to the even more complex work of negotiating a management agreement with a casino operator.

That's when I made the decision to leave my position with the Tribal attorney's office and take the job as executive director of the Cherokee Tribal Gaming Commission.

It was a risk. But I knew where the future was. The future was gaming.

One of the best decisions I made early on was bringing in Tonya "Sunshine" Toinetta as my executive assistant. She became my office manager in every sense of the word—she made sure the other employees showed up on time, did their work, and stayed accountable. She sat through every commission meeting and took the minutes. She kept my schedule straight, kept me on time, and kept the mountain of paperwork flowing the way it needed to flow. As the operation grew from four people in a living room to a fully staffed regulatory agency, Sunshine was the one who made sure the office actually ran. She was my confidant, my springboard, and for the better part of two decades, the person who knew where everything was and how everything worked. In an operation built on regulatory credibility, the person who holds the office together matters more than most people ever know.

My first priority was the same thing I had been focused on since 1993: getting our independence locked into law. We had been operating under interim rules, patched-together resolutions, and the goodwill of the Tribal Council.

But goodwill isn't a foundation. Law is.

The Blueprint from Washington

In April 1994, the National Indian Gaming Commission had released NIGC Bulletin 94-3, providing guidance on the structure of Tribal Gaming Commissions.

I read that bulletin the way some people read Scripture: carefully, repeatedly, looking for meaning in every sentence.

The bulletin laid out what independence required: funding that wasn't subject to annual appropriation battles, authority to make rules and issue licenses without interference, and protection from political retaliation. Commissioners needed to be able to make tough calls without worrying that they'd lose their jobs for doing the right thing.

I compared it to what we had been doing in Cherokee and realized: We were close, but we needed to formalize it. We needed to lock it into law.

The Per Capita Ordinance

Before I could finalize the Gaming Commission ordinance, there was another critical piece of legislation.

In September 1995, the Tribal Council passed Ordinance No. 582, the Per Capita Ordinance. It established the framework for distributing gaming revenue directly to enrolled members of the Tribe, ensuring that every Tribal member would benefit from gaming, not just the government.

The US Department of the Interior approved it on October 30, 1995. That approval was critical: under IGRA, any distribution of gaming revenue to tribal members must be approved by the Secretary of the Interior. Cherokee met all the requirements, and the foundation was in place for a per capita distribution system that would become a model across Indian Country.

Ordinance No. 238

With the Per Capita Ordinance approved, I turned my full attention back to the Gaming Commission structure.

I spent months working on that ordinance. Late nights. Long weekends. Drafts and redrafts. I consulted with the commissioners, reviewed ordinances from other tribes, and studied the federal regulations line by line.

In July 1996, I presented Ordinance No. 238 to the Tribal Council.

The ordinance established an independent Cherokee Tribal Gaming Commission, separate from the Tribal Council, separate from the Principal Chief's office. It created independent funding through a percentage of gaming revenue, allocated automatically, not subject to annual appropriation votes. It gave the Commission rule-making authority, licensing authority, and enforcement authority. And it protected commissioners from political interference; they could only be removed for cause, following a formal process with due process protections.

The Tribal Council passed it in July 1996.

Two months later, Phil Hogen at the National Indian Gaming Commission released a memo titled "The Perfect Tribal Gaming Commission." When I read it, I smiled—it described almost exactly what we had just built in Cherokee.

The Second Board

By 1996, we were deep into negotiations with Harrah's Entertainment for a management agreement. And Harrah's made something very clear.

They needed two things to operate successfully: a truly independent regulatory body and a separate business oversight board that could make business decisions based purely on business considerations: no political pressure, no election-year promises, no family favors.

Harrah's had seen what happened when tribal politics interfered with casino operations. They had seen councils micromanaging operations, making decisions based on votes instead of revenue. They knew that model didn't work.

Chief Joyce Dugan liked the idea immediately. So did I.

I drafted the ordinance establishing the Tribal Casino Gaming Enterprise Board in 1996. Five members appointed by the Principal Chief. Independent authority over business operations. No overlap with the Gaming Commission. No interference from the Tribal Council.

The five members of the original TCGE Board were Brenda Ocumma, Eddie Huskey, Hillary Osborne, Jim Smith, and John Houser. Five people with different backgrounds, different skills, but all committed to doing what was best for the Tribe's business interests.

One of the most important decisions we made was establishing independent funding for both boards. We wrote it into the management agreement—a percentage of casino operations revenue would go directly to the Gaming Commission for regulatory activities, and funding for the TCGE Board would be built into the casino's budget structure. Both boards would have the resources they needed to function independently.

The Structure That Lasted

Looking back now, I see those years, 1993 to 1996, as the years when we built the skeleton that all else would hang on.

The casino opened in 1997. The revenue poured in. The Tribe grew wealthier than anyone had imagined. But none of that would have been possible without the structure we built first.

J.L. Burgess, Tom Haigler, and Robert "Birdie" Saunooke served as commissioners for over twenty years. That kind of stability is almost unheard of in tribal government. It happened because we built a system where commissioners were protected from political interference, funding was secure, and authority was clear.

The TCGE Board provided the business oversight that kept operations focused and profitable. Regulatory decisions stayed with the Gaming Commission. Business decisions stayed with the TCGE Board. Each group did what it was supposed to do, and because each group stayed in its lane, the whole system worked.

I've seen tribes where the Tribal Council tries to do it all: regulate the casino, run the casino, oversee compliance, approve every contract. And every single time, it ends badly. Because when you mix regulatory authority, business management, and political power in the same hands, you create conflicts of interest that can't be resolved.

Cherokee didn't make that mistake.

Because of that dual structure, Cherokee became a model. Other tribes studied our ordinances. Federal regulators pointed to Cherokee as an example of how to do it right. State officials trusted us because they saw that we could regulate ourselves.

And the casino grew, from sixty thousand square feet to one of the largest gaming operations in the United States—without ever losing the regulatory standards or business discipline that made it possible.

CHAPTER 10

THE MANAGEMENT AGREEMENT

"Trust, but verify."

— Ronald Reagan

Casino companies came courting the Tribe with chartered jets and lavish parties. My job was to see through the spectacle and evaluate what was real.

◆　◆　◆

AS SOON AS WORD spread that the Tribe was serious about gaming, as soon as the compact was signed and we started soliciting proposals, they came. Not one or two companies. Several. Some were legitimate, experienced casino operators with national reputations. Others were opportunists, investors, and middlemen who saw Cherokee as a chance to cash in on the next big thing in Indian gaming.

The tactics they used ranged from professional to shameless.

Casino Magic was one of the most aggressive. They operated a casino in Biloxi, Mississippi, and they wanted Cherokee badly. Their strategy was simple: impress us with spectacle.

They chartered planes and flew nearly two hundred Tribal members—Council members, Tribal employees, staff, even custodians—to Biloxi for all-expenses-paid weekends. Luxury hotel rooms. Prime rib buffets. Entertainment. Cash handed out "to sample the games."

It was a full-court press designed to win hearts, minds, and votes.

I went on one of those trips. Not because I supported Casino Magic, but because I needed to see what was happening. I needed to understand what Council members were being exposed to, what promises were being made, what pressures were building.

The trip was exactly what I expected: flashy, loud, designed to dazzle.

But one moment from that trip stands out in my memory—less for the spectacle than for the warning it carried.

There was a young Cherokee man on the trip, someone who worked for Tomahawk Gaming, one of the local operations that had been pushing hard for Casino Magic. He was there as part of the Casino Magic delegation, enjoying the perks, soaking up the atmosphere.

And at some point during the night, he drank too much. He got intoxicated, caused a scene at the casino, and was arrested by Biloxi police. They threw him in jail.

The next morning, people came to me in a panic.

"Patrick, you've got to do something. He's in jail. We're supposed to fly home in a few hours. Can you get him out?"

I wasn't there as an attorney handling criminal cases in Mississippi. I was there observing, just like everyone else. But they didn't have anyone else to turn to.

So I went down to the courthouse, worked with local officials, helped secure his release, and got him back to the airport just in time for both of us to catch the flight home. The charges were eventually dropped. The whole thing was handled quietly.

But it stayed with me. Because it was a reminder of what happens when money, influence, and excess mix with politics. Things get messy. And if we weren't careful, Cherokee could end up in a partnership built on spectacle instead of substance.

The Jet to South Dakota

Casino Magic wasn't the only company flying people around.

One day, I found myself on a private jet headed to South Dakota. The trip was organized by Sodak, a division of International Game Technology, one of the largest slot machine manufacturers in the world. Sodak was their Indian gaming arm, and they wanted to show us a new product: a horse-racing game they thought would be perfect for Cherokee.

The jet was small, maybe ten seats, and the passenger list was carefully chosen: Principal Chief Ed Taylor; Chairman William "Bill" Taylor; Dan McCoy; Chief Taylor's wife, Cleo; and me.

It was a quick trip. We flew out, toured the facility, saw the game, and flew back, either the same day or the next. I honestly can't remember if we stayed overnight. It was that fast.

The game itself didn't end up being part of Cherokee's future. But the trip was another reminder of how aggressive the courtship had become. Companies were pulling out all the stops. Private jets. Luxury trips. High-pressure presentations.

Everyone wanted a piece of Cherokee.

Harrah's—The Quiet Professional

And then there was Harrah's.

Harrah's didn't charter planes full of Tribal members. They didn't hand out cash at the casino. They didn't throw lavish parties or pay for weddings.

They comped a few hotel rooms. They provided meals. And that was it. Nothing more.

At first, I didn't fully understand why they were so restrained while their competitors were spending money like water.

But as I learned more about Harrah's—about their operations in Las Vegas and Atlantic City, about the strict regulatory environments they operated under—it became clear.

Harrah's was licensed by the Nevada Gaming Commission and the New Jersey Casino Control Commission, two of the toughest gaming regulators in the world. One misstep, one questionable gift, one envelope of cash, one appearance of impropriety, and they could lose it all. Their licenses. Their reputation. Their entire business.

So they didn't take risks. They didn't try to buy influence. They didn't play games.

They operated with discipline and professionalism.

And I noticed. I respected it. And later, it would matter.

Gridlock

By late fall of 1994, the Tribal Council was deadlocked.

The courtship phase was over. Now it was time to make a decision. And the Council couldn't agree on anything.

Some members pushed hard for Casino Magic. They had been wined and dined, flown to Biloxi, impressed by the spectacle. They believed Casino Magic was the best choice.

Others wanted a merit-based process, a fair, transparent system that would evaluate companies based on their qualifications, not their marketing budgets.

Still others had their own preferred companies, their own alliances, their own reasons for supporting one bidder over another.

The result was paralysis. Meetings stalled. Votes failed. The Council lost quorum. Chairman Bill Taylor refused to call votes without a clear process in place. And the entire government drifted toward dysfunction.

Meanwhile, the pressure was relentless. Phones rang at all hours. Council members were pulled aside for private conversations. Accusations flew, about favoritism, about influence, about who was getting what from whom.

The atmosphere inside the Council House was toxic. Hope mixed with suspicion. Ambition mixed with fear. Everyone knew this decision would shape the Tribe's future for decades. And no one wanted to be the person who made the wrong choice.

Something had to break the deadlock.

And during the quiet days between Christmas and New Year's, I decided to try.

Resolution 370

I didn't go home much during the holidays that year.

Cyndi understood. She always did. She was, and is, a great partner, a great mother. She took care of the kids, kept the house running, and gave me the space I needed to work.

I tried to keep work at the office. I didn't want to bring the stress, the late nights, the endless legal drafts into our home. I wanted home to be home—a place where I could be a husband and a father, not just a lawyer drowning in Tribal politics.

So I stayed at the office. Late into the night. Through the holidays. Alone in the Council House with a stack of legal pads, the compact, the proposals from every company, and the weight of knowing that if I didn't find a solution, the Tribe might never move forward.

And somewhere in those quiet hours, the answer came to me.

A process. A fair, structured, merit-based process that would remove politics from the equation and force companies to prove they could deliver.

I drafted a resolution, assigned as Resolution 370 (1995).

The concept was straightforward. The Tribal Council would rank all the companies: first, second, third. Then we would negotiate exclusively with the top-ranked company for thirty days. During that window, the company had to produce two things: a $100 million letter of credit, irrevocable and guaranteed, and an irrevocable Letter of Intent proving financial capacity.

If they failed to meet the requirements, we would automatically move to the second-ranked company. No need to go back to the Council. No new vote. No political battles. If the second company failed, we'd move to the third. If all three failed, we'd reevaluate the criteria and start over.

It was brilliant in its simplicity.

It gave the Council the political cover to vote for their preferred company. But it also created objective standards that couldn't be gamed or manipulated. If a company couldn't produce the financing, they were out. Automatically. No exceptions.

I drafted the resolution over the Christmas holidays. When it was done, I called Chairman Bill Taylor and explained the concept. Walked him through the process. Answered his questions.

He immediately saw its value.

"This could work," he said. "This could actually get us unstuck."

I also called Ben Bridgers, even though he was home recovering, even though I hated bothering him during the holidays. I needed to know if the idea was legally solid.

"Ben," I said, "I think I have a way forward. But I need you to tell me if it's sound."

I explained the concept.

There was a long pause on the other end of the line.

Then Ben said, "Yes. Definitely. Get it drafted for when the Council reconvenes in January. We'll put it to a vote."

On January 5, 1995, the Tribal Council passed Resolution 370. Only three members opposed it.

Cherokee finally had a clear path forward.

Casino Magic Fails

The vote wasn't even close.

When the Council ranked the companies, Casino Magic came in first. Their marketing had worked. Their trips to Biloxi had paid off. They had the votes.

And under Resolution 370, that meant we would negotiate exclusively with Casino Magic for the next thirty days. All they had to do was produce the financing.

They couldn't.

Within days, maybe a week, Casino Magic showed they did not have the financial capacity to meet the Tribe's requirements. No $100 million letter of credit. No irrevocable financing guarantee. No proof they could actually build and operate a casino at the scale Cherokee needed.

The flashiest bidder in the room collapsed under the weight of real standards.

On February 4 or 5, 1995, we reported to the Council that Casino Magic had failed to meet the requirements. Under Resolution 370, we automatically moved to the second-ranked company.

Harrah's.

And from the first conversation, Harrah's was ready.

They didn't hesitate. They didn't complain. They didn't ask for more time. They got to work.

Within the thirty-day window, they produced everything we asked for: the full $100 million letter of credit, irrevocable financing guarantees, proof of operational capacity, and regulatory credentials from Nevada and New Jersey.

They weren't just bidding. They were ready to build.

Loan Security and Collateral

In a move that surprised Harrah's, the Tribe decided to set, as a baseline, all of the best provisions of the Casino Magic proposal and all the best provisions of Harrah's proposal. The thirty-day window was open and time was of the essence. Harrah's was, at the time, the only publicly traded gaming company with investment-grade debt. It's offer on the development agreement, in line with its other agreements in Indian Country, provided that the Tribe would borrow directly from whatever bank was mutually agreed upon, all moneys the two parties agreed was needed on a completely unsecured basis. The debt would be secured by Harrah's guaranty, which allowed the Tribe to borrow at the same interest rate available to Harrah's without markup. In one fell swoop, the Tribe had access to all the money it would need to develop and open its casino at borrowing rates unavailable to anyone other than those with the country's best credit rating.

It took a lot of explaining to the Tribal members before they understood that the Tribe had no real monetary risk as, in case of failure, the bank would get its money back from Harrah's and the Tribe had limited Harrah's source of recovery from the Tribe for the amounts it guaranteed only to net revenues from gaming.

In March 1995, I drafted Resolution 427—the formal authorization of the development and management agreements with Harrah's, operating under the name Promus Companies at the time.

There was grumbling from the Casino Magic supporters. Some Council members were still unhappy. But the process had been followed. The standards had been met. The vote was clear.

The Tribal Council passed Resolution 427.

For a moment, just a brief, hopeful moment, it felt like the hardest part was behind us.

The Veto

Then the floor dropped.

I was in the Council House when word came through. Someone walked into the room, I don't remember who, and said, "Chief Taylor vetoed Resolution 427."

I stood there, not quite processing what I had just heard.

"He did what?"

"Vetoed it. The whole thing. It's dead."

Without warning. Without consultation. Without any indication it was coming. Principal Chief Ed Taylor had vetoed the management agreement with Harrah's.

I walked outside and stood in the parking lot, trying to make sense of it. The air was cold. The mountains in the distance looked gray and indifferent.

Why would he do this?

Chief Taylor had been one of the strongest advocates for gaming. He had fought for the compact. He had pushed for economic development. He had championed the idea that Cherokee could build its own future.

And now, after all the work, after all the negotiations, after Resolution 370 had created a fair process and Harrah's had met every requirement, he was killing it.

With a veto. No explanation. No amendments. No path forward.

Just: No.

The community was stunned. Council members were furious. Rumors exploded overnight. Was it outside pressure? Political resentment? A breakdown in communication? Something deeper?

To this day, only a few people know for certain.

But what everyone knew was this: The Tribe was now split cleanly in two. And the political foundation we had been trying to build was cracking.

The Override

Chairman Bill Taylor didn't hesitate.

He reconvened the Council immediately. The agenda was clear: Vote to override the veto.

I was in the room that day. The Council House was packed—Council members, staff, community members who had heard what was happening and come to witness it. The air was thick with tension, with anger, with the weight of everything that hung in the balance.

The debate was intense. People spoke with passion, with frustration, with the knowledge that whatever happened in this room would shape the Tribe's future for decades.

One Council member, I won't name him but his voice still echoes in my memory, stood up and said, "We have worked too hard to let this die. We have followed the process. We have done everything right. And I will not let one veto undo what this Council has built."

Another member defended the Chief. "He has his reasons," she said. "We should respect the office, even if we disagree with the decision."

But the momentum in the room was clear. Too many people had invested too much. Too many hopes were riding on this moment. Too much was at stake.

When the vote came, the Council overrode the veto.

I don't remember the exact count. But I remember the feeling in the room when it was done. Relief. Exhaustion. And the quiet knowledge that something had broken that could not be repaired.

The Aftermath

The veto override didn't end the chaos. If anything, it intensified it.

Chief Taylor was angry that his veto had been overturned. The Council was angry that he had issued it in the first place. Accusations flew. Investigations were launched. Political alliances fractured.

Over the next few months, we finalized the contract with Harrah's. It was signed in July 1995.

But the damage to Cherokee's government was already done.

The primary election, the first in Cherokee history, reshaped the political landscape. Joyce Dugan was elected as the first woman Principal Chief.

And in September 1995, just two weeks before Chief Taylor's term was set to end, the Tribal Council voted to impeach him.

To this day, I believe that impeachment was unnecessary. He had already lost the election. He had two weeks left in office. The new administration was ready to take over.

But the Council insisted on moving forward.

And on September 15, 1995, Principal Chief Ed Taylor became the first—and at that time, only—Principal Chief in Cherokee history to be impeached.

The Lesson

Through all of it—the negotiations, the gridlock, the veto, the override, the impeachment—I kept thinking about my mother.

With Ben gone, I had to live by her lesson every single day. And somehow, it was enough.

The Choice That Defined Us

Looking back now, the management agreement battle was about far more than choosing a casino partner.

If Cherokee had chosen Casino Magic, if we had let the spectacle

win, our future would have unfolded very differently. But we chose
Harrah's. We chose the company that refused to buy votes. We chose
integrity.

And that choice built everything that came after.

CHAPTER 11

1995: THE YEAR EVERYTHING CHANGED

"There are decades where nothing happens; and there are weeks where decades happen."

— Vladimir Lenin

Five months from compact signing to machines on the floor—a timeline gaming professionals today don't believe. Sometimes history compresses, and 1995 was that year.

◆ ◆ ◆

THE COMPACT WAS SIGNED on August 11, 1994. Five months later, we had machines running.

People who work in gaming regulation today hear that timeline and don't believe it. Standing up a Certification Commission, classifying games, securing compliant equipment, building a count room, installing surveillance, hiring staff, and opening the doors to a legal Tribal casino, all of it from scratch, all of it over the holidays, in five months.

But that's what we did.

The compact required a Certification Commission—an independent body authorized under state law to classify which games could be offered. The chairman had to be mutually agreed upon with the state. The state had its own representative on the Commission. It was designed to be a legitimate, independent regulatory process, and we built it that way from the start.

The Commission held its first meeting in December 1994. The central question was whether video poker met the compact's standard for authorized games—games "involving the use of skill or dexterity."

That language was critical. The prior state law had permitted only games "based on" skill or dexterity—a much higher bar. The compact language was different: "involving the use of." It didn't specify how much skill or dexterity had to be involved. Just that the game had to involve some.

And video poker did.

The reasoning was straightforward. In video poker, you're dealt a hand. You decide what to hold and what to discard. Those decisions matter. A player who understands the game—who knows the odds, who recognizes the best options for a winning hand—is going to do better than someone pressing buttons at random. It's not pure chance. Skill is involved.

One person who was critical to establishing that point was James Maida, the founder and president of Gaming Laboratory International (GLI) out of New Jersey. Maida was the gold standard in the industry for certifying gaming equipment and the software that ran it. His testimony and certification letters carried weight—not just with our commission, but with regulators nationwide—commercial as well as in Indian Country.

The commission heard the testimony, reviewed the evidence, and in early December 1994 issued orders classifying video poker as meeting the compact's criteria.

Now we needed machines.

We had two sources—both confiscated from the illegal operations we'd shut down. Cherokee Bingo had yielded thirty-eight machines. TeePee Village Casino had given us about seventy-six. But the TeePee Village machines were noncompliant—no shockproof cabinets, didn't meet NIGC regulations or our own standards for patron safety. They weren't operable under any legitimate regulatory framework.

The thirty-eight machines from Cherokee Bingo, however, were compliant.

We still had them in compound. We entered an agreement with the owners of those machines, made arrangements to operate them legally, and moved them over to the Tribal bingo hall.

The First Tribal Casino

The bingo hall had a small side entrance that opened into a nonsmoking area—just large enough to hold the thirty-eight machines. That was our casino.

Through the holiday period of 1994, we set up everything. Count room. Surveillance. Central reporting system. Procedures for the drop, the count, all the regulatory requirements. A small staff to run the operation.

All of this happening while we were simultaneously working on the management agreement—ranking the companies, dealing with Casino Magic, watching that whole process unfold. It was all running at the same time.

On January 25, 1995, we opened the doors.

We chose a midweek opening deliberately—a soft opening to avoid weekend traffic and give us time to get all thirty-eight machines operational. We didn't run twenty-four hours. Daytime through early evening only.

That first morning, at ten o'clock, we had fifteen machines ready. Fifteen. That's all we had hooked up to the central reporting system with full surveillance in place.

The first person through the door was Teresa McCoy. She walked in with her quarters in hand, sat down at a machine, and placed the first legal bet in the history of Cherokee tribal gaming.

We operated until eight o'clock that evening. Then we closed the doors, practiced the drop, ran the count room procedures on whatever had come in that first day.

We made several thousand dollars.

The next day, we had twenty-five machines running. By the third day, all thirty-eight were in operation.

The response was overwhelming. Within weeks, we were ordering new machines. By midsummer of 1995, we moved bingo out of that building, across the road into a small convention center, and took over the entire bingo hall for casino operations.

By the end of 1995, we had close to two hundred machines running. By the end of 1996, three hundred. And in November 1997, we opened the permanent facility under the Harrah's management agreement and transferred all the equipment we'd purchased for the Tribal casino into that new operation.

But all of that growth came later. First, we had to survive.

The State's Challenge

Less than two weeks after we opened, the state sent a letter ordering us to cease all gaming activities.

Their position was that our operations were not compliant under the compact and violated state law. They didn't believe video poker qualified.

The timing wasn't a coincidence. I think it shocked people in Raleigh that we were up and running so fast. The compact had been signed in August. By January, we had machines on the floor, a regulatory commission in place, and revenue coming in. They hadn't expected that.

The legal issue came down to the same distinction the Certification Commission had already addressed—"based on" versus "involving the use of."

There was a particular individual who had lost a case dealing with video poker under the prior state law—the old standard that required games to be "based on" skill or dexterity. Under that standard, video poker didn't qualify. But our compact wasn't written under that standard. The compact authorized games "involving the use of" skill or dexterity.

That distinction was everything.

When the state's letter arrived, we moved immediately. I called an emergency assembly of the Certification Commission.

We brought everyone back. We got James Maida back down from New Jersey. We re-heard the testimony. We walked through the legal analysis again—this time with a specific eye toward the state law question, addressing point by point why these games were authorized under the compact as signed.

The commission reached unanimous agreement. All members—including the state's own representative, sitting on an independent body established under state law with a mutually agreed chairman—found that the games were valid under the compact.

We wrote it up in a full legal response and sent it to the state.

They accepted it.

And we never heard another word about it.

No follow-up letter. No legal challenge. No second attempt to shut us down. The process we had built—the independent commission, the legal framework, the regulatory structure—had held under pressure on its very first test.

We'd been open less than a month, and we'd already survived the one thing that could have ended it all before it started.

The importance of the credibility of the Commission and GLI to the success of the casino cannot be understated. I don't think any game ever approved for play was by less than unanimous vote of the Commission. Likewise those games that were not approved.

The Saturday Meeting

The office was quiet that Saturday morning.

January light filtered through the window overlooking the parking lot on the first floor of Ben Bridgers's law office in Sylva. I had the space to myself, the office was closed on weekends, and the building carried that particular silence that only comes when no one else is around.

I was working on gaming matters. Always gaming matters in those days. Drafting regulations, reviewing contracts, building the legal framework that would have to hold under pressure we couldn't yet fully imagine.

The phone rang.

"Patrick, it's Bill. What are you doing?"

William "Bill" Taylor from Big Cove, Chairman of Tribal Council. The man who had held the government together through the most chaotic year in Cherokee's modern history.

"I'm at the office," I said.

"Mind if I stop by? I need to talk to you about something."

"Sure. Come on over."

When Bill walked through the door twenty minutes later, I could see it immediately: He had a lot on his mind.

It was January, cold enough that he wore his usual jacket, the kind he always wore during winter Council sessions. But it wasn't the cold that made him look tense. It was something else.

Bill Taylor was a serious man. Always had been. He didn't waste time on small talk, didn't joke around much, didn't soften hard truths with pleasantries. When Bill had something to say, he said it. When he saw a problem, he moved to fix it.

That's what made him effective as chairman. And that's what made him dangerous to the status quo.

He sat down across from me, his expression carrying the weight of concern, not panic, but the steady, grinding worry of a man who could see trouble coming and couldn't figure out how to stop it.

"I'm worried about the election," he said.

I nodded. "A lot of people are."

"It's the system," he continued. "The way it works now, it's not fair. You can have ten candidates running for Chief. Somebody can pay filing fees for people just to split the vote. The incumbent only needs to be the top vote-getter, even if that's twenty percent. Somebody with real support could finish second or third and never get a fair shot."

He wasn't wrong.

Cherokee's election system at that time was winner-take-all. No runoffs. No primaries. Just one election in September, and whoever got the most votes won, even if "the most" was barely a plurality.

It was a system ripe for manipulation.

And Bill Taylor, sharp, strategic, always thinking three moves ahead, could see exactly how it would play out.

"If we could just get it down to two people," he said, leaning forward. "Head-to-head. Then you'd see who really has the support of the people. No vote-splitting. No games. Just a clear choice."

I listened.

"What if we created a primary?" he asked. "Like the state does. Like the federal system. What if we had an election in June to narrow it down to two candidates, and then the general election in September?"

The idea hung in the air between us.

It made sense. It was fair. It would force candidates to build real coalitions instead of just hoping the vote split the right way. And, though neither of us said it out loud, it would give Bill Taylor a fighting chance to beat Ed Taylor in a head-to-head race.

"I think you should draft it," Bill said. "An ordinance creating a primary election. June for the primary. September for the general. Top two vote-getters in the Chief and Vice Chief races advance. Top four in the Council races advance."

I nodded slowly, already turning the structure over in my mind.

"It's a good system," I said. "Cleaner. Fairer."

"Will you do it?"

"Yeah," I said. "I'll draft it."

Bill stood up, shook my hand, and walked back out into the cold January afternoon.

And I sat back down at my desk and started writing the ordinance that would create Cherokee's first primary election.

What Bill Taylor didn't count on, what neither of us fully anticipated, was that the system he created would be the very system that ended his political career.

The Kroll Investigation

While I was drafting the primary election ordinance, another storm was building across Cherokee.

Chairman Bill Taylor, using contacts he had developed through his political work in Washington, DC, had brought in Kroll Associates, a high-powered investigative firm used by Fortune 500 companies and major government agencies.

Their mandate was clear: Investigate issues surrounding Chief Taylor's office.

There were suspicions. Rumors. Whispers that had been circulating for months about the use of government resources, government travel, government property. Questions about why Chief Taylor had vetoed the Harrah's management agreement. Questions about who was influencing decisions behind the scenes.

The Kroll investigation was designed to get answers.

But what it created, more than anything, was fear.

I didn't deal directly with the investigators. I didn't testify. I didn't provide documents. My role was legal counsel to the Tribe, not a participant in the investigation.

But I saw the effects.

People were terrified.

Cherokee is a small community. Everyone knows everyone. And when outside investigators, men in black suits carrying briefcases and legal pads, start showing up unannounced to ask questions, the fear spreads like smoke through timber.

Tribal employees were approached. Questioned. Asked about what they had seen, what they had heard, what they had been asked to do. I heard about it in whispers. In hallways. In careful conversations where people looked over their shoulders before speaking.

One custodian—a man who had worked closely with Chief Taylor, doing whatever tasks were asked of him—became so anxious during the investigation that he had to go to the hospital and be treated for his nerves.

That's how heavy the atmosphere was.

When employees came to me asking what to do, my answer was always the same: "Be truthful. Cooperate. Things will be fine."

I believed that. I still do.

But the truth is, people weren't just scared of the investigation. They were scared of the politics.

There's been a fear of politics on the Qualla Boundary for as long as I can remember. A fear of saying the wrong thing, supporting the wrong person, being on the wrong side when power shifts. People were scared of losing their jobs. Scared of retaliation. Scared of being caught in the middle of something they didn't fully understand.

That fear, born into the atmosphere here, constant and heavy, never fully goes away.

And in the winter and spring of 1994–1995, it was everywhere.

The Primary

The Tribal Council passed the primary election ordinance in early 1995.

It was exactly what Bill Taylor had asked for: a primary election in June to narrow the field, then the general election in September as usual. Top two vote-getters in Chief and Vice Chief races advance. Top four vote-getters in the Council races advance.

Clean. Fair. Democratic.

A system designed to prevent vote-splitting and ensure that whoever won had real, head-to-head support from the people.

Bill Taylor believed, genuinely believed, that if he could stand head-to-head against Ed Taylor, he would win. The people would see the choice clearly. The reformer versus the incumbent. The future versus the past. And Bill would prevail.

I was at the Council House on primary election night, watching the results come in.

And when the numbers became clear, I felt something I didn't expect: surprise and not-surprise, both at the same time.

Bill Taylor had come in third place.

Ed Taylor finished first. Joyce Dugan, an educator, a school administrator with years of experience at Cherokee Central Schools, smart, credentialed, and well-respected, finished second.

Bill Taylor, the man who had created the primary system, was eliminated by it.

He would not advance to the general election for Chief. And because he had stepped out of the legislative race to run for the executive seat, he wouldn't be advancing to the Council ballot either.

His political career was over.

I was surprised, because Bill was a strong leader, and I knew he had support.

But I wasn't surprised, because I also knew the landscape.

Joyce Dugan was coming on strong. People were excited about her. The possibility of electing the first woman Chief in Cherokee history carried real energy.

And Bill had made enemies. Not out of malice. But out of necessity.

As chairman, Bill had ruled with authority. He held tight reins on the Council. He didn't let meetings drift into chaos. He didn't let political gamesmanship derail important business.

That made him effective. It also made him unpopular.

Council members who had been accustomed to operating with more freedom resented his discipline. Constituents who wanted favors or special treatment found him unmovable. And in a small community where personal relationships shape politics as much as policy, those resentments accumulate.

Bill had a tough election ahead of him no matter what. But I don't think he expected to be eliminated in the primary he himself had created.

To his credit, Bill handled it with grace. He was disappointed, of course he was. But he didn't lash out. He didn't blame the system. He didn't undermine the process.

Instead, he did what statesmen do: He worked to create a smoother transition for the new administration. He helped ensure that whoever won in September would inherit a functioning government. He stayed professional, steady, honorable, right up until his final day as chairman.

That's the Bill Taylor I remember. A serious man who believed in good government. A reformer who perhaps pushed too hard, too fast, and paid the political price. Bill passed away on October 1, 2002. A man of integrity to the end.

The General Election

The general election in September 1995 was historic.

Ed Taylor versus Joyce Dugan. Head-to-head. Just like the system was designed.

And Joyce Dugan won.

I didn't know Joyce well before the election. I knew of her; everyone in Cherokee knew of her. She had spent years working at Cherokee Central Schools as an administrator. She was intelligent, educated, respected.

But I hadn't worked closely with her. Our paths hadn't crossed much in my legal work for the Tribe.

Still, I could see why people were drawn to her candidacy. She campaigned on structure, on accountability, on openness. She talked about running the government in a better fashion, more honest, more transparent, more responsible with the people's money and resources.

She wasn't running against Ed Taylor as much as she was running toward a vision of what Cherokee government could be.

And the people responded.

On election night, September 1995, there was a celebration at Joyce's house. I heard about it later, people gathering in her neighborhood, the energy of history being made, the excitement of electing the first woman Principal Chief in the history of the Eastern Band of Cherokee Indians.

I wasn't there. I chose, as always, to stay out of election night events. My job required neutrality. I needed to be able to serve whoever won, without the perception that I had taken sides.

But I felt the significance of the moment even from a distance. Something was shifting. Not just in who held power. But in what the people expected from their government.

And the shift went deeper than the Chief's race.

Out of twelve Council seats up for election, ten flipped. Out of fourteen total elected seats—Chief, Vice Chief, and twelve Council members—eleven changed hands.

The only survivors were Gerard Parker as Vice Chief, Teresa McCoy from Big Cove, and Marian Teesateskie from Painttown.

Everyone else, gone.

It was the largest political turnover in modern Cherokee history.

Looking back now, I understand why. The year 1995 had been too much. Too much chaos. Too much uncertainty. Too much talk about gaming companies and management agreements and leather jackets and paid-for weddings and free trips and money flowing in ways people didn't understand.

The compact had been signed. The future was opening. But the people had lost faith in the leaders who had brought them to that moment.

They wanted a clean slate. They wanted to believe that the new era would be different.

So they voted out nearly everyone and started over.

September 15, 1995

Between the September general election and the first Monday in October, when the new administration would be sworn in, there was about a month for the outgoing Council to wrap up unfinished business.

One piece of that unfinished business was whether to hold an impeachment vote against Principal Chief Ed Taylor.

Most people assumed the impeachment would move forward only if Chief Taylor won reelection. If he lost, which he did, the assumption was that the matter would die on the vine.

Why impeach a man who had already been defeated by the voters and had less than a month left in office?

But there was energy around it. Excitement. A large push to "close the chapter" and show the people that the old politics were over.

And so, on September 15, 1995, the Tribal Council convened to vote on the impeachment and removal of Principal Chief Jonathan L. "Ed" Taylor.

I was present in the Council Chambers that day.

The room was the same one I had sat in hundreds of times—the rectangular chamber with the open end where the podium stands, the chairman seated at the far end, the Council members arranged in what we call "the horseshoe."

But the atmosphere was different. Somber. Heavy. Almost angry.

The previous weeks had been full of heated arguments about the Kroll investigation findings. There were reports about Tribal employees doing private work for the Chief—mowing grass, running errands—small things that weren't criminal but still crossed ethical lines.

Nothing super serious in the grand scheme of things. But enough to fuel the narrative that it was time for accountability.

Chief Taylor came into the Council Chambers that day and did something unexpected.

Before the proceedings even started, he tendered his resignation.

He stood at the podium and basically told the Council: Don't do this. I'll resign. I have two weeks left anyway. Let it end here.

It was an offer of peace. A way out. A chance to avoid the spectacle of impeachment and let him leave with whatever dignity remained.

But the Council refused.

Not with sympathy. Not with reluctance. With anger.

They wanted him to answer for what he had done. They wanted to show the people that they were starting on a clean foot, that the old politics were finished, that there would be accountability.

So they refused his resignation.

And Chief Taylor, defeated, exhausted, humiliated, left the Chambers.

The vote happened in his absence.

I don't remember the exact count, but I believe it was unanimous or close to it.

The room was tense. The air felt thick. This wasn't a careful deliberation. This was a ritual. A performance. A statement being made.

And when the vote was called, it was over in minutes.

Principal Chief Jonathan L. "Ed" Taylor was impeached and removed from office.

Immediately after the vote, they brought in Vice Chief Gerard Parker. He stood at the podium, the same podium where Ed Taylor had stood just minutes before, and was sworn in as Acting Principal Chief.

The Council ordered the Tribal marshal to inform Chief Taylor that he needed to collect his things and leave the Council House. Leave his office. Turn over the keys.

It was done.

People left the Chambers quietly. There was no celebration. No cheering. Just a somber, heavy silence.

I walked out into the late-afternoon light and felt something I couldn't quite name at the time. Sadness, yes. But also something darker.

A sense that what had just happened was unnecessary. Mean-spirited.

Chief Taylor had already been defeated by the voters. He had already offered to resign. He had two weeks left in office.

But that wasn't enough.

The hunt was still on. The crowd had taken over. And sometimes, I don't fully understand why, human nature seems to enjoy that kind of thing. The chase. The fall. The final blow.

I didn't speak to Ed Taylor in those final two weeks before Joyce Dugan took office. It would be months, maybe even a few years, before I saw him again.

When I did, we were friendly. We still are.

I still believe he did a lot for the Tribe. I still believe he was caught up in the atmosphere of that time, just like everyone else.

But I also believe the impeachment was wrong.

He made mistakes.

But kicking someone when they're already down doesn't serve justice. It serves something else. Something Cherokee should have learned to resist.

The First Per Cap

While the political upheaval of 1995 played out in the Council Chambers and at the ballot box, something quieter was happening in the Finance Office.

Revenue was coming in.

The credit for pushing that ordinance through the Council belongs to Dan McCoy, who championed it from the floor and never let it die. Without his persistence, the checks never would have gone out.

From January 25 forward—from those first fifteen machines through the expansion to thirty-eight, then to one hundred, then to two hundred by year's end—money was flowing into Tribal accounts for the first time from legal gaming operations. We'd drafted the Per Capita Ordinance and gotten it approved, establishing the framework for distributing gaming revenue directly to enrolled members of the Eastern Band.

The credit for pushing that ordinance through the Council belongs to Dan McCoy, who championed it from the floor and never let it die. Without his persistence, the checks never would have gone out.

But having an ordinance on paper and actually getting checks into people's hands are two different things.

Cyndi was working in the Tribal Finance Office at the time, running the front office. She was assigned the job of putting together the distribution list—compiling the names, verifying enrollment, making sure every eligible member of the Tribe was accounted for.

It was detailed work. Painstaking work. The kind of work that doesn't make headlines but makes everything else possible.

In December 1995, the first per capita checks went out.

Five hundred and ninety-five dollars.

That was the number. The first per cap check in the history of the Eastern Band of Cherokee Indians: $595, drawn from $56 million in gaming revenue generated in our first year of legal operations.

Five hundred and ninety-five dollars doesn't sound like much today—not when you know what came after, not when you've seen what Cherokee gaming grew into. But in December 1995, for families on the Qualla Boundary, that check meant something. It meant groceries. It meant a light bill getting paid. It meant Christmas presents for children who might not have had any otherwise.

It meant the promise was real.

All of it—the compact, the Certification Commission, the fifteen machines on opening day, the fight with the state, the management agreement battles, the political chaos—all of it had led to this: a check in the mail with your name on it, proof that the Tribe's future was changing.

And it was just the beginning.

CHAPTER 12

THE FIRST INAUGURATION

"We do not inherit the earth from our ancestors; we borrow it from our children."

— Native American Proverb

Joyce Dugan's inauguration was the first public ceremony for a Cherokee Principal Chief. She understood that leadership is stewardship, not ownership.

◆ ◆ ◆

OCTOBER 1995 ARRIVED WITH the turning of leaves and the turning of power.

For the first time in Cherokee's modern history, the swearing-in of a new Principal Chief would not happen quietly inside the Council Chambers with a handful of family members holding a Bible and a judge administering the oath.

This time would be different.

Joyce Dugan—the first woman elected Principal Chief of the Eastern Band of Cherokee Indians, had decided that the moment deserved ceremony, public witness, and celebration.

She called it an inauguration. And she meant it.

In the past, what we called a "swearing-in" was exactly that: a functional, almost private event held inside the Council House. The new Chief or Council member would stand at the podium in front of the horseshoe, raise their right hand, take the oath, and sit down.

Family attended. A few friends. Maybe a handful of employees.

No speeches. No program. No tents or stages or public gathering.

Just the oath, the handshake, and the work beginning immediately.

But Joyce understood something the Tribe had forgotten: Transitions matter. Symbols matter. The people deserve to witness the peaceful transfer of power.

So on the first Monday in October 1995, the Tribe gathered at the ceremonial grounds directly across from the Council House, a large, open outdoor area with an amphitheater-style setup.

Large tents were pitched to provide shade and shelter. Food was prepared for the public. A formal program was printed with the order of speeches, prayers, and the administration of the oath.

It felt different. Bigger. More public. And right.

Joyce Dugan was signaling to the Tribe that this administration would operate differently, more transparent, more accountable, more connected to the people.

I was there that day, standing in the crowd with everyone else. I wasn't invited to take part in the ceremony. I had no role on the stage. I was simply another Tribal member watching history unfold.

And I was fine with that.

Because I understood what was happening. The old era—the era of backroom deals, vetoes, investigations, and impeachment—was ending. A new era was beginning.

And whether I had a role in it or not, I was witnessing something important.

The New Structure

One of Joyce Dugan's first major decisions was structural.

She eliminated the position of Tribal attorney, the outside legal counsel structure that had existed for decades, and replaced it with an in-house Attorney General position.

It was a bold move.

The Tribal attorney system had worked for decades. Ben Bridgers had served in that role with distinction. I had stepped into it when Ben fell ill, and I had done my best to hold the government together through the most turbulent year in Cherokee's modern history.

But Joyce wanted something different. She wanted legal counsel that answered directly to the Chief, operated inside the government structure, and functioned more like a cabinet position.

It made sense.

And when she appointed Brad Letts as the Tribe's first attorney general, I thought it was a good choice. Brad was sharp. Intelligent. Thoughtful. I wondered if the new structure would work—moving from an independent outside counsel model to an internal AG model always carries risks.

But I supported the concept. And I believed Brad would do the job well.

For me, the transition was smooth but strange.

I had spent the better part of a year serving as the Tribe's primary legal counsel—handling everything from gaming regulations to impeachment proceedings to federal negotiations to Tribal Council legislation, hospital contracts, school board matters, and housing law. I had to handle it all. Alone.

Now, that role was ending.

The new administration wanted a new structure.

And that was their right.

I had set up a small office in the old log cabin beside the Council Chambers. The cabin had originally served as the office for the Save the Children program. I had later turned it into a legal aid service office, and it would eventually become the original office for the Tribal Gaming Commission before we moved to the Frontier Shopping Center. Years later, the log cabin was taken over as the TOP office, and though it burned and was rebuilt, it still serves as the TOP office today.

As the new attorney general's office took shape, I handed over most of the ongoing legal work, case files, contracts, pending matters, and institutional knowledge.

It wasn't dramatic. It wasn't painful. It was just the natural transition that happens when administrations change.

By the holidays that year, most of my responsibilities had already been transferred.

And I was preparing for what came next.

The Opportunity

In the fall of 1995—while the political chaos of the impeachment and election swirled around Cherokee—the Tribal Gaming Commission had quietly begun advertising for a position that had never existed before: executive director of the Cherokee Tribal Gaming Commission.

The ordinances I had drafted earlier that year had created the role. But no one had ever filled it.

The position remained open through the election, through the transition, through the uncertainty of what the new administration would bring.

And in late 1995, after Joyce Dugan took office, the Commission formally opened the application process.

I applied. So did three others.

I wasn't sure what to expect.

Ben Bridgers, my mentor, the man who had taught me nearly everything I knew about tribal law, did not want me to apply.

He wanted me to stay in private practice with him. He believed I could build a better legal career by staying outside the tribal government structure, representing clients, handling a variety of cases, and maintaining independence.

He thought stepping into the executive director role would limit my options. Narrow my focus. Tie me to one institution for years.

And in a way, he was right.

But I saw something different.

I saw the future of the Tribe. I saw that gaming, if done right, if regulated with integrity, if built on a foundation of law and discipline—could transform Cherokee in ways we couldn't yet imagine.

And I saw that the person who led the Gaming Commission would play a defining role in that transformation.

I wanted that role. Not for power. Not for prestige. But because I knew I could do it well. And because I believed it mattered more than anything else I could do.

Chief Dugan didn't encourage me to apply. She didn't discourage me either. She simply let the Commission make the decision independently, exactly as the system was designed.

But the three gaming commissioners, J.L. Burgess, Tom Haigler, and Robert "Birdie" Saunooke, wanted me to apply.

They had worked with me for years. They knew my knowledge of IGRA, the compact, the regulations, the history. They knew I understood the legal framework better than anyone else available.

And they trusted me.

The application process was formal. Full interviews. Written materials. Evaluation of qualifications. The other candidates were strong.

Serious. Qualified.

But I had one advantage no one else could match: I had been there from the beginning.

I had drafted the ordinances. I had written the compact language. I had built the regulatory framework from scratch. I knew the systems inside and out, not because I had studied them, but because I had created them.

When the Commission finished their deliberations, they informed me verbally first, then officially by letter: I had been selected as the first executive director of the Cherokee Tribal Gaming Commission.

I called Cyndi that evening and told her.

She was happy—she knew it meant I would be closer to home.

Ben's office in Sylva had been a twenty to thirty-minute drive each way, every day. Long hours, time away from the family, the wear of constant travel.

Now, I would be working right here on the Boundary. Closer to home. Closer to the people. Doing work that mattered more than any courtroom case ever could.

The First Day

My first day as executive director came in early 1996.

The office wasn't glamorous.

We had leased space in the Frontier Shopping Center—an old bank building that had sat empty for a while. The Gaming Commission assumed the lease, and I moved in with nothing but a desk, a phone, and the enormous responsibility of building a regulatory system that didn't yet exist.

There was no staff. No policies. No manuals. No one to train me, because no one had ever done this job before.

Just me, an empty office, and the knowledge that when Harrah's Cherokee Casino opened its doors on November 13, 1997, everything we built in the next eighteen months would determine whether Cherokee gaming succeeded or failed.

The first tasks were basic but critical.

I had to organize the office, set up filing systems, establish procedures, create a workspace that could handle the volume of work coming.

I needed to find an assistant, someone who could manage the administrative load, handle correspondence, keep the office running while I focused on building the regulatory infrastructure.

I had to draft job descriptions for all the positions we would need: licensing clerks to process background investigations, gaming agents to monitor the casino floor, compliance officers to enforce standards, support staff to handle daily operations. Every position had to be defined, advertised, and filled before the casino opened.

And I had to write the regulations, internal control standards, licensing procedures, surveillance protocols, cash-handling rules, jackpot procedures, vendor requirements. Every system had to be documented, approved, and ready to enforce.

People sometimes ask me what those early months felt like.

The answer is simple: overwhelming, exciting, and absolutely essential.

I was building the backbone of Cherokee gaming from nothing. No blueprint to follow. No predecessor to call for advice. No model to copy.

Just federal law, best practices from other jurisdictions, and the knowledge that if I got this wrong, the consequences would be catastrophic.

The Work Before the Doors Opened

Most people think the casino's story began on opening night in November 1997.

But the real story began two years earlier.

Because before a single guest could walk through those doors, before a single slot machine could be played, before a single dollar could be wagered—we had to build the regulatory foundation that would make it all possible.

Under NIGC regulations, no casino can operate without a facility license issued by the Tribal Gaming Regulatory Authority. That meant the Cherokee Tribal Gaming Commission had to certify that the building met all safety codes, surveillance systems were adequate, security protocols were in place, emergency procedures were established, fire safety standards were met, and the facility was structurally sound and safe for public use.

We couldn't just rubber-stamp it. We had to inspect. Verify. Document. Test. Every system. Every camera. Every exit. Every alarm.

And if something wasn't right, we had the authority, and the responsibility, to delay the opening until it was fixed.

Harrah's was hiring fast. Dealers, cage cashiers, security officers, housekeeping staff, restaurant workers, slot technicians, managers, supervisors. Thousands of people.

And under IGRA, every single person who worked in or around the gaming operation had to be licensed by the Tribal Gaming Commission. That meant background investigations, criminal history checks, employment verifications, reference checks, fingerprinting, credit checks for key employees, and review and approval by the Commission.

We processed thousands of applications in those two years. Some were approved immediately. Some required additional investigation. Some were denied.

And every decision had to be defensible, documented, and consistent with our licensing standards.

We worked directly with Harrah's corporate team to develop the Internal Control Standards—the policies and procedures that would govern every aspect of casino operations. How jackpots are paid. How hoppers are filled. How cash is transported. How surveillance monitors the floor. How financial records are maintained. Who signs. Who counts. Who verifies.

Harrah's brought their corporate standards, polished, tested, refined over decades in Las Vegas and Atlantic City. We reviewed them. Strengthened them. Adapted them to Cherokee's specific needs.

And then we formally adopted them as our standards, enforceable under Tribal law. Not Harrah's rules. Cherokee's rules.

That distinction mattered.

Every company that did business with the casino had to be licensed. Slot machine manufacturers. Food suppliers. Uniform companies. Maintenance contractors. Security firms. Linen services. Everyone.

We conducted background investigations on vendors, reviewing ownership structures, financial stability, criminal histories, regulatory compliance records. Some vendors had never been through this level of scrutiny before.

But this was Indian gaming. Federal law required it. And we took it seriously.

Over the years, the vendor licensing model we built became a template used by tribes across the country.

The Construction Challenges

Building the casino wasn't simple.

Early in construction, workers discovered a layer of blue clay deep in the ground—a type of unstable soil that couldn't support the weight of a building the size of what we were planning. It had to be excavated, removed, and replaced with stable fill. The process delayed construction by weeks and added significant cost.

But it had to be done right.

Then came the discovery that stopped everything.

During excavation, construction crews uncovered archaeological remains, graves on the site. Cherokee land. Cherokee ancestors.

Federal law—specifically the Native American Graves Protection and Repatriation Act, NAGPRA—requires that any discovery of Native American remains be handled with respect, consultation, and proper procedures.

Work halted. Tribal elders were consulted. Federal officials were notified.

Decisions had to be made about how to proceed, whether to relocate the remains, whether to redesign the building footprint, how to honor those who had been laid to rest on that land generations before.

It was handled carefully. Respectfully. Lawfully.

And eventually, construction resumed.

But it was a reminder: We were building something modern on land that carried history, memory, and the presence of those who came before us.

Preparing for the Unknown

By the fall of 1997, everything was in place.

The building was finished. The machines were installed. The employees were trained. The facility license was issued. The surveillance systems were operational. The internal controls were documented and enforceable.

Harrah's was ready. The Tribe was ready. And the Cherokee Tribal Gaming Commission—the independent regulatory body that would protect the integrity of everything we had built, was ready.

But none of us understood what was coming.

We had projections. Forecasts. Market studies.

We knew gaming could be successful. We believed it would generate revenue. We hoped it would create jobs and opportunity.

But what we didn't know, what we couldn't know, was that we were standing on the edge of a transformation that would reshape and sustain Cherokee's economy, Cherokee's future, and the lives of every enrolled member for generations to come.

All I knew was this: The work mattered. The Tribe needed it done right. And I was ready.

CHAPTER 13

THE EXPLOSION: OPENING NIGHT

"If you build it, they will come."

— W.P. Kinsella

Traffic backed up before 7:30 AM on opening day. Every skeptic who said the Cherokee couldn't fill a casino in the Smoky Mountains got their answer that morning.

◆ ◆ ◆

I BARELY SLEPT THE NIGHT before.

By 7:30 a.m. on November 13, 1997, I was already pulling into the parking lot near my office on the lower end of the property—a good distance from where the casino sat gleaming and ready.

And already, at seven thirty in the morning, the traffic was already starting to back up.

Cars slowed to a crawl on the road toward Soco. Headlights cutting through the early fog. Engines idling. People waiting.

I had a hard time even getting to my own office.

Fortunately, we had a side street with a gate, authorized access for staff, that let me avoid most of the entrance traffic. But even using the back route, I could feel it: Something massive was building.

And no one, not the analysts, not the consultants, not Harrah's corporate, not the Tribe, truly understood how big it was going to be.

The Ribbon Cutting

By midmorning, the crowd had already gathered at the front entrance.

Guests had parked, wherever they could find space, and walked up to the doors, waiting for the official opening. There was a formal ribbon-cutting ceremony. A couple of short speeches. The usual words about partnership, opportunity, and the future.

But you could feel the impatience in the crowd. People weren't there for speeches. They were there to get inside.

Leading up to opening day, the newspapers had been full of speculation. Would it work? Would people really come to the mountains of North Carolina for a casino? Was this sustainable, or just opening day curiosity?

The Tribe had been authorized under the compact to build sixty thousand square feet of gaming space.

But someone on Harrah's side had gotten cold feet.

They decided to pull back: to build the full sixty-thousand-square-foot shell, but NOT to finish and equip all of it—only fifty thousand square feet A solid wall stood between the public gaming floor and the unfinished ten thousand square feet.

The logic was simple: save on front-end costs, see if demand justified the space, and expand later if needed.

It was a cautious, conservative, reasonable decision.

And by 10:00 a.m. on opening day, it was already clear: It was the wrong decision.

The Lightning Bolt

One of the most memorable features of that original casino was a design element running down the center of the ceiling—a long corridor lit with neon effects that created a visual centerpiece for the entire floor.

This wasn't just decoration. It was connected to the jackpot reporting system.

Whenever a guest hit a jackpot large enough to require a hand pay—when the machine couldn't pay out from the hopper and a gaming host had to come and manually deliver the winnings—the system would trigger a lightning bolt effect that lit up the entire center of the casino.

Everyone in the building would know: Someone just won.

Nearly thirty years ago, that was high-tech. That was spectacle. That was theater.

And on opening day, we were eager to see if it actually worked.

It worked. Oh, it worked.

From the moment the doors opened, jackpots started hitting across the floor. And the lightning bolts started flashing. Again. And again. And again.

The crowd went wild every time. People cheered. People clapped. People would glance around to see who had won, hoping they'd be next.

The energy in that room was unlike anything I had ever experienced. It wasn't just excitement. It was electricity.

The Flood

Within an hour, the casino floor was at total capacity.

Fire code restrictions meant we could only allow a certain number of guests inside at any given time. So we started metering entry. One guest leaves, one guest enters.

And the line outside started growing.

It grew out into the parking lot. It wrapped around the building. It kept growing.

By midmorning, the queue outside looked like something you'd see at a theme park on a holiday weekend, except this wasn't a ride. This was a casino in the mountains of North Carolina that nobody was sure would even survive its first year.

When the doors first opened that morning, the crowd let out a cheer that could probably be heard all the way from Soco to Birdtown. A roar. Not polite applause. A roar.

And it didn't stop. The energy just kept building, kept humming, kept pulsing through every corner of that building.

I was on the floor most of the day. So were the Harrah's executives, the supervisors, the gaming hosts, the security staff—everyone who had any responsibility for keeping things running. We were all there, moving through the crowd, watching the systems, making sure procedures were followed, trying to keep up with the sheer volume of activity.

Our internal control procedures, the hand-pay requirements, the jackpot documentation, the hopper fills, the cash counts, were being tested on day one. And they were being tested hard.

By 11:00 a.m., the floor was humming.

We still didn't serve alcohol on the gaming floor, and honestly, that was probably a good thing, because I don't know what would have happened if you'd mixed alcohol with the energy already in that room.

It was already chaos. Controlled chaos, but chaos.

Midnight

By midnight, I knew we were in trouble.

Not the kind of trouble that comes from things going wrong. The kind of trouble that comes from things going too right.

People had been working nonstop since 7:00 a.m. The gaming hosts were stretched to their absolute limit. The line outside still wrapped around the building, no letup, no slowdown. The casino floor was still packed wall to wall.

And the jackpots kept hitting. Lightning bolt. Lightning bolt. Lightning bolt.

Every flash meant another hand pay. Every hand pay meant cash leaving the cage. Every guest cashing out meant quarters, dimes, and nickels flooding back into the system, coins that had to be counted, bagged, and redistributed back into the hoppers.

In those days, slot machines didn't use tickets. They used coins. Real, physical, heavy coins.

And we were running out.

At midnight, a call went out to all senior management staff: Report to the cages immediately. Help with fills and emergency drops.

And they came. Every one of them.

Carlos Tolosa, the area-wide president for Harrah's, was on the floor doing manual hopper fills at midnight. The casino general manager, Jerry Egelus, was helping with emergency drops and bank fills. Bruce Johnson, the director of operations, was right beside him. Executives in suits, sleeves rolled up, hauling coins.

Customers sat at machines waiting an hour or longer for someone to approach them with a jackpot payoff. The backlog was overwhelming. Gaming hosts were running from machine to machine, but there were simply too many jackpots and not enough hands.

By 2:00 a.m., the situation was critical. We didn't have enough cash in the cage to pay the jackpots. The hoppers were empty. The coins were still being counted, thousands and thousands of quarters sitting in bins, waiting to be processed and redistributed.

The system was overwhelmed. And something had to give.

The Call

I had gone home around midnight, exhausted after seventeen hours on my feet. I planned to grab a couple hours of sleep, a quick shower and change of clothes, and get back there to help.

Cyndi was up waiting for me. She had watched the eleven o'clock local news, and they were showing the huge crowds, the long lines wrapping around the building, the spectacle of opening night. She knew I would be tired. She knew I probably hadn't eaten.

So she had some of her homemade soup simmering on the stove.

She got me a bowl the moment I walked in, and we sat at the kitchen table talking about the day, the crowds, the energy, the lightning bolts flashing across the ceiling, the chaos we hadn't anticipated.

Then the phone rang.

It was Harrah's management. They had made the call: They needed to shut down temporarily. Clear the floor. Catch up. Restock the cages. Fill the hoppers. Get the system back in order.

But they needed my authorization.

Under the regulatory structure we had built, the Gaming Commission had authority over operational decisions that affected the integrity of the gaming floor. Closing the casino, even temporarily, required commission approval.

I called J.L. Burgess, the chairman, and we discussed it. We both agreed. I called management back and gave the authorization.

All customers were asked to leave and come back later. By 4:00 a.m., the casino was empty.

And every available person—executives, managers, hosts, cage staff—threw themselves into the work. Counting coins. Filling hoppers. Restocking the cage. Resetting the systems. Getting ready to reopen.

I slept for a few hours. Maybe.

By early morning, I was back, making sure the regulatory side stayed solid even in the chaos.

By 10:00 a.m., we were back up to speed. The machines were filled. The cage was restocked. The coins were counted and bagged. Everything was ready.

The line outside had died down a bit, still people waiting, still people eager to get inside, but not the overwhelming crush from the night before.

We opened the doors again.

And we haven't closed them since—except when COVID forced a brief shutdown more than two decades later.

Total shutdown time on opening night: about six hours. Just long enough to catch up with demand no one ever saw coming.

The Wall Must Come Down

Immediately, within days, we knew the truth: The wall separating the unfinished ten-thousand-square-foot section had to come down.

But we tested it for a while. We wanted to be sure demand wasn't just opening day curiosity.

We gave it six weeks.

By New Year's, the answer was undeniable.

The decision was made: Fast-track the expansion. Get the wall down. Get the other ten thousand open.

This was a joint decision, the Tribal Council, the Chief's office, and the Tribal Casino Gaming Enterprise Board working together.

The Gaming Commission's role at that point was regulatory: make sure procedures were followed, ensure the expansion met all licensing and surveillance requirements, verify that the new space was safe and compliant.

Business decisions belonged to TCGE and the Tribe. Regulatory oversight belonged to us. And we made sure the line stayed clear.

The expansion happened fast. Within a few months, the unfinished space was fully fitted with proper finishes, machines installed, surveillance operational, everything blended seamlessly with the original floor.

By May 1998, the wall was gone. The full sixty thousand square feet was open. And the place was humming.

It's been gangbusters ever since.

CHAPTER 14

THE BAKER'S DOZEN

"The only thing necessary for the triumph of evil is for good men to do nothing."

— Edmund Burke

A thirty-second hallway whisper led to the discovery of an internal theft ring. I could have looked the other way—instead, thirteen people were prosecuted.

◆ ◆ ◆

IN THE EARLY YEARS of our casino—when the lights were bright, the systems were new, and the excitement of a growing industry filled every corner of the gaming floor—the Tribal Gaming Commission carried a simple but heavy mandate: protect the Tribe, protect the public, protect the integrity of the games.

Most people who worked in that building treated that mandate with respect. But not everyone.

What came to be known as "The Baker's Dozen" began quietly, almost invisibly, but ended as one of the most significant internal fraud cases in the early history of Indian gaming. It became a teaching case across the country. And it changed how we regulated jackpots forever.

It started with a conversation that lasted no more than thirty seconds.

It was about 9:00 p.m. one evening in 1998. I was in the back of the casino, walking through the hallway between the Gaming Commission agents' office and the wardrobe section, down the hall from security, an area most guests never see. I was there to check on the agents and handle some other business.

That's when one of the casino hosts stopped me. A good employee. Former law enforcement. He had worked for other tribes in different areas and brought real experience to the job.

We stood there chatting, the kind of quick, casual conversation you have in hallways when you're both heading somewhere else.

And then he said it.

"Patrick . . . something's not right."

I stopped. "What do you mean?"

He looked around, not paranoid, but careful. "There's a group of people," he said. "Casino employees. They're living it up. Throwing lavish parties. Spending money like water."

He gave me examples. A rented minivan—they took eight to ten people on a trip to the beach, partied for several days, all expenses covered. Lavish parties with T-bone steaks and expensive alcohol, the kind of spending that didn't match their salaries. Flashy purchases, things that stood out, things that didn't add up.

"Something just doesn't feel right," he said.

I thanked him. I told him I'd been checking, and everything looked in order on the surface, nothing out of sorts in the reports, the audits, the systems.

But as I walked away that night, his words stayed with me.

I went home. I went to bed. But I couldn't stop thinking about it.

The next morning, I kept replaying the conversation in my head. How could it possibly happen? If something was going down, how would they be doing it? Where's the vulnerability?

And then it hit me.

Jackpots.

The Investigation Begins

I called in my senior agent, Rick Saunooke, and my director of finance for the Commission, Lee Dillard. I laid out what I wanted them to check.

"Pull the jackpot payoffs. Look at any that were manual-pay jackpots. Match them to the system records. See if there's anything we missed."

We pulled the past day's jackpot slips, then several days' worth. We started matching automated jackpot slips, paid through the system, against manual jackpot slips, hand-paid by gaming hosts when the automated system malfunctioned.

Everything should have matched. One slip per jackpot. Either automated or manual, never both.

And then we started catching it.

Jackpots that showed paid from the system with an automated slip generated, and also paid manually with a hand-pay slip filled out.

The same jackpot. Paid twice.

"Oh crap," I said.

Rick looked at me. Lee looked at the slips. We all knew what we were looking at.

The Conference Room

We took over a conference room in the casino. We pulled all the old jackpot payout records from storage, paper slips, signed forms, everything we had kept. We pulled all the computer printouts showing jackpots paid through the system. And we started matching them up.

First, we went back six months.

And we found more. A lot more.

Then we asked the question: How far back does this go? At that point we had been open for just over one year.

So we went back as far as our storage records would allow, pulling every slip we had, matching them to every system payout. Hours and hours. Days and days. Just me, Rick, Lee, and two other agents, sitting in that room, going through thousands of slips, building the case line by line.

It was quiet work. Methodical work. The kind of investigation that doesn't make for good TV, no chases, no confrontations, no dramatic moments. Just paper. And patterns. And the slow, grinding certainty that we had been right.

Something was going down. And we were about to catch every single person involved.

The Flaw They Found

Here's how the scam worked.

In those early years, our slot payout system had a vulnerability—a weakness that no one on the regulatory side had yet fully recognized.

When a machine hit a jackpot, the system generated an automated jackpot slip. A gaming host took the slip to the cage, collected the cash, and paid the guest.

But there was also a manual jackpot option, used when the automated slip malfunctioned.

The problem was there was no mechanism to cancel a jackpot once paid, link an automated payout to a manual payout, or flag that the two slips were for the same jackpot.

That tiny gap, less than a line of code, was all a small group needed to exploit the system.

Gaming host number one paid a legitimate jackpot using the automated slip. Gaming host number two, also in on it, used a manual jackpot slip signed by a corrupt supervisor. The cage paid the manual slip, believing the automated slip had failed. The group pocketed the second payout and split the money.

No guest complained. No jackpot went unpaid. Nothing appeared wrong on the surface.

But on the back end, they were duplicating jackpots.

They started small. Then they grew bolder. Soon they were replicating payouts across multiple shifts, multiple hosts, and multiple machines.

Their spending became reckless. And recklessness leaves footprints.

Bringing In the FBI

We didn't confront anyone.

Once we had the pattern documented, once we knew the scope, we went straight to the FBI.

I contacted Special Agent Andy Romagnuolo, the FBI agent assigned to our region. He came to the casino. We brought him into the conference room where we had been working. We showed him the process: the automated slips, the manual slips, the duplicates, the timeline, the pattern.

He looked at the evidence spread across the table, stacks of paper, highlighted records, timelines mapped out on whiteboards.

"This is solid," he said.

He took the information back to the FBI field office.

A few days later, he called me.

"We're moving forward. Federal charges. Felony arrests."

The Arrests

The FBI came early in the morning, close to Christmas 1998.

Early morning raids. Coordinated arrests. All thirteen of them, The Baker's Dozen, taken into custody.

I wasn't present during the arrests. But I heard about it quickly.

The casino floor was buzzing. Employees were shocked—some of them had worked alongside these people for years.

But mostly, the reaction was relief.

People came up to me in the days that followed and said things like: "I'm glad you caught them."

"This proves the system works."

"Now everyone knows—you can't cheat here and get away with it."

Employees felt vindicated. Because they had been doing it the right way. And now the bad apples were gone.

The People Behind the Numbers

I didn't know most of the thirteen personally. But some I did. Some I would even call friends—or at least friendly acquaintances. People I still speak to today, even though they were arrested, charged, and convicted.

There was no happiness about getting them arrested. No satisfaction in watching people I knew face federal prosecution.

But there was relief. Relief that the system we had built—the controls, the documentation, the oversight—had worked.

It didn't catch the fraud immediately. It didn't prevent it from happening. But it detected it. And it allowed us to stop it, document it, and hold people accountable.

That distinction mattered. Because we didn't frame this as a failure. We framed it as the system worked. The integrity held. And the people responsible were caught.

The Convictions and Restitution

Every single one of the thirteen was charged and convicted in federal court. Federal felonies. Theft from an Indian casino. Embezzlement. Fraud.

The total stolen: $187,000.

The federal court ordered restitution—repayment through

garnishment of their per capita payments. For enrolled Tribal members involved, that meant a portion of their per capita checks would be withheld each distribution until the debt was paid.

It lasted for several years. Until it became politically untenable.

Some of the individuals had child support payments or other garnishments already in place. The finance side of the Tribe eventually ordered us to stop the per capita garnishments. So we never recovered the full amount.

But the message had been sent.

Changing the Rules

The Baker's Dozen case didn't just expose wrongdoing. It changed the blueprint of tribal gaming regulation.

We immediately implemented stricter jackpot protocols, mandatory cancellation systems so that once a jackpot is paid it's locked in the system, a two-step verification where automated and manual systems cross-check, reinforced cage procedures, enhanced surveillance requirements, and cross-checks between automated and manual payouts.

But we didn't stop there. We documented the entire case—the vulnerability, the pattern, the detection method, the solution—and shared it.

I presented the Baker's Dozen case at tribal gaming conferences across the country. I taught it in regulatory training sessions. I sat on panels with other tribal gaming commissioners and federal regulators, walking them through exactly how the scam worked and exactly how we caught it.

The response was immediate.

Tribes started updating their systems. Regulators started implementing dual-verification protocols. Surveillance teams started watching for the patterns we had identified.

The NIGC incorporated lessons from our case into the MICS (Minimal Internal Control Standards) we were helping to write.

Cherokee's experience became a national teaching case, because we caught it, documented it, and fixed it.

The Jurisdictions That Ignored Us

But not everyone listened.

Some commercial jurisdictions, state-regulated casinos, particularly in the Northeast, dismissed the warning. Maybe it was pride. Maybe they didn't want to admit they could learn something from Indian Country. Maybe they thought their systems were different, more advanced, less vulnerable.

Whatever the reason, they didn't act.

And years later, five, six, seven years after we caught and prosecuted the Baker's Dozen, those same jurisdictions fell victim to the exact same scam.

Duplicate jackpot slips. Manual overrides exploiting automated systems. Gaming hosts splitting payouts. The same pattern. The same vulnerability. The same fraud.

When I heard about it, I felt two things: frustration, because we had warned them, we had documented it, we had shared the solution; and vindication, because it proved once again that Cherokee wasn't just keeping up with the industry, we were leading it.

That hallway conversation, thirty seconds on a random evening, led to one of the most significant regulatory victories in Cherokee's gaming history.

CHAPTER 15

> *"Courage is not the absence of fear, but the triumph over it."*
>
> — Nelson Mandela

This chapter carries two threads: the painstaking work of drafting national gaming standards, and the morning of September 11, when I was in Syracuse and the world changed. Mandela's words bridge both.

◆ ◆ ◆

WHEN THE NATIONAL INDIAN Gaming Commission asked me to serve on the committee to draft the MICS, I understood immediately that this was history.

For the first time, tribes and the federal government were sitting shoulder to shoulder to build the framework that would govern gaming across Indian Country. These standards would determine how every casino in America protected its money, its integrity, and its people. And they would last for decades.

I took the responsibility seriously. I also knew it would be work, long, technical, exhausting work. But I never imagined that the most significant moment of my service on that committee would have nothing to do with regulations at all.

The MICS were not guidelines. They were the backbone of tribal gaming oversight. They dictated how money was counted, how surveillance operated, how jackpots were processed, how cage operations were secured, how slot systems were audited, how every tribe protected itself from fraud, theft, and manipulation.

Before MICS, regulations varied wildly from tribe to tribe. Some did it well. Some didn't. And without consistent minimum standards, the entire industry remained vulnerable.

When the NIGC first promulgated the MICS in 1999, tribes nationwide finally had consistent minimum standards to work from. By the time I joined the committee, we were refining and strengthening those standards—building on the foundation that had already been laid.

The Committee

Serving on the committee wasn't glamorous. It was hours upon hours of technical debates, line-by-line drafting, reconciling sovereignty with federal oversight, reviewing decades of industry data, and arguing over definitions, commas, thresholds, and procedures.

We traveled all over the country so tribes from each region could attend—New Orleans, Seattle, San Diego, Washington, DC, New Mexico, Syracuse, and several more.

The committee brought together some of the sharpest minds in Indian gaming—people who had built regulatory systems from scratch, people who had seen what worked and what failed, people who understood that what we were writing would shape the industry for decades.

There were tribal gaming commissioners from large operations and small ones. There were NIGC staff members who had spent years in the field. There were technical experts and attorneys who understood both the law and the politics. We didn't always agree. But we all understood the stakes.

The MICS covered everything: surveillance standards, cash-handling procedures, jackpot protocols, slot machine controls, cage operations, licensing requirements. Every line mattered. Because these weren't suggestions—they were minimum standards that every tribal gaming operation in the United States would be required to meet.

Get it wrong, and you either create loopholes that invite fraud—or you create burdens so heavy that small tribes can't comply. We had to get it right.

The hardest debates were about how much federal oversight was appropriate. Tribes are sovereign nations. We regulate ourselves. But the MICS were being written by the federal government, and some tribes rightfully worried these standards could become a tool for federal micromanagement. So we fought, line by line, to preserve sovereignty while creating standards strong enough to protect industry integrity.

I brought something to that table that many others didn't have: real-world experience building a regulatory system from scratch. When debates arose about whether a standard was realistic, whether a procedure was enforceable—I could speak from experience. Not theory. Experience.

The meetings always started at 9:00 a.m. But before the formal sessions began, we'd gather for coffee and muffins, casual conversation, people going over notes, preparing for another day of dense regulatory work.

That's where we were on the morning of September 11, 2001, in Syracuse, New York. Standing around. Drinking coffee. Talking. Normal.

September 11, 2001

It was about ten till nine when someone came by, I don't even remember who, and said: "A plane hit the World Trade Center. It's on fire."

Everyone rushed to the TV. We turned it on and saw Tower One smoking, thick, black smoke pouring out of the upper floors, flames visible, chaos on the streets below.

The newscasters were still trying to figure out what had happened. Pilot error, they said. A terrible accident. How could a pilot let the plane get so close to the tower?

For the first ten or fifteen minutes, I think most people thought that's what it was, a tragic, inexplicable accident. Even the people in my group. Even me.

And then, at 9:03 a.m., we watched, live, in real time, with the rest of the country, as the second plane came in and struck the second tower.

Everything changed.

The room went silent. Then someone gasped. Then someone else started crying. And we all knew—instantly, deeply, horrifyingly—that something very serious was happening. Something that would change the world.

Immediately, everyone started trying to call home.

I got through to Cyndi. She was already up. The TV was on. She was scared to death.

"Can you get home?" she asked.

"I'm going to try," I said. But even as I said it, I knew it wasn't going to be easy.

We kept watching the TV. Around 9:30 a.m., we watched Tower One fall. Just collapse. Gone. Half an hour later, Tower Two fell. The same way. Just gone.

It was total chaos. The flights were grounded, all of them, nationwide, immediately. And even if they hadn't been, I didn't want to get on a plane at that moment. Nobody did.

People started scrambling for rental cars. Within an hour, every rental car in the Syracuse area was gone, snapped up by people desperate to get out, to get home, to get back to their families.

I stayed in the same hotel for those extra couple of days, trying to figure out how to get home.

Stranded

The next few days are a blur, but certain moments stand out with terrible clarity.

Those of us who remained in Syracuse, workers, employees, stranded travelers like me, did the best we could. The hotel staff tried to maintain normalcy, but you could see the strain on their faces. Everyone was glued to the TV. Every new piece of information, the Pentagon attack, the plane that went down in Pennsylvania, the rising death toll, the search for survivors, felt like another blow.

People sat in the lobby for hours, just watching, unable to look away.

We found food when and where we could. The first day, some restaurants were still open. By the second day, much of Syracuse had shut down. I remember one afternoon, I think it was the next day, walking around trying to find something to eat. The city had shut down. So I went to a convenience store and bought chips, crackers, some snacks. That was dinner.

It sounds small. But in that moment, standing in a convenience store in upstate New York, hundreds of miles from home, buying chips for dinner because the world had stopped, it felt surreal.

I called Cyndi every day. Sometimes multiple times a day. Just to hear her voice. Just to make sure she and the kids were okay. Gina was fourteen. Nelson was thirteen. They were old enough to understand what was happening, and that made it harder.

She was holding it together, she always did, but I could hear the strain.

"When are you coming home?" she asked.

"As soon as I can," I said. But I didn't know when that would be.

On the second or third day, I don't remember exactly when, Chief Leon Jones called me.

"Patrick," he said, "you need to be home with your family. Everyone should be home with their family at a time like this."

He paused.

"I'll send a driver to come pick you up."

From Cherokee to Syracuse, nearly fifteen hours each way. A thirty-hour round-trip just to bring me home.

It was one of the kindest offers ever made to me.

"Chief," I said, "don't worry about it. A driver would take longer to get here than it would for me to wait for the flights to get rescheduled. I'll be fine."

That gesture, in the middle of a national crisis, when everyone was terrified and uncertain, meant more than Chief Jones probably realized. It reminded me that even when the world feels like it's falling apart, there are people who care. People who look out for each other.

The Flight Home

By Thursday evening, September 13, the airlines began repositioning aircraft—flying empty jets to reset the system because planes had landed wherever they could during the shutdown.

I finally got a flight out on Saturday, September 15, 2001.

The flight was eerie. There was one other passenger on the plane besides me. We may have exchanged pleasantries—I don't remember. But mostly, we both just sat there in shock.

The stewardesses were polite, professional—but you could see it on their faces too. Fear. Uncertainty. Grief.

Everyone at the airport, everyone on that first flight back, had the same look: shock. And the weight of knowing the world had changed.

The pilot said very little. Just that they were repositioning the plane—getting aircraft back in place so the system could restart.

I sat in my seat and looked out the window as we flew over the land below. And I remember thinking: How much change is coming? What does this mean for the country? What does this mean for the world?

I felt fearful, not of the flight itself, but of what lay ahead. For all of us.

Returning to the Work

Our committee paused our work during those dark days. But not our resolve.

When meetings resumed weeks later, the work felt different. We understood, more than ever, how fragile systems could be. How vital strong controls were. How much was at stake.

And so we pressed forward.

Months later, we finished what we started. The MICS were finalized, published, and implemented across Indian Country.

25 CFR Part 542 became the regulatory foundation for tribal gaming nationwide.

And the standards we wrote, born out of years of experience, shaped by debate and compromise, tested by real-world application, are still in use today.

In 2006, the Colorado River Indian Tribes case changed things. The DC Circuit Court ruled that the NIGC lacked authority to enforce or promulgate Class III MICS. But by then, it didn't matter in the way some might have expected. The standards were already in place. Most tribes had already adopted them. They worked. And tribes continued to follow them, not because they were forced to, but because they understood the value of what we had built.

Cherokee's regulatory model influenced those standards. The internal controls we built. The licensing procedures we developed. The surveillance protocols we implemented. The standards we refused to compromise.

All of it fed into the national framework that now governs hundreds of tribal gaming operations across the United States.

That's fact, not pride.

And it's a reminder that the work we do—even the unglamorous, technical, tedious work of writing regulations—matters. It protects people. It protects money. It protects the integrity of an industry that transformed Indian Country.

And when I finally made it home, when I walked through the door and saw Cyndi and the kids, I didn't talk about the committee. I didn't talk about the regulations. I just held them.

CHAPTER 16

THE DAY WE LAID DAD TO REST

*"When someone you love becomes a memory, the
memory becomes a treasure."*

— Unknown

Thanksgiving Day, 2007. A cold morning, a simple casket, no
headdress—just Dad. Sometimes the simplest words carry the
most weight.

◆ ◆ ◆

THE MORNING WE BURIED my father was cold, the kind of cold that
sinks through your coat and settles somewhere deep in the chest. It
was Thanksgiving Day, November 22, 2007—a date that should have
held warmth and family and the smell of dinner filling the house. Instead,
it was the day we lowered Henry Lambert into the ground.

He wasn't dressed in his regalia. No headdress. No beads. No
feathers. Just Dad—in the same everyday clothes he wore in life. That
was how he wanted it. How we wanted it. Honest. Simple. True to who
he was.

The sky hung gray over the mountains, a muted Carolina blue buried
behind thick clouds. The leaves had fallen early that year, carpeting the
earth around his grave in a blanket of reds and browns—as if the land
itself had laid something down to comfort him.

I remember the quiet most of all.

My sisters stood close, some holding hands, some holding
themselves upright through sheer force of will. Our mother, Patsy, stood
between us, her shoulders squared, her chin trembling only when she
thought no one was looking. She had spent her whole life holding our
family together. Even here, even now, she was doing it again.

Funerals tell you a lot about a man. And Dad's told the story of a life
bigger than most people ever knew.

People showed up from everywhere—Cherokee, Bryson City,

Maggie Valley, Birdtown. Men he had worked with decades ago. People he had taken photos with thirty years earlier. Elders who remembered him as the young "Chief Henry" along the roadside. Tourists who had come through town once and never forgotten him, as if they owed him a final visit.

They lined up to touch his hand one last time, or lay a hand on his casket, or whisper, "He was a good man" in that soft way people from home say things that carry weight.

And he was. He truly was.

He had his struggles, everyone knew that. He fought hard battles with alcohol, the kind that take a toll on a family but never defined his heart. He never raised a hand to any of us. Never once. Even in the hardest chapters of his life, kindness lived in him like a permanent tenant.

People loved him because he loved people, openly, easily, without judgment.

And he was handsome, too, movie-star handsome, the kind of face that ended up on postcards across America and once in a full feature in *National Geographic*. He kept a shelf in the house with stacks of those cards, proud as could be. Not prideful, proud. There's a difference. Prideful is ego. Proud is gratitude.

As the minister read the final Scripture, my mind drifted, not in grief, but in memory.

Fishing with Dad on Hazel Creek. The way he'd stand knee-deep in the cold water, patient as a stone, waiting for the trout to rise. He never rushed anything. Never forced it. He understood that the river had its own rhythm, and a man who fought against it would always lose.

Hiking along the ridge above Goose Creek. His hand on a moss-covered stone, telling me it had been there longer than any of us and would remain long after we were gone. Teaching me that some things endure not because they're strong, but because they're patient.

Watching him charm strangers from Ohio or Florida or Germany who stopped to take a picture, only to leave talking about Cherokee history they never knew until he told them. He had a gift for that—making people feel like they'd learned something important, like their brief encounter with him had been more than just a tourist transaction.

Hearing him laugh, that wide, warm laugh that could fill a room. The sound of it was medicine. Even now, years later, I can still hear it when I close my eyes.

My father was born August 5, 1935, and lived seventy-two years on this earth, a man shaped by land, by culture, by hardship, and by heart. And that morning, standing by his grave, I felt something I didn't expect: a shift inside myself. A realization that everything he had been, the good, the flawed, the strong, the soft, lived in me. And now it was mine to carry forward.

As we lowered him down, I made him a promise, one he would never hear, but one that changed my life anyway.

I would quit smoking.

I had smoked for twenty-two years. Started young, the way too many people do, and never found the will to stop. Cigarettes were my constant companion through law school, through the early years of marriage, through building the Gaming Commission, through every late night and early morning of a life that never seemed to slow down.

But watching lung cancer take my father piece by piece broke something open inside me. The disease didn't kill him quickly. It was slow, methodical, cruel—stealing his breath a little more each day until there was nothing left to steal. The cancer had spread throughout his body by the end.

I had watched him shrink. Watched the man who once filled a room with his presence become fragile, diminished, fighting for air. And I knew, standing there in the cold quiet of that Thanksgiving morning, that I was looking at my own future if I didn't change.

"Dad," I whispered, so softly that no one else could hear. "I'm done. I'm finished with it."

Three months later, on February 22, 2008, I smoked my last cigarette. I chose that date intentionally—exactly three months from the day I made my promise at his graveside. The twenty-second would mean something now.

It wasn't easy. Anyone who tells you quitting is simple has never been addicted. The cravings came in waves, sometimes manageable, sometimes overwhelming. There were moments when I wanted to give in more than I wanted almost anything else.

But every time that urge hit, I thought about my father. About the way his lungs had failed him. About the promise I made at his graveside. And somehow, that was enough to get me through one more hour, one more day, one more week.

Every year since, on February 22, I run one mile for every year smoke-free. It started as a way to mark the anniversary—a physical reminder that I had kept my promise.

The first year, I ran one mile. The second year, two. And so on, adding a mile each year like compound interest on a debt I owed to myself.

By the time I turned sixty, I ran sixteen miles on that day. Not fast, not gracefully, but steadily—the way my father taught me to approach everything worth doing.

At seventy, I will run a full marathon—26.2 miles for twenty-six reclaimed years. It will be my twenty-sixth year smoke-free, and I will honor my father with every step. It seems impossible now, but so did quitting in the first place. And if I've learned anything, it's that impossible things become possible when you refuse to give up.

The running isn't really about fitness. It's about honoring him. It's my way of saying: Your life changed mine. Your death taught me something. And every mile I run is a mile I wouldn't have had if I'd kept poisoning myself the way you did.

I wish he could see it. I wish he could know that his struggle became my salvation.

But maybe he does know. Maybe somewhere in the mountains that raised us both, he's watching. Maybe that's enough.

In the weeks after the funeral, something else changed too.

The business we had built, Chief Henry's Gifts and More, was named after him. It carried his name, his legacy, his image on the sign out front. With him gone, something about running that store didn't feel the same anymore.

The craft shop business was already declining anyway. Tourists were changing. Online shopping was eating into retail. The numbers told a story we couldn't ignore.

So Cyndi and I decided we would close the craft shops and focus on the car wash and the laundromat, two businesses that didn't rely on tourist trends, that served locals and visitors alike, that generated steady income without requiring us to be on-site every single day.

It was the right call, financially. But it was also an emotional closing—the end of a chapter that had begun when my father was still alive, still posing for pictures, still filling the world with that wide warm laugh.

I still think about him almost every day. Not with the sharp grief of those first months, but with a quieter kind of presence.

When I'm hiking in the backcountry, I hear his voice pointing out the way the light falls through the trees. When I'm working through a difficult problem, I remember his patience, his refusal to force things before they were ready. When I'm with my grandchildren, teaching them about the land and our history, I feel him standing beside me, not as a ghost, but as a continuation.

Parents don't just raise you while they're living. They raise you long after they're gone.

And on February 22 of every year, when I lace up my running shoes and step out onto the road for another mile, another year, another proof that I kept my promise—I know that somewhere in the mountains, my father is proud.

Not prideful. Proud.

There's a difference.

And he taught me that, too.

CHAPTER 17

HARRAH'S

"Character is doing the right thing when nobody's looking."

— J.C. Watts

While other companies flew Council members on chartered jets and handed out gifts, Harrah's showed up with spreadsheets and a track record. They won by integrity, not spectacle.

◆ ◆ ◆

FROM THE VERY BEGINNING, Harrah's stood apart from every other company that came courting the Eastern Band of Cherokee Indians.

Long before the casino opened its doors, before the tourism boom, before the expansions, before the profits reached numbers we could have never imagined—Harrah's made a quiet but significant choice: They refused to buy their way into Cherokee.

They didn't fly Council members across the country on chartered jets.

They didn't hand out leather jackets, cash, or gifts. They didn't throw catered parties, cover weddings, or host political allies.

I watched other companies try all of that. I saw the gifts arrive. I heard the promises made behind closed doors. I witnessed the subtle and not-so-subtle attempts to curry favor with decision-makers through personal generosity that always came with strings attached.

Harrah's didn't play that game.

They stood on their reputation. They stood on their regulatory discipline. And they stood on integrity.

That restraint—at a time when other companies were competing with extravagance—said something about who they were and, more importantly, who they intended to be. It told me early on that if the Tribe partnered with Harrah's, we weren't just signing a management agreement. We were setting the tone for an entire future.

I remember sitting in meetings during the selection process, watching how the different companies presented themselves. Some came in with flash and promises of quick riches. Some came with political connections they implied could smooth over any regulatory obstacles. Some came with thinly veiled suggestions that the right people could be taken care of.

Harrah's came with spreadsheets, compliance records, and a track record of working successfully with tribal nations. They came with a plan. They came with discipline. And they came with respect.

That difference mattered more than any of us fully understood at the time.

The People Who Made It Work

Over twenty-one years as executive director, I worked with dozens of Harrah's executives, some briefly, some for years, some who became more than colleagues.

A few stand out. For their character, not their titles.

If I had to name one person who exemplified everything a gaming executive should be, it would be Bill Buffalo.

Bill served as general counsel for Harrah's North Carolina Casino Indian Gaming Division. But his responsibilities extended far beyond Cherokee. Bill also served as the chief regulatory compliance officer for all of Harrah's, both domestic and international operations. And during various periods, he served as general counsel to the entire corporation. His boss at the time was Carlos Tolosa—the president of Harrah's eastern division and someone I came to respect deeply, both professionally and personally.

But Bill was the one I worked with most closely. And I can say without hesitation: Bill Buffalo set the standard.

What made Bill different, what made him exceptional, was his honesty. In all my years of regulatory work, I never met another corporate attorney quite like him.

I'll never forget the times he would come to me and self-report issues.

Things that weren't quite according to regulation. Small things, sometimes, procedural missteps, minor deviations, paperwork errors.

The kind of things that most companies would hope never came to light.

The kind of things that corporate attorneys are specifically trained to minimize, deflect, or bury.

But Bill didn't wait for us to catch it. He came to us first.

"Patrick," he'd say, walking into my office, or in just a phone call, "we need to talk about something."

And then he'd lay it out—what happened, why it happened, what they were doing to fix it. No spin. No excuses. No carefully worded statements designed to provide legal cover. Just facts.

The first time it happened, I was surprised. By the third or fourth time, I understood: This wasn't an exception for Bill Buffalo. This was how he operated. This was who he was.

That level of honesty, especially from in-house counsel for a company as large as Harrah's, was rare. Most corporate attorneys are trained to protect their clients, to minimize exposure, to say as little as possible. Their job is to shield the company from liability, not to volunteer information that could create problems.

But Bill understood something deeper: Long-term partnerships are built on trust. And trust requires transparency. Even when it's uncomfortable. Even when it might create short-term difficulties. Even when the easier path would be to stay quiet and hope no one noticed.

Bill was always protective of Harrah's, that was his job, and he did it well. But he was also always up-front with the regulators he had to work with. He kept us fully informed of any changes, any challenges, any situations that might require our attention. He never left us blindsided. He never let us walk into a situation unprepared.

And because of that, we trusted him.

When Bill Buffalo told us something, we knew it was true. When he said Harrah's would handle something, we knew they would. When he gave us his word, we could take it to the bank.

That kind of credibility can't be bought. It has to be earned. And Bill earned it, every single day, for years.

Over time, Bill and I developed more than a professional relationship. I came to know his family. We kept in touch over the years, even after roles changed and people moved on. I would call it a friendship, the kind built on mutual respect, shared values, and years of working together toward something bigger than either of us.

The Leaders Who Set the Tone

Bill's boss, Carlos Tolosa, was someone I considered more than just a Harrah's executive.

Carlos was a leader—the kind of person who understood that success in Indian Country required more than business acumen. It required respect. It required cultural sensitivity. It required understanding that the Tribe wasn't just a client. The Tribe was a sovereign Nation.

And Carlos never forgot that.

In every meeting, every negotiation, every conversation we had over the years, Carlos treated the Eastern Band with the respect that sovereignty demands. He didn't talk down to us. He didn't try to explain away our concerns. He didn't treat our regulatory requirements as obstacles to be overcome.

He treated them as legitimate expressions of tribal authority, because that's exactly what they were.

Carlos and I also developed a close professional relationship, one I would term as a friendship. We worked together through expansions, through compact amendments, through regulatory challenges, through moments when the partnership was tested and had to be strengthened.

There were times when Harrah's corporate interests and Tribal regulatory requirements didn't perfectly align. Times when the company wanted to move faster than our processes allowed. Times when decisions made in corporate boardrooms had to be reconciled with decisions made by the Tribal Gaming Commission.

And through all of it, Carlos remained steady, principled, and committed to doing things the right way. He never pressured us to cut corners. He never implied that our friendship should translate into regulatory favors. He understood the difference between personal relationships and professional obligations.

I got to know his family too. We kept in touch over the years. And I will always be grateful for the way he led Harrah's engagement with Cherokee, not as a company extracting profit, but as a partner building something that would last.

Another executive who stands out in my mind is Darold Londo, who served as senior vice president and general manager from 2006 to 2011.

Darold was a West Point graduate. And you could tell.

He was organized. Disciplined. Particular about making sure rules were followed and regulations were adhered to. He ran the casino with military precision. He didn't tolerate sloppiness. He didn't allow corners to be cut. And he expected excellence from everyone around him, not in a harsh way, but in a way that elevated the entire operation.

I really appreciated Darold's service. He brought a level of professionalism and structure that made our regulatory oversight easier, not harder. Because when the general manager is committed to compliance, the entire organization follows. When the person at the top sets the standard, everyone else rises to meet it.

During Darold's tenure, we went through some of our most significant expansions. The pressure to cut corners, to speed up processes, to look the other way on minor issues—that pressure is always greatest during periods of rapid growth. But Darold never wavered. He understood that the integrity of the operation was more important than any timeline.

I also got to know Jerry Egelus and Bruce Johnson very well—two of the first Harrah's executives on the ground in Cherokee.

Jerry was the first general manager assigned to the property. He set up an office in a temporary location to get the management team rolling here in town, long before the casino was even built. Those early days were chaotic, uncertain, and full of challenges that no playbook could have prepared us for.

Jerry was the one laying the groundwork, hiring the first employees, building relationships with the Tribe, establishing the systems that would eventually become a billion-dollar enterprise. He was working out of makeshift spaces, dealing with construction delays, navigating Tribal politics he was still learning to understand, and trying to build something from nothing.

I got to know Jerry very well during those early years. He was always trying to do the right thing. Always focused on building something sustainable, not just something profitable. He understood that the decisions made in those first months would echo for decades.

Bruce Johnson was part of that early team as well, another executive committed to doing things right. Both men left a lasting mark on the foundation of Cherokee gaming. And I will always remember them for the way they approached the work, with respect, with discipline, and with a genuine desire to see the Tribe succeed.

The Ownership Changes

Over the years, Harrah's went through multiple corporate transformations: Promus Companies when we first negotiated, then Harrah's Entertainment, which is the name most people know, then Caesars Entertainment after the acquisition.

Each time the name changed, people asked: Will this affect the relationship? Will the new ownership honor the commitments? Will they try to renegotiate the terms?

The concern was understandable. In Indian Country, we had seen too many examples of corporate promises that evaporated when ownership changed hands. New executives would come in, review the existing agreements, and suddenly discover that the previous commitments were no longer convenient.

The answer, every time, was no.

None of the name changes affected our relationship with the company. We continued under the same management contract. The same management terms.

The same commitments. Just with a new name on the letterhead.

Each of those transitions required regulatory approval. Every corporate restructuring, every change in ownership, every shift in the parent company had to be reviewed, documented, and approved by the Tribal Gaming Commission. We didn't just rubber-stamp the changes. We examined them carefully, asked hard questions, and made sure that the new corporate structure would honor the obligations of the old.

And each time, Harrah's, or Caesars, or whatever name they were operating under at that moment, worked with us transparently and professionally. They provided the documentation we requested. They answered our questions directly. They didn't try to use the corporate restructuring as an opportunity to renegotiate terms or diminish commitments.

I remember sitting down with Phil Satre, who served as chairman of the board for Harrah's Entertainment for many years. We met several times over the course of the partnership, and I always found him to be exactly the kind of leader you want at the top of a company you're doing business with.

We talked about the changes. The acquisitions. The corporate restructuring. The pressures that public companies face from shareholders and analysts who don't always understand the unique dynamics of tribal partnerships.

And he assured me, directly, personally, that none of these transitions would impact the relationship with Cherokee.

"We're committed," he said. "That doesn't change."

And it didn't.

Why This Partnership Succeeded

Many tribal-casino partnerships around the country collapsed under mismanagement, political interference, failed oversight, corruption, personality conflicts, compact disputes, or economic downturns.

Ours did not.

Cherokee and Harrah's faced difficult moments. There were disagreements over expansion pacing—times when the company wanted to move faster than the Tribe was comfortable with, or times when the Tribe was ready to expand before the company had secured the financing. There was hesitancy by governors to approve table games, years of frustration as we waited for live dealers while watching other jurisdictions move ahead. There were obstacles with state lottery politics, shifting administrations in Raleigh, national recessions that tightened credit markets, evolving gaming technology that required constant adaptation, and political volatility at home that threatened to destabilize relationships we had spent years building.

But through all of it, we endured because the foundation was built right.

Integrity at the center. Compliance at the core. Respect as the operating principle.

Harrah's succeeded with Cherokee because they respected sovereignty and never tried to circumvent Tribal authority. They never meddled in Tribal politics or tried to influence elections or Council decisions. They honored regulation and treated the Gaming Commission as a partner rather than a threat or obstacle to be managed. They believed in long-term trust rather than short-term profit maximization. They invested heavily, consistently, and professionally in the property and the community. They valued our people and our reputation. And they kept their promises, even when cheaper options existed, even when corporate pressures might have justified cutting corners.

And we held up our end of the bargain: strict regulation, disciplined licensing, uncompromising enforcement, professional independence, political neutrality within the Gaming Commission, and high expectations that were consistently met.

This created something rare: a tribal-corporate partnership built on trust instead of leverage.

And that foundation changed everything.

The Transition

In many ways, the partnership with Harrah's marked the end of Cherokee's proving years.

We had shown the State of North Carolina that we could be trusted to regulate our own gaming industry. We had shown the federal government that tribal sovereignty and regulatory excellence could coexist. We had shown ourselves that we could build something world-class without losing our identity.

CHAPTER 18

LIVE CARDS

"Sovereignty is not given. It is exercised."

— Wilma Mankiller

The battle for live table games was sovereignty in action—not a principle discussed in classrooms, but a right asserted across six governors and two decades. Mankiller understood that distinction as well as anyone.

❖ ❖ ❖

THERE ARE MOMENTS IN a tribe's history when sovereignty is not simply asserted, it must be proven.

Most people, including legislators, lawyers, and even many in our own Tribe, had no idea that the key to our future was hidden in a line of federal law so obscure that ninety-nine out of a hundred attorneys never read it.

The rule under IGRA is simple, but powerful: If a state "permits or regulates" a form of gaming for any person, organization, or purpose, then a federally recognized tribe may negotiate a compact for that same game.

That's the exact principle affirmed in *Artichoke Joe's v. Norton* and embedded into the very architecture of IGRA.

For years, I educated lawmakers, attorneys, governors, and their staff on this point: Video poker, video blackjack, and video table games were already legal in North Carolina; therefore, the games themselves were not prohibited.

If the game was not prohibited, then under federal law the tribe had the right to negotiate for it, whether in video or live format.

It was not a loophole. It was the law.

And it became the cornerstone of our strategy.

Six Governors

Across my twenty-one-year span as executive director, I worked, directly or indirectly, under six different North Carolina governors: Jim Martin, Jim Hunt, Mike Easley, Beverly Perdue, Pat McCrory, and Roy Cooper.

Each one shaped the path in a different way, some helpful, some hostile, some cautious, some visionary.

But every one of them met the Cherokee Tribe, in negotiation, in litigation, or in quiet political moments behind closed doors.

I never actually met Governor Martin. By the time the first compact negotiations were happening in the early 1990s, I was working with Ben Bridgers, providing input, building the legal arguments, but Ben was the lead attorney dealing directly with the governor's office.

Governor Martin refused to negotiate. So we filed suit.

And when Governor Hunt returned to office, everything changed.

Governor Hunt was someone I had a kind of family connection with, though maybe I shouldn't phrase it that way.

When I was a young boy, Governor Hunt came to Cherokee. He had his picture taken, along with his wife and children, with my father, Chief Henry, at the roadside stand where my father worked with the public.

I still have a copy of that photograph. Governor Hunt standing with my father in front of the stand, both men smiling, tourists and family gathered around.

Decades later, I would sit across the table from that same man, no longer a boy watching from the sidelines, but a Tribal attorney negotiating the future of Cherokee gaming.

The arc of that story still amazes me.

Governor Hunt honored his promise to negotiate in good faith. He didn't just meet with us, he listened. He understood. He worked with us as partners, not adversaries.

What began as adversarial litigation under Martin transformed into the opening that would make everything else possible.

The Governor's Mansion

One of my favorite memories from all those years of negotiation happened at the governor's mansion in 1999—sitting around a large round table with Chief Leon Jones, Ben Bridgers (who passed away on July 9, 2016), Bill Buffalo, Phil Carlton, Jack Stewart from the governor's legal team, Governor Hunt, and me.

We were discussing extending the compact term from seven years to thirty years, necessary for financing the first hotel tower.

It showed something important: Governor Hunt understood politics. He understood loyalty. And he understood that moving forward required protecting the people who had stood with us in the past.

That provision has stood for many years. And the Cherokee Preservation Foundation he envisioned became a transformative philanthropic force in Western North Carolina, funding education, cultural preservation, and community development projects that continue to this day.

The Breakthrough Years

I didn't know Governor Easley before he became governor.

But once he took office, I developed a very close working relationship with him and his staff, particularly Hampton Dellinger and Andy Vanore, two of the sharpest legal minds I ever worked with.

Together with Chief Leon Jones, we worked through the first major 4(B) Compact Amendment. Section 4(B) is a provision in the compact that allows the Tribe to request amendments, with authority for the governor to approve them based on prior legislative approvals—without requiring the full legislative process every time.

My push to utilize the never before used Section 4(B) created the real breakthrough: video raffles.

Under North Carolina law, raffles were legal and regulated. And under IGRA, if the state permits raffles, the Tribe can conduct raffles.

So we made the argument: If we structure our video slot machines as raffles, with the proper legal framework, then we can offer the full library of games from IGT and other manufacturers.

The full range: the standard video slot machines people recognize everywhere, cherries, bells, whistles, sevens, all the classic imagery and game types.

It was a legal and technical breakthrough that opened up an entirely new world of gaming options.

Governor Easley's administration understood the argument, worked with us in good faith, and approved the amendment.

And just like that, Cherokee gaming expanded exponentially.

The Historic Moment

Beverly Perdue became the first woman governor of North Carolina.

I remember the time she came to the casino. She smiled as she placed the chips on the table. The dealer dealt the cards. The crowd around us, Tribal officials, Harrah's executives, media, guests, watched in silence.

The hand didn't turn out in her favor. Everyone laughed, including the governor.

She placed a couple more bets. Won a hand or two. The tension broke into celebration.

But the moment itself, that first bet, that first hand, that crossing of a line we had fought for two decades to reach, was something I will never forget.

It was about sovereignty. About proving that a small mountain Tribe could negotiate as equals with a state government, assert rights under federal law, and win.

The Difficult Years and Restoration

After Governor Perdue came Governor Pat McCrory.

His term was one where the Tribe didn't have a whole lot of success. He was difficult to work with, not hostile, exactly, but distant. Unengaged.

There was one meeting with him when I went down to Raleigh, expecting to meet in his office. Instead, he wanted to meet at the governor's mansion.

We sat down in the mansion, and I waited for the substantive conversation to begin.

It never did.

Governor McCrory wanted to talk about issues and events that weren't even germane to what we were there to discuss: gaming, compact amendments, regulatory concerns.

The meeting was polite. Professional. But ultimately, not substantive at all.

I left that day knowing that this administration was not going to be a partner the way the others had been.

Following McCrory came Governor Roy Cooper. And immediately, the relationship improved.

I had known Roy Cooper for years, long before he became governor. When he served as attorney general, I met with him personally several times in the AG's office. We had built trust, respect, and a working relationship grounded in mutual understanding of the law.

When he became governor, that trust carried forward.

The Real Argument

One of the biggest misunderstandings in North Carolina was this: Legislators thought "live blackjack" was fundamentally different from "video blackjack."

They aren't.

We brought in experts, gaming scientists, industry specialists, who testified that the mathematics are the same, the risk model is the same, the betting mechanics are the same, the regulatory standards are the same. Only the delivery mechanism differs.

Video poker is still poker. Video blackjack is still blackjack. Video roulette is still roulette.

And under IGRA, if the game is allowed in any format, then it is not prohibited.

This argument, simple and undeniable, eventually broke the state's resistance.

Sovereignty Exercised

Looking back, the fight for live gaming wasn't about blackjack tables or roulette wheels.

It was about recognition.

It was about teaching a state government, one governor at a time, that the Cherokee people are a sovereign nation with rights defined not by politics, but by law.

It took six governors, more than twenty years, litigation, lobbying, statutory education, constitutional arguments, federal precedent, Tribal unity, and relentless persistence.

But we did it.

We transformed Cherokee from a video poker outpost into the most successful gaming destination in the Southeast.

And we did it legally. Honorably. Strategically. And with the full force of our sovereignty.

Six governors. Two decades. And still the same lesson: Sovereignty is exercised, not given.

The Shift

By the time we won the legal battles that brought live table games and modern Class III gaming to Cherokee, something larger was already happening, something you could feel in the homes, the schools, the businesses, and in the way our people walked with their heads a little higher.

Before gaming, the economy ran on a simple, harsh reality. The Tribe employed fewer than two hundred people total. Employment was scarce, fiercely protected, and a dead end: you got hired as a custodian, you stayed a custodian. There was no career ladder, no advancement, no pension. Poverty wasn't occasional; for most families, it was generational. Your parents struggled. Their parents struggled. And unless something changed, something big, you would struggle too.

I'll never forget one afternoon in the early 1990s when the Tribe had to borrow $50,000 from a local businessman just to make payroll. That's how thin the margins were. That's how much power the local business community held.

Gaming changed all of that, steadily, year after year. Today, between 7,500 and 10,000 jobs exist because of gaming revenue. The Tribal government alone employs over 1,200 people. But what the numbers can't capture is the transformation in how people lived. Families moved from substandard housing to homes they owned. Reliable vehicles appeared in driveways. Heat that worked. Roofs that didn't leak. College went from a distant dream to an expectation, parents began saying "when you go to college," not "if." Families took vacations for the first time. Christmas meant real gifts under the tree.

I watched people who started as dealers become pit bosses. People who started in housekeeping become department directors. Young people entered at the ground floor and worked their way up until they were running entire departments, not because they had connections, but because they worked hard and earned it. That belief, that your effort will be rewarded, is the foundation of every healthy economy. For the first time in Cherokee's modern history, we had it.

And the generation that grew up with gaming didn't have to leave. For generations, the most ambitious Cherokee young people had no choice; if you wanted education, a career, opportunity, you left the Qualla Boundary. But these children could stay. They could build careers here, raise families here, contribute to their community here. That shift—from a people defined by what we lacked to a people defined by what we were building, was perhaps the greatest transformation of all.

The Resistance

Not everyone saw the change as progress. For decades, local business owners who catered to tourists had sustained the Tribal government through the levy. These weren't just business relationships, they were lifelines. When talk of expansion began, especially building a hotel, many of those owners felt betrayed.

One particular family patriarch contacted Governor Hunt directly, lobbying against the Tribe building a tower. The governor listened. When we negotiated the extended-term compact, he insisted on an unusual requirement: 7,500 complimentary room nights per year guaranteed to local hoteliers. Gaming comp nights written into a state compact, unheard of. But without it, he wasn't moving.

We agreed. We were already purchasing tens of thousands of room nights to house our guests. The 7,500 comp nights were a fraction of what we were already doing. That provision still exists in the compact today.

The Balloon That Touched the Sky

The day we broke ground on the first hotel tower in 2002, the casino brought a massive balloon and lifted it twenty-one stories high. Standing on the ground, watching it rise above the tree line, Something settled in me that I hadn't expected. Before that moment, the tallest building anywhere in the area was three stories, and we were about to eclipse that by seven times.

The balloon stayed up for weeks. People brought their children to see it. For a people who had once been removed from their homeland at bayonet point, who had walked the Trail of Tears, who had fought for generations just to survive—the sight of a Cherokee-built tower rising toward the sky meant something more than just revenue. It meant we were rising too.

The first tower didn't just succeed, it transformed everything. Demand exploded. From there, expansion came in waves: the second hotel tower, high-limit rooms, restaurants, entertainment venues, construction phases year after year. Each expansion required regulatory review, licensing, compact compliance, surveillance updates. As the buildings rose, our regulatory system had to rise with them.

CHAPTER 19

THE RESERVES

"Sunlight is the best disinfectant."

— Louis Brandeis

I discovered millions hidden from our people through an illegal fund born from a dinner conversation. Brandeis was right—the only cure was daylight.

◆　◆　◆

THERE ARE MOMENTS IN a regulator's career when the job becomes personal. Not emotional. Not vengeful. But personal—in the sense that you realize the system you built, the independence you fought for, the integrity you refused to compromise—all of it is about to be tested in a way you never imagined.

For me, that moment came in June 2004.

I discovered that the Tribal government—the very entity that created the Gaming Commission to regulate the gaming revenues—had been withholding millions of dollars from the enrolled members. Illegally. Quietly. And with no intention of stopping.

I was reviewing the gaming financial reports from January through May 2004 when I saw it. A line item that didn't belong. A "Special Reserve Fund"—accumulating at a rate of approximately $1.3 million per month. By June 2004, the fund had grown to over $6 million.

I stopped. I read it again. Read it a third time. And I felt something cold settle in my chest.

Under Cherokee law, specifically our Revenue Allocation Plan and our Gaming Ordinance, 50 percent of net gaming revenues must be distributed to Tribal members as per capita payments. Not 45 percent. Not 47 percent. Fifty percent. That wasn't a suggestion. That was Tribal law, approved by the Department of Interior, codified in our ordinance, and binding on everyone, including the Tribal government itself.

I called my director of finance, Lee Dillard, and my senior agent,

Rick Saunooke, the people I trusted most. "We need to investigate this. Quietly. Thoroughly. And fast."

Building the Case

Over the next few weeks, we pulled every financial document we could access. What we found was troubling.

The Special Reserve Fund had originated back in 1999, from a dinner discussion. Not a Council session. Not a formal proposal. A dinner discussion. Someone had floated the idea, and somehow that conversation had turned into policy without ever being brought before the Tribal Council, incorporated into the Revenue Allocation Plan, or receiving the legal authorization that Tribal law required.

The TCGE Board of Advisors had implemented the reserve as if it were legitimate, pitched as prudent financial management, a safety net. It sounded reasonable. But it was illegal. The Revenue Allocation Plan didn't allow for discretionary reserves that reduced per capita distributions. That requirement couldn't be changed by a dinner conversation. It could only be changed through a formal amendment approved by the Tribal Council and submitted to the DOI.

None of that had happened.

For five years, money had been quietly diverted. Each enrolled member would have received approximately $3,200 in the June 2005 distribution. Because we discovered the illegal reserves and forced their return, the distribution became over $5,200, an extra $1,800 or more per person. For a family of four enrolled members, that's over $7,000. Multiply that by thousands of enrolled members, and you're talking about tens of millions of dollars withheld from the people who legally owned it.

The Public Confrontation

On July 19, 2004, I submitted my formal investigation report to the Gaming Commission Board. The findings were unambiguous: The fund was created without legal authority, violated the Revenue Allocation Plan and Gaming Ordinance, and must be immediately discontinued with all withheld funds returned to the people.

I requested a closed session with the Tribal Council to present my findings privately. I wanted to give them the opportunity to correct the problem quietly.

The Council chairman refused. "We'll stay live," he said.

So I presented my findings in an open, public Council session, cameras rolling, Tribal members watching, everything on the record. I stood at the podium and laid out the facts. I had prepared a document to ensure I stayed on message. The key points were these:

"The Gaming Commission is here to protect the Tribe and this includes ALL the enrolled members."

"Our Ordinance is structured to give the commission the power and independence to make the tough decisions when needed without the fear of reprisal from the government."

"Our duty to protect the Tribe and its members may at times mean that we have to make a ruling against the Tribal government itself in order to enforce Tribal law and the rights of enrolled members."

The room was silent. Then the questions started. Some Council members were angry, at me, for making this public. Some were defensive. But I didn't back down.

"This isn't about politics," I said. "This is about law. And the law is clear."

The NIGC Intervenes

Shortly after my public presentation, I reported the violations to the National Indian Gaming Commission. I didn't do this lightly. Bringing in federal regulators is a serious step. But the Tribal government was violating its own laws and refusing to correct the problem. I had no choice.

On September 1, 2004, the NIGC sent a formal letter to Principal Chief Michell Hicks indicating they had received information that the Tribe's per capita payments may not be consistent with its revenue allocation plan, and that they intended to commence an examination.

The letter was signed by Philip N. Hogen, chairman of the NIGC. And here's the irony: Philip Hogen was the author of a paper called "The Perfect Tribal Gaming Commission." He had literally written the manual on how tribal gaming commissions should operate. And now he was coming to Cherokee because the Tribal government was violating the very principles he had championed.

On September 15, 2004, Chairman Hogen and his team met with

Chief Hicks, the Tribal Council, and me. I remember sitting in that meeting, watching Hogen review the documents, ask questions, and occasionally glance my way with something that felt like quiet approval.

The NIGC made its position clear: The reserves were not consistent with the Tribe's approved plan, the money must be returned, and the Tribe must comply with its own laws.

And then Hogen said something I will never forget. He looked at the Tribal Council and said, as I recall his words, "You built a strong Gaming Commission. This is what that looks like."

The Victory

Within weeks, the Special Reserve Fund was discontinued. The withheld money was returned. Every enrolled member received an extra $1,800 or more because the Gaming Commission did its job.

When the checks arrived, most people were happy. But few understood why the checks were bigger. The Tribal government didn't publicize what had happened. They just distributed the money and moved on.

But what mattered most wasn't recognition. The system worked. The people got their money. And Cherokee proved, to the federal government, to ourselves, and to anyone watching, that we could regulate ourselves.

The reserves fight confirmed something I had been feeling for years. Protecting the Tribe from the outside wasn't enough. Sometimes the threat came from within, from the very people entrusted to lead. And the closer I looked, the more I saw a government that needed someone willing to challenge it from the top.

The Hallway

It didn't happen the way people think it did. There was no grand announcement, no sudden epiphany. The decision to seek the highest office in our Tribe didn't come from ambition or calculation.

It came from a brief encounter in a hallway. A simple hallway in our casino, tile floors, fluorescent lights, the hum of slot machines in the distance.

A young employee, maybe only a few months on the job, stopped me.

"Mr. Lambert . . . can I ask you something?"

I nodded.

"You're the only one I see who walks around here like this belongs to the people. You're everywhere, checking everything. I wish someone like you was running the whole Tribe."

I smiled, thanked him, and continued down the hallway. But I could not forget it.

The Voices

That hallway conversation happened in 2004—right after I forced the Tribal government to return millions in illegally withheld per capita funds. People had seen the results in their checks. And some of them knew where it came from.

After that, people began to see me differently. Not as a regulator. As someone they could trust, someone who couldn't be bought, pressured, or silenced. Everywhere I went, the message was the same: "Patrick, you should run for Chief."

Cyndi heard it as much as I did, maybe more. People stopped her at the store, at events, at Tribal gatherings. She'd come home and tell me. Different people. Different places. Same message.

It wasn't just employees or young voters. One evening after a community meeting, an elder waited until everyone left, walked up slowly, and placed her hand on my arm.

"Son, I've watched you your whole life. You've spent twenty years protecting the Tribe from the outside. Maybe it's time to protect us from the inside."

She squeezed my arm once, gently, and walked away. I stood there alone in the empty room, her words echoing.

There were so many others. Elders from Big Cove, from Snowbird, from every community. Many of them have passed now. But their words still stick with me.

The Decision

Somewhere in 2006, after two years of hearing the same message from hundreds of people, Cyndi and I went to dinner at the Grove Park Inn in Asheville.

I laid it all out: the pressure, the voices, the sense that I was being called to something I hadn't asked for. But there was something else. From my position as executive director, I had a unique vantage point into how the Tribal government operated, not the public face, but the machinery behind it. Waste. Favoritism. Opacity. Good people pushed out because they wouldn't play the game.

"I think I can make a difference," I said. "I think I can bring the same discipline we built in the Gaming Commission to the entire Tribe."

She listened. She didn't interrupt. And then she leaned forward, looked me in the eyes, and said:

"Patrick, you know that whatever you decide to do, I will be one hundred percent with you."

That's how we operate. I generally don't make a move without first consulting Cyndi. If she's not fully with me, I know there's something I need to reconsider.

"Let's do it," she said.

The Three Campaigns

In 2007, I entered a crowded field. I made it through the primary easily and campaigned through the summer—home visits, porches, living rooms. The reception was overwhelmingly positive.

I lost by seven votes. Chief Michell Hicks defeated me by the narrowest of margins, after a court skirmish over ballot procedures. It was tough. But I accepted it and went back to work.

In 2011, I ran again. Same close race, same razor-thin margin, less than 1 percent, essentially a tie that went to the incumbent.

After the 2011 election, Hicks signed an amendment to the Gaming Ordinance requiring any Gaming Commission employee running for Principal Chief to resign before filing. To my knowledge, I was the only employee in Tribal history required to resign their job to run. No one before me. No one after me. It was designed to stop me.

It just made the decision clearer.

The Landslide

In January 2015, I resigned. After twenty-one years as executive director, I left the Gaming Commission, not because I wanted to, but because the amendment required it.

This time, I campaigned full-time. I set up headquarters in the hotel Cyndi and I owned. I hired Sage Dunston as campaign manager, a young man, my son's age, but brilliant and possessing keen political instincts from his experience in DC and Raleigh. I knocked on doors, sat on porches, and promised transparency, accountability, and a government that serves the people.

On election night, the results were overwhelming. Over 71 percent of the total voting population selected me as Principal Chief. In Cherokee elections, 60 percent is considered a strong victory. Over 70 percent is unprecedented.

People weren't just voting for me. They were voting for a track record—two decades of work that spoke louder than any campaign speech.

I stood there on election night, surrounded by Cyndi, my family, my supporters, and I felt the weight of it. Not the victory. The responsibility. Because I knew what that 71 percent meant.

PART III

WHEN THE WALLS CLOSED IN

CHAPTER 20

LET IT BEGIN

"They tried to bury us. They didn't know we were seeds."

— Mexican Proverb

I walked into a gutted office on my first day—no files, no furniture, no transition. What was intended to bury me only planted me deeper.

◆　◆　◆

I **ARRIVED AT THE TRIBAL** Council House early on my first official day as Principal Chief, before most of the staff had filtered in. I wanted a quiet moment to stand in the space where I would serve our people and let the weight of it settle before the chaos of governance began.

I opened the door to the Executive Office and stopped cold.

The room was barren. Not empty in the way an office might be between occupants. Barren in a way that felt deliberate. No chairs. A desk with drawers hanging loose, one leg propped up unevenly. No pens, no paper, no staplers. Supply cabinets standing open and empty. No artwork on the walls. No files, no records, no transition documents, no briefings, no contact lists. Nothing that would help a new Chief understand the current state of Tribal operations.

The office had been gutted. Whether done out of spite, panic, or a desperate desire to erase any record of how the previous administration had operated, I'll never know. But it was a message delivered before I'd spent one hour in the position: You're on your own, and we're not going to make this easy.

I'd be lying if I said it didn't hurt. Not for myself, I'd survived worse than an empty office, but for what it said about how little respect some people had for the democratic process, for the peaceful transition of power that's supposed to be sacred in any government.

I pulled out my phone and called Sage. "I need you to come to the

Executive Office."

He arrived five minutes later, walked through the door, and stopped in the same spot where I'd stopped. He looked around slowly.

"They really did a number on this place," he said.

"Where are the files?" he asked, already knowing the answer.

"There are no files."

"None?"

"None. No transition documents. No briefings. No contact lists. Nothing."

We stood there together in the empty office, and I could see him running through the same calculations I'd already made: How many weeks to rebuild basic institutional knowledge from scratch? How many phone calls to department heads? How many requests for documents that should have been waiting for us?

"All right," I finally said. "We've got work to do. Let's get started."

The First Battles

For the first several months, we worked out of the Emergency Operations Center while the Executive Office underwent a long-overdue renovation, fully approved by the Tribal Business Committee, documented, lawful, and routine. Yet even that became a target. "What's he renovating? How much is he spending? What's he trying to hide?" The questions were accusations dressed as questions.

As winter approached, the signs grew harder to ignore. People who had been warm during the campaign were suddenly cautious. Staff who once spoke freely now chose their words carefully. Routine requests that should have taken a day took a week. People don't shift this way on their own. Not this quickly, not this systematically. It wasn't me they feared. It was what transparency would reveal.

The Hallway

One evening after a particularly tense Council meeting, Tommye Saunooke, the Painttown representative, approached me privately. She looked nervous, glancing over her shoulder.

"Chief, they told me if I support you, I'll be the next one removed. They said they'd come after my seat. Is that true?"

"No. That's not true. Council members can only be removed for cause through a legitimate process. But the fact that they're saying it—that tells you everything you need to know about what's happening here."

She nodded slowly. "I thought so. But I wanted to hear it from you."

When Resistance Becomes Conspiracy

The impeachment didn't begin with paperwork or formal charges. It began with these moments: the gutted office, the whispers that turned allies into neutrals, and the pressure applied to vulnerable Council members.

All of it was laying the groundwork for what came next.

The storm had not yet struck in its full fury. But the air had changed. The machinery of resistance had been built and set in motion, waiting only for the right moment to be deployed.

CHAPTER 21

FOR THE RECORD: CHEROKEE FAMILIES FIRST

"The measure of a man is what he does with power."

— Plato

Ninety-seven million in debt eliminated. Twenty million in waste cut. Services expanded, not reduced. This chapter answers Plato's question.

◆ ◆ ◆

WHILE THE POLITICAL MACHINERY churned behind closed doors, I was doing what the people elected me to do, governing.

I want to pause the story here and lay something down for the record. Not to boast. Not to campaign. But because what was accomplished during my shortened tenure deserves to be documented before the noise of impeachment drowns it out. The people who elected me asked for specific things. They asked me to cut the wasteful spending, pay down the debt, root out corruption, and put Cherokee families first. I want the record to show what happened when I worked to keep those promises.

The Budget

The first thing I did was tear the budget apart and rebuild it.

I walked into office and inherited a Tribe that was $96 million in debt with no clear plan to address it. The previous budget had been built on the same assumptions it had been built on for twelve years—assumptions that prioritized politics over families. I gave direct instructions to the Tribal Finance team: we are going to dramatically improve the integrity and accountability of how this Tribe spends its money, and we are going to cut every dollar of waste we can find without reducing a single service to our people.

They delivered. We redrafted the entire FY2016 Tribal Budget, including a comprehensive revision of the Revenue Allocation Plan Ordinance. When we were finished, we had recovered over $20 million in savings—not by cutting programs, not by reducing services to enrolled members, but by eliminating the bloat, the redundancy, and the carelessness that had become routine. We restructured Tribal Divisions into a common model. We kept 100 percent support going to Tribal members and the community. We even increased revenues flowing into the Endowment, Debt Service, and Tribal Growth funds.

Twenty million dollars reduced. In the first budget. And not a single Cherokee family lost a service.

Paying Off the Debt

But cutting waste was only the beginning. The real anchor around the Tribe's neck was the debt—nearly $97 million spread across the new hospital project, the Wastewater Treatment Plant, and casino enterprise obligations under the Harrah's Management Agreement.

I created a Debt Service Task Force to research every component of that debt—what we owed, to whom, on what terms, and what it was costing us in interest and fees every year. The answer was staggering. Millions of dollars a year were leaving our Tribe and going straight to bankers.

I submitted and pushed legislation to pay off the two Tribal elements of the debt pool—the hospital and the Wastewater Treatment Plant. And we did it. We paid off the Tribal debt in the amount of nearly $97 million, saving over $6 million in annual interest payments to banks. That money didn't leave Cherokee anymore. It stayed home, where it belonged.

That single act, getting the bankers off our backs, may have been the most consequential financial decision in a generation. Every dollar saved in interest was a dollar that could go to elder services, child welfare, police coverage, infrastructure. The compounding effect of that payoff would benefit Cherokee families for decades.

Cutting Waste

I also went after the day-to-day spending that had become a culture of entitlement in the previous administration. We tracked every category and measured it against the prior year's numbers. The results spoke for themselves:

Travel expenses: cut by $893,673.

Credit card expenses: cut by $712,120.

Fuel expenses: cut by $350,368.

In total, we cut over $1.9 million in waste in the first year, a 42.5 percent reduction compared to the previous administration. That wasn't accounting magic. That was discipline. That was leadership saying no, you don't need to fly somewhere on the Tribe's dime when a phone call will do, and no, you don't get to swipe a credit card for personal expenses and call it government business.

Cherokee Families First

But the numbers only tell part of the story. What mattered most to me was what we were building for our people.

Public Health and Human Services was the heartbeat of the Cherokee Families First agenda. I added twenty-six new positions to PHHS and directed them to begin transitioning vital services from county and state oversight to Tribal control—adult and child welfare, supplemental nutrition, Medicaid eligibility, the Low Income Home Energy Assistance Program, and early education. These were services that affected our most vulnerable families, and for too long they had been administered by outsiders who didn't understand our community.

Starting in October 2015, we assumed authority for child welfare services—the provision of services for child maltreatment, foster care, and adoption—from the State of North Carolina. In those first months alone, we received 226 new child welfare referrals. Twenty-one children were placed in foster care. Three were returned to safe homes. Seven Cherokee foster homes were approved and licensed. Twenty-eight cases were transferred to our Family Safety program from neighboring counties.

We investigated 2,836 Indian Child Welfare notices involving potential Tribal member children across thirty-eight states. We verified seventeen were EBCI members. That work had never been done with that level of focus before. Those were our children, scattered across the country, and for the first time someone was paying attention.

I negotiated directly with North Carolina so that all previous Social Services funding—money that had been flowing to Swain and Jackson counties—was redirected to the Eastern Band. That secured approximately $402,000 for the current year and up to $708,000 annually going forward. That was Cherokee money going to Cherokee families instead of county governments.

We entered a formal Title IV-E agreement for direct federal funding. We completed the new Family Safety facility and saved $340,000 on construction costs through collaborative cost management. We relocated Temporary Assistance for Needy Families (TANF) and Child Support Enforcement under PHHS. We merged the Handicap, Elderly Living Program (HELP) into the Housing Rehabilitation Division.

And we doubled Senior Christmas checks from $250 to $500.

Public Safety

On day one, I eliminated the position of Deputy Marshall and hired a Chief of Police. My directive was simple: Get our officers back on our land, bust the drug dealers, track down the thieves, and be professional about it. I wanted a visible police presence in our communities—not officers sitting in offices, but officers on the roads, in the neighborhoods, earning the community's trust.

We increased twenty-four-hour patrol coverage. We refocused the Narcotics Division to concentrate its investigations on Tribal lands. We restructured the entire Public Safety Division, placing the jail, dispatch, Natural Resources Enforcement, Child Advocacy, and Animal Control under the same branch so communication and coordination were seamless.

Most importantly, we created twenty-four-hour police coverage for our Snowbird and Cherokee County communities—families who had been underserved for years finally had officers on the ground around the clock.

I restructured EMS, Fire, and Emergency Management into a single department for better accountability and coordination. That restructuring proved itself almost immediately when severe weather hit and the unified response was faster and more effective than anything the Tribe had managed before. We entered a mutual agreement with Cherokee County EMS and Fire that saved the Tribe over $13 million in the first year. We reached agreements for fire protection covering Cherokee families in Grape Creek, Peachtree, Valleytown, and Hanging Dog.

And at Cherokee High School, we instituted a new EMT curriculum.

Thirteen students completed it. That was the future being built, one class at a time.

Constituent Services

One of the things I noticed immediately was that regular enrolled members had no real pathway to get help from their own government. They would call the Executive Office with a problem—a land transfer question, an emergency housing need, a need for a wheelchair ramp for a disabled elder—and there was no system for following through. People fell through the cracks because nobody's job was to catch them.

So I created the Constituent Services Office inside the Executive Office. Charlotte Saunooke served as director, leading a team of three representatives, Denise Walkingstick and Rosie McCoy each charged with daily caseloads. Their job was simple: When a Cherokee person has a problem with their government, fix it.

By the time I was removed from office, that team had resolved over 2,400 individual cases. Housing issues, land transfers, benefit questions, referrals, phone calls made on behalf of elders who didn't know how to navigate the system. Twenty-four hundred families who got help because somebody finally built a door they could walk through.

Infrastructure and Public Works

I created a new Department of Administration and Public Works, assembling under one roof all the programs that delivered public services—water, sewer, Tribal construction, sanitation, and facilities. I was tired of seeing trash piled up and infrastructure neglected. Our communities deserved better than that.

We merged Site Prep into Tribal Construction, which immediately improved efficiency. We combined Recycling, Compost, and Sanitation into a single unit. We completed projects on water mains, bridge replacements, new raw water intakes, and revised our Forest Management Plans and Fish and Wildlife Service policies.

I wanted our town and our streets to be clean, safe, and something our people could be proud of. That wasn't a luxury—it was a statement about how we saw ourselves.

Beyond the Boundary

I didn't just govern inside the Qualla Boundary. I took the Tribe's voice to places outside our Tribe..

I met with North Carolina's governor and attorney general. I attended United South and Eastern Tribes (USET) as a new board member. I testified before the House Indian Affairs Subcommittee on the Lands Reacquisition Act. I met with the presidents of Duke Power and Verizon about improving electrical and communications infrastructure on Tribal lands. I signed a 638 contract with the BIA for the Jail and Justice Center. I negotiated a $1.7 million settlement with Duke Energy for damages from a 2009 fire in Big Cove.

And I had the honor of speaking with President Obama. The first thing I mentioned to him was the access road beside Cherokee School—a simple but important issue for our families. I also spoke to him about the right of the Eastern Band to continue traditional harvesting in the Great Smoky Mountains, because that land is traditional Cherokee land, and our people should never have to ask permission to gather from it.

I led the fight to ensure that Swain County continued offering the Cherokee language as a foreign language course rather than demoting it to an elective. That may sound like a small thing. It wasn't. Language is culture. Culture is survival. And every time someone tries to reduce our language to something optional, they're telling our children that being Cherokee is optional too.

The Legislation

In my time in office, I introduced more legislation to Tribal Council than any Principal Chief in recent memory. Much of it passed. Some of it was blocked. All of it was aimed at building a government that worked for its people instead of for itself.

The Legal Division

One of the accomplishments I'm most proud of—and one that has proven its value every year since—was the complete restructuring of the Tribe's legal division.

When I took office, the Attorney General's office was understaffed and stretched thin. There was no Legal Services office. There was no Public Defender. Cherokee families who needed legal help navigating Tribal systems, who couldn't afford private counsel, had nowhere to turn within their own government. That wasn't right. And it wasn't sustainable for a nation growing as fast as ours was.

So we fixed it.

I expanded the Attorney General's office, adding attorney positions to meet the actual legal demands the Tribe faced. I created the first Legal Services office in the Tribe's history—giving enrolled members access to legal assistance they had never had before. And I established the first Public Defender's office, ensuring that Tribal members facing charges in Tribal Court had someone in their corner.

The most satisfying part? We didn't go looking for new money to fund it. Every dollar came from the waste and abuse we had already cut from the budget. No new burden on the Tribe. Just a reallocation of resources from what was being squandered to what actually served the people.

That structure is still standing today. Still serving Cherokee families. Built on savings. Built on principle. Built to last.

Among the legislation that passed: creation of a Tribal Constitution process, authorization of a full Tribal Census, reinstatement of the 5 percent 401(k) match for all employees, a 2.5 percent cost of living raise and 3 percent merit increase retroactive to October 1, the restructuring of minors' per capita into staggered payments to protect their money, the creation of a Department of Justice, term limits for Chief and Vice Chief, a new election ordinance, a $500 per capita loan program at zero percent interest to help families in times of need, authorization to build a homeless shelter and soup kitchen, and the launch of forensic audits to uncover wrongdoing from previous administrations.

I also proposed and pushed for a drug treatment and rehabilitation center, a new Senior Center and Child Care Center in Snowbird, a bowling center and community building, and the Big Cove Child Care Center.

Additional Milestones

- Organized a Legal Summit bringing together Tribal legal leaders
- Hosted a Heroin Summit to address the opioid crisis on Tribal lands
- Established a Project Development Working Group for long-range planning

• Launched improvements to the Cherokee Veterans Memorial Park

• Met with Park Service officials on traditional gathering regulations

• Created monthly Bingo games for elders

• Published the first-ever *First 100 Days Report* and *Six-Month Report* to the people

• Hosted community events including the Graduate Awards Dinner, Easter Eggstravaganza, Mother's Day Celebration, Spring Garden Fair, Keeping Cherokee Beautiful Street Sweep, Father's Day Festivities, Summer Splash, Back to School Bash, Community Prayer Circle, and Community Day

• Rode with the Sanitation crew on their morning route to see the work firsthand

• Increased criminal penalties for drug offenses in Cherokee communities

• Began 638 contract process with BIA for expanded Tribal self-governance

• Received the Jedi Award from the *Smoky Mountain News* for the marijuana veto—a moment of levity in an otherwise relentless schedule

The Record Stands

I share all of this not to dwell on what was, but because the record matters. When the impeachment story is told, and it will be told many different ways, I want the full picture to be available. I want the Cherokee people to know what their government was doing for them during those months. I want them to see the trajectory, the momentum, the direction we were heading before it was interrupted.

Every one of these accomplishments was real. Every dollar saved was documented. Every program created served actual families. Every piece of legislation went through proper channels and was voted on by Tribal Council.

This was not a Chief sitting in his office collecting a paycheck. This was a government working at full speed, trying to make up for many years of lost time, trying to build something that would outlast any one person's tenure.

And for a while, it did.

Cyndi once said it best. She wrote an open letter during my first year that captured what those days felt like from the inside:

"He has so many ideas that can bring so much good to our Tribe, and just maybe he will not run out of time to get them done."

We did run out of time. Not because the work failed, but because it succeeded—and that success threatened the people who had built their power on the old way of doing things.

But the record stands. And the record is this: In less than two years, working from a gutted office with no transition documents and mounting political opposition, we saved over $20 million in the first budget, paid off $97 million in Tribal debt, cut $1.9 million in wasteful spending, assumed child welfare from the state, expanded police coverage to communities that had been forgotten, resolved over 2,400 constituent cases, and passed more legislation than any administration in recent memory.

No impeachment vote can erase what we built in twenty months.

CHAPTER 22

THE AUDITS

"Three things cannot be long hidden: the sun, the moon, and the truth."

— Buddha

When I hired independent auditors to examine every corner of Tribal finances, the people with nothing to hide looked relieved. The people with plenty to hide looked terrified.

◆　◆　◆

DURING THE CAMPAIGN, TRIBAL members repeatedly pulled me aside with quiet questions that carried years of frustration behind them.

"Chief, where is all the money going?" they would ask in low voices at community gatherings, glancing around to make sure no one was listening. "Why do some departments never get audited? Why are certain people protected no matter what they do? Why does no one check the books?"

These were the questions of people who had watched programs struggle while certain individuals prospered, who had seen contracts awarded to the same connected families, who had heard rumors about credit cards and travel expenses and housing loans that didn't quite add up—but nobody in power seemed interested in looking too closely.

On Inauguration Day, standing before the people who had given me this responsibility, I spoke one simple promise that would change everything: "We will follow the truth wherever it leads."

That line landed softly in the crowd, just one sentence among many. But for some people listening that day, it landed hard. They understood exactly what I was promising and what it would mean for their comfortable arrangements.

RGL Forensics—A Turning Point No One Saw Coming

One of my first major decisions as Principal Chief, long before calling the FBI, was to hire RGL Forensics, a national, independent auditing firm with no connections to Cherokee politics. They were professionals who had conducted similar work for governments across the country, and their reputation depended on accuracy and independence.

Their assignment was simple: Follow the money. All of it. Document what you find. Report it accurately.

For the first time in our Tribe's history, an audit would fully examine every corner of Tribal finances—Executive Office credit cards, Council credit cards, Qualla Housing Authority, the ABC Board, contracting practices, internal controls.

When I announced the engagement, I watched certain faces in the room change. The people who had nothing to hide looked relieved. The people who had plenty to hide looked terrified.

The Work Begins—January 2016

In January 2016, RGL began their work. Within weeks, I began noticing small tremors inside the system.

The truth had started to move.

The First Reports—April 2016

By April 2016, the first reports came back.

I sat alone at my desk late at night, and I read every page.

The patterns were unmistakable: credit card expenditures with nothing to do with Tribal business, personal expenses charged to the Tribe without justification, weak internal controls that allowed abuse to continue unchecked because nobody was watching.

The misuse wasn't universal; plenty of people were doing their jobs honestly. But the problems were systemic enough that I knew immediately what had to happen next.

There was no hesitation in my mind. The law was clear. My duty was clear.

I turned the audit findings over to the FBI and the United States Attorney's Office.

I gave them the full file, every document, every finding, every detail, exactly as the law required. No filtering. No political calculations about who might be protected.

The Federal Partners

The FBI agents I worked with on this matter were professionals I had known for years through my work with the Tribal Gaming Commission. Special Agent Andy Romagnuolo and Agent Bill Gang had both worked with Cherokee on previous investigations related to casino operations, and they had earned my respect through their professionalism and thoroughness.

They knew how seriously we took our responsibilities at the Gaming Commission. They knew we weren't the kind of people who made accusations lightly or wasted federal resources on political vendettas. When I called them with the audit findings, they understood immediately that I was bringing them something real.

The United States attorney overseeing the case was Jill Westmoreland Rose from the Western District of North Carolina. Her office received the materials we provided and began their own assessment of what the audits had revealed.

The process was professional, methodical, and completely appropriate—exactly how cooperation between tribal and federal authorities should work when potential crimes have been discovered.

Their response was simple and professional: "Thank you, Chief. We will handle it from here."

I hung up the phone, and for the first time since taking office, I felt the full weight of what was coming.

Not fear. Not regret. Just clarity—the understanding that the people who had benefited from the old system would never forgive me for exposing it, and the fight ahead would be unlike anything I had faced before.

The DOJ Letter—October 4, 2016

On October 4, 2016, the investigation became official and undeniable.

The United States Department of Justice sent a formal letter to the director of Qualla Housing Authority, notifying her that the federal government was conducting an investigation into possible criminal conduct in the housing organization.

The letter was direct and unmistakable in its language: "By this letter, the United States Department of Justice is notifying you that it is conducting an investigation regarding possible criminal conduct related to certain loans and loan applications, among other matters, involving the Qualla Housing Authority. The allegations under investigation include possible violations of federal program fraud, mail fraud, and wire fraud."

The letter instructed Qualla Housing personnel not to tamper with, destroy, or alter any documents, including loan applications, customer files, banking records, grant information, and all other business records.

This was no longer a Tribal matter being handled internally. This was the full weight of the federal government focused on potential violations within Cherokee governance.

The DOJ letter confirmed what the audits had already suggested: There were serious problems at Qualla Housing, problems that went beyond poor management or sloppy recordkeeping, problems that potentially rose to the level of federal crimes.

And the same audit process that had uncovered those problems was continuing to examine other areas of Tribal operations—including the credit card expenditures of Council members who would soon be voting on my impeachment.

My Report to the Tribal Council—October 10, 2016

Six days after the DOJ letter arrived, on Monday, October 10, 2016, I stood before the Tribal Council during their regular session and made a public statement about what was happening.

I told them directly and completely.

"Mr. Chairman, I just want to mention that I think the word has filtered throughout the community about the letter and notification from the IRS asking for substantial records, particularly including payments to Tribal employees and Tribal officials," I said. "At the same time, we have been officially notified that there is a federal criminal investigation of Qualla Housing and HCD files and actions."

I explained that I had instructed the secretary of treasury, the attorney general, and the secretary of housing to compile all of the documents that had been requested in the federal investigations.

And then I issued a direct challenge to every member of the Tribal Council: "I just ask that each member of the Tribal Council join me this morning in pledging to provide all of the documents requested and to cooperate fully with the investigations."

The room was silent.

Some Council members shifted uncomfortably in their seats, avoiding my eyes. Others stared straight ahead with expressions that revealed nothing. A few nodded in what might have been agreement or might have been acknowledgment that they had no choice but to agree publicly, whatever their private feelings.

The message was clear: The federal government was investigating Cherokee operations. I was cooperating fully. And I was asking, in front of cameras, in front of the public, in a way that would be recorded and remembered—for every Council member to commit to the same cooperation.

Later, I issued a public statement to the press that reinforced the same message: "My office is taking the investigation conducted by the US Department of Justice, US Attorney's Office, and the IRS very seriously. Cherokee families deserve a government that is open, honest, and aboveboard. That is why I have directed all Tribal departments and programs that are involved to fully cooperate and provide all information needed to conduct a thorough investigation into all wrongdoing."

More Audits, More Exposure, More Panic

RGL continued their work throughout 2016 and into 2017, and every system they touched revealed deeper problems.

Housing showed loan irregularities and weak controls that had allowed questionable transactions to proceed without proper oversight. The ABC Board had compliance issues that should have been caught years earlier. Internal controls across multiple departments were inconsistently enforced, creating opportunities for abuse that some people had apparently exploited. Council credit card records showed personal expenditures, noncompliant transactions, and practices that had been normalized through years of repetition until people forgot, or pretended to forget, that they were wrong.

Nothing was hidden anymore. Nothing was protected by the comfortable silence that had prevailed for so long. Every finding was documented, every irregularity was noted, and every report was submitted to the FBI and the US Attorney's Office exactly as the law required.

A Normal January—Until It Wasn't

Early in the new year of 2017, something changed. The resistance that had been diffused suddenly became organized and focused. Opposition stopped being a collection of individual complaints and became a coordinated plan with a timeline that was planned to culminate in my removal from office.

Every January, I attended the Walt Disney World Marathon Weekend in Florida with my family—one of the few times each year when I stepped away from the constant demands of public life. After months of political warfare, those few days felt like oxygen.

At the very same time, a group of Council members and the Vice Chief traveled to Washington, DC, for USET Impact Week—ostensibly routine government business.

In reality, it became something very different.

The Washington Trip

Through documented accounts and direct conversations with one of the Council members who refused to participate, I learned what happened during that January trip.

They weren't just attending the official meetings. They were interviewing attorneys.

Not attorneys for legislation or federal advocacy. They were interviewing attorneys to serve as prosecutor in an impeachment proceeding they had already decided to pursue, against me.

No charges existed. No allegations had been formally made. No investigation. They were shopping for a prosecutor before the first accusation was ever written.

I came to believe the decision to remove me had been made long before the first charge was ever written. I cannot prove this conclusively, but the sequence of events—attorney meetings in January, formal charges months later—led me to that conclusion.

From my perspective, the impeachment wasn't a response to wrongdoing, it was a strategy to stop the audits, protect the people those audits were exposing, and eliminate the Chief who had promised transparency and was actually delivering it.

Everything that came after—the formal allegations, the investigation, the hearing itself—felt to me like theater designed to justify a conclusion that had already been reached in Washington.

Who Went to Washington

The group that traveled to DC for Impact Week included the key architects of what would become the impeachment coalition.

Vice Chief Richard G. Sneed was there—the man who would become Principal Chief the moment I was removed, who had the most direct personal interest in seeing me gone, and who had been quietly building alliances against my administration since the first weeks of my term.

Dennis "Bill" Taylor from Wolfetown was there, serving as both Council member and chairman of the Qualla Housing Board—the same Qualla Housing Authority that was already under federal investigation, the same organization whose problems the audits had helped expose.

Brandon Jones, vice chairman of the Council and representative from Snowbird, was there. He was one of the key figures in the coalition that formed against my administration.

Travis Smith from Birdtown was there—the loudest and most aggressive voice against my administration, the man who would attack me publicly at every opportunity but who, when voters had their say, would be rejected soundly at the polls in his next election.

Richard French from Big Cove was also present on the trip. But he later told me directly, looking me in the eye with the kind of honesty that was increasingly rare in Cherokee politics: "I didn't attend the attorney meetings. I wasn't part of that."

He saw what was happening. He understood that this wasn't about legitimate oversight or genuine concerns about my conduct in office. He recognized it for what it was—a coordinated plan to remove an elected official for political and personal reasons—and he wanted no part of it.

Three Council members, Richard French, Teresa McCoy, and

Tommye Saunooke, would eventually stand against the impeachment when it came to a vote. And all three of them had seen the coordinated plan to remove me forming in real time, had been invited to participate, and had refused.

What They Were Looking For

The attorneys they interviewed in Washington weren't being hired for Tribal business in any normal sense. They were being hired to build a case against me—to take the predetermined conclusion that I needed to be removed and work backward to construct charges that might justify that conclusion.

What they wanted was someone who had no connection to Cherokee politics, or did not care about politics, no existing relationships that might complicate their willingness to do what was asked, or not care about existing relationships and just do it for the money. They needed someone who could give the impeachment the appearance of legitimacy, who could stand in front of cameras and a packed Council Chamber and present accusations with the authority of an expert.

They didn't find anyone in Washington. Instead, they turned to a local hotshot.

They retained Rob Saunooke to serve as the prosecutor. He is an attorney with a commanding courtroom presence, and he became the face of the prosecution—the person who stood before the Council and the cameras and presented the charges against me.

The charges he presented did not reflect any actual wrongdoing. The allegations were legally insufficient and the process fundamentally flawed. But at that moment, his role was to give the proceeding the appearance of a legitimate legal process.

The FBI Raid—February 2, 2017

In February 2017, everything came to a head.

Without warning, the FBI raided the Qualla Housing Authority, executing a search warrant that had been issued based on the evidence the audits and ongoing investigation had developed. Federal agents walked into the offices, secured the premises, and began boxing up records and evidence.

They confirmed through their actions what the RGL audits had already revealed: There were serious financial problems at Qualla Housing—problems some people desperately hoped would never see daylight.

That same day, while FBI agents were carrying boxes out of Qualla Housing, a Council meeting happened to be underway at the Tribal Council House. When word of the raid reached the Council Chamber, the atmosphere changed instantly.

Phones buzzed with text messages as the news spread. Council members exchanged looks of panic rather than the righteous outrage you might expect if they had nothing to hide. Whispers circulated through the gallery as observers tried to understand what was happening.

And in the middle of that fear-filled moment, Vice Chief Richard G. Sneed stood up and asked for a motion that would change everything: "I request a move that we investigate the Chief."

No allegation of wrongdoing. No evidence of misconduct. No formal complaint from anyone. No justification beyond the obvious desire to change the subject from the FBI raid to something else, anything else, that might distract attention from the people who may have actually been under federal investigation.

February Council—The Ambush

The February Council meeting where the investigation into my office was launched didn't announce itself as anything special. Nothing on the published agenda hinted at what was coming. Nothing in the routine proceedings suggested that this session would be different from any other.

I arrived expecting normal Tribal business—the kind of discussions and votes and administrative matters that filled every Council meeting.

Then, without warning, the Vice Chief stood up and began a tirade against me, complaining about a personnel matter. Then, on cue, Travis Smith asked to be heard and said that he thought there should be an Internal Audit investigation against me. He made a move and it passed.

His timing was perfect, coming immediately after the FBI raid, when fear was highest and the need for a distraction was most acute.

He asked the Tribal Council to direct Internal Audit to investigate my office.

No prior notice to me. No specific allegation of wrongdoing. No discussion with me or my staff about whatever concerns might exist. No due process. No reasoning grounded in any actual policy violation or legal issue.

Just a sudden, coordinated motion to put me under investigation.

It was a test balloon, the first official step in their plan. If the Council approved the investigation, they could use whatever they found, no matter how innocent, as the basis for impeachment charges. If they didn't find anything problematic, they could keep investigating until they did, or simply reframe ordinary decisions as misconduct and dare anyone to challenge their interpretation.

In hindsight, the intention was unmistakable: launch an investigation to create the appearance of scandal, then use that appearance to justify the impeachment they had already decided to pursue. All of it executed on the same day federal agents raided offices.

The Four-Month War Begins

From that moment in February until the impeachment hearing in late May, my administration was forced into a constant defensive posture.

Every day brought new battles, new accusations, new procedural attacks that had to be answered and documented and defended against. It wasn't one fight; it was dozens of overlapping conflicts, each designed to consume time and energy that should have been spent governing.

There were sudden requests for documents that should have been readily available but were framed as if I were hiding something. Political maneuvering behind closed doors as Council members traded favors and made deals about how they would vote when the time came. Procedural traps set up to make routine decisions look suspicious. Accusations whispered into community ears, spreading through the Boundary like poison, turning neighbors against each other and making people afraid to be seen as supportive of the Chief.

Alliances solidified among Council members who had never agreed on anything before.

The pressure escalated week by week, each new attack building on the last, each accusation amplified by the machinery they had built in Washington.

The investigation they had launched wasn't designed to discover wrongdoing. It was designed to manufacture it.

The Charge They Dropped

There was one article of impeachment they drafted but never brought to the hearing.

It accused me of notifying federal authorities and inviting them to investigate Tribal operations.

The charge was dropped before the hearing—once the optics proved devastating. How do you stand in front of the Cherokee people and argue that a Principal Chief should be removed for inviting law enforcement to investigate potential corruption?

But that dropped charge forced me to do something I hadn't done enough of: reflect.

I had moved too fast.

Twenty-one years in gaming regulation had trained me to identify problems and fix them—immediately, systematically, without hesitation. When you see cash sitting unguarded on a counting room table, you don't form a committee. You act. When you catch a jackpot scam, you don't wait for political consensus. You call the FBI.

But tribal government doesn't move like a regulatory commission. Politics has its own rhythm—slower, more cautious, built on relationships and recognition and the careful balancing of interests. I knew that intellectually. I had watched it for decades. But when I became Chief, I governed like a regulator, not a politician.

I ordered forensic audits within months of taking office. I instituted accountability measures across Tribal programs. I pushed for transparency in areas that hadn't seen the sunlight in years. All of it was right. All of it was necessary. And all of it made me enemies faster than I made allies.

Some of those enemies might have been allies if I had moved differently. Not slower on the substance—the problems were real and needed fixing. But slower on the politics. More attentive to the people who needed to feel included, consulted, respected. More willing to let others share credit for reforms they hadn't initiated but could have supported.

I didn't do that. I just moved. And I left a lot of people behind—some of them angry, some of them scared, some of them looking for any way to stop what I had started.

What Happened to the Federal Investigation

Here is a bitter irony that history should record.

The federal investigation that prompted so much panic, the FBI raid that triggered the motion to investigate me, the DOJ letter that confirmed that possible criminal conduct was being examined—all of it seemed to simply evaporate after I was removed from office.

I don't know what negotiations or conversations took place after my impeachment. I don't know whether the new administration cooperated with federal investigators the way I had, or whether they found ways to slow things down, limit access, or make the investigation less of a priority. Also remember, a new Trump administration was making a lot of changes to US Attorney offices, and in fact Jill Westmoreland Rose was replaced about this time. Andy Romagnuolo was up for retirement as well.

I was on the outside by then, fighting for my own vindication, with no visibility into what was happening with the federal case.

I want to be clear that I have no inside knowledge of why the investigation appeared to slow. But from my outside perspective, the urgency that drove the FBI to execute a search warrant in February 2017 seemed to disappear once I was gone. The investigation that had been moving forward with purpose and momentum appeared to lose steam. The consequences that some people clearly feared, the consequences that may have driven them to remove me from office, never seemed to materialize in any public way.

Whether that represents a failure of federal follow-through, a change in prosecutorial priorities, personnel changes at the US Attorney's office, or something else entirely, I genuinely cannot say. I make no accusation of impropriety. What I can say is that the audits revealed real problems, the FBI took those problems seriously enough to raid Qualla Housing, and somehow the whole thing faded from public view after the person who had initiated the transparency was removed from power.

A Quiet Moment Before the Storm

That night, after the FBI raid and the Council motion to investigate me, I just drove through the familiar roads of the Boundary, watching the mountains pass in the darkness, trying to process what had happened and what it meant for everything ahead.

Cyndi was waiting at the kitchen table when I walked in. She didn't ask what happened, she could read it on my face, in the way I carried myself, in the heaviness that had settled over me like a weight I couldn't put down.

We sat for a long time without speaking. Finally, she said quietly, "Whatever they're afraid of . . . it must be big."

I nodded. She was right. The reaction was so extreme, so coordinated, so obviously panicked, that it revealed the depth of what they were trying to protect. Nobody launches an impeachment as a distraction unless they're terrified of what happens if attention stays focused where it should be.

And for the first time, I said out loud what I had only thought in the privacy of my own mind. "They're going to come after me, Cyndi. Not because of anything I've done wrong. Because they can't stop the federal investigation, but they think they can stop me."

She reached across the table, took my hand, and said, "Then you stand your ground."

I will never forget that moment, her hand in mine, her voice steady, the storm gathering overhead.

CHAPTER 23

THE GRAND COUNCIL OF 2017

"When the people lead, the leaders will follow."

— Mahatma Gandhi

Over 1,300 Tribal members gathered for the first Grand Council in two decades—not a rally, but the oldest expression of Cherokee democracy. The people led, and the leaders who opposed them were exposed.

◆ ◆ ◆

FOR THE FIRST TIME in more than two decades, the Cherokee people gathered in the Grand Council, not for ceremony or celebration, but to confront a constitutional crisis.

The gymnasium at Cherokee Central Schools filled with citizens who understood that something fundamental was at stake, something that transcended the particulars of my situation and touched the deepest questions about who holds power in our Nation and how that power should be exercised.

I did not call that meeting lightly. The authority to convene a Grand Council is one of the oldest and most sacred powers of the Principal Chief, a power that predates the modern Tribal Council, predates our court system, predates all the governmental structures we have built over the past century. It stretches back to our earliest traditions, when the people themselves, not institutions, not elected representatives, not appointed officials, held the final say on matters of greatest importance.

The Grand Council represents the original source of Cherokee sovereignty: the gathered voice of the people speaking as one.

And in April 2017, the people needed to be heard. They needed a forum to express what they thought about the impeachment process that was grinding forward despite mounting evidence that it was politically motivated rather than justified by any actual misconduct. They needed to exercise the democratic voice that the Tribal Council seemed determined to silence.

Why a Grand Council Was Necessary

As the impeachment machinery ground forward through the spring of 2017, it became increasingly clear that this was no longer a conflict the Tribal Council could resolve fairly or honestly.

Too many members appeared compromised by their own conduct or their alliances. Too many had already made up their minds about my guilt before any hearing was held or any defense was offered.

The normal checks and balances of Tribal government had failed. The Council that was supposed to provide oversight had, in my view, become the instrument of a political vendetta. And the people whose votes had put me in office were being systematically excluded from any meaningful voice in what happened next.

The Grand Council was the people's last constitutional safety valve, the ultimate expression of Cherokee democracy, the recognition that when institutions fail, the people themselves retain the authority to speak and be heard.

And the moment had come to open that valve before it was too late.

I stood on the authority given to the Principal Chief in Article 10 of the Charter and Governing Document, which states clearly: "The Principal Chief shall have the right to call a Grand Council of all enrolled members . . . and he shall preside over such meeting."

The intention behind that constitutional provision was unmistakable—when government fails to act with integrity, when elected representatives abandon their duty to the people who elected them, the citizens may gather in one body to express their will and attempt to correct the course of their Nation.

For generations, this power had been used sparingly, reserved for moments of extraordinary need when the normal processes of government had proven inadequate. But if ever there was a moment worthy of invoking that ancient authority, this was that moment.

I set the date for April 18, 2017. I set the location at Cherokee Central Schools gymnasium, the largest indoor gathering space available.

I opened the doors to every Tribal member regardless of their township, their family connections, or their political stance. And I prepared myself for whatever judgment the people would deliver.

The People Arrive

In the afternoon of April 18, 2017, something extraordinary happened on the roads leading to Cherokee Central Schools.

Traffic backed up more than a mile along Big Cove Road, a river of vehicles moving slowly toward the gymnasium as Tribal members from every corner of the Boundary made their way to participate in the first Grand Council in over twenty years.

The line of cars stretched farther than anyone had anticipated, filled with elders who remembered previous moments of Tribal crisis, young families with children in car seats, single mothers taking time off work, veterans wearing caps from their military service, employees of Tribal programs, teenagers old enough to vote for the first time, and old-timers who had lived through the 1995 impeachment of a previous Chief and recognized the patterns repeating.

By the time the meeting was called to order, over 1,300 Tribal members had filled the gymnasium and the overflow areas. It was the highest gathering of Cherokee people for a political decision in modern history, a turnout that exceeded anything the organizers of the impeachment had expected or wanted.

The setup reflected the seriousness of the occasion and the commitment to democratic process. Tribal enrollment staff were stationed at the entrance with the official enrollment books, checking identification and verifying that each person seeking to vote was an enrolled member of the Eastern Band of Cherokee Indians. Anyone who wanted to attend could come in and witness the proceedings, but only verified enrolled members received the colored dots that would allow them to cast ballots on the measures before the people.

Green dots for enrolled members eligible to vote. Red dots for non-enrolled attendees invited to witness but not participate in the voting.

The rules were explained clearly: one person, one voice, three minutes to speak on any issue, with the majority determining the outcome on each question.

But the heart of that day was bigger than any procedural detail. This was the Cherokee people gathering to exercise their sovereign authority, to speak directly about what was being done in their name, to make their voices heard when their elected Council seemed determined to ignore them.

The People Speak

One by one, for hours, Tribal members rose and took the microphone.

The diversity of voices was remarkable: different ages, different townships, different life experiences, different relationships to Tribal government. Some spoke softly, their voices trembling with emotion as they described what the impeachment process had meant to them and their families. Some spoke with fire, generations of frustration behind their words as they denounced the political manipulation they were witnessing.

Some spoke with the measured tones of elders who had seen similar crises before and recognized the patterns of power being abused.

But the overarching message across all those voices was unmistakable: The impeachment was unjust. The process was politically motivated. The people who had voted to put me in office had not been consulted about removing me. And accountability, real accountability, the kind I had promised and was delivering through the audits, had finally begun under my administration.

The corruption being exposed wasn't mine. It appeared instead to belong to the people trying to remove me before the investigations could go any further.

Elders stood and spoke about Cherokee traditions of justice and fair dealing, about how the process being used against me violated everything they had been taught about how leaders should be treated. Employees of Tribal programs stood and described the improvements they had seen under my administration, the reforms that were making government work better for the people it was supposed to serve. Parents stood and talked about what kind of example the impeachment was setting for their children about how politics worked in Cherokee. Young men and women stood and expressed their disillusionment with a Council that seemed more interested in protecting itself than in serving the people.

A woman from Birdtown took the microphone and said bluntly what many were thinking: "We see accountability now. Where was it before? This impeachment is payback, pure and simple. They're not going after the Chief because he did something wrong. They're going after him because he caught them doing something wrong."

Another citizen from Big Cove said: "The Council's been on a witch hunt for our Chief forever, and everybody knows it. Everybody sees what's happening. They think we're too stupid to figure it out, but we know exactly what they're doing."

Even those who had policy disagreements with my administration, who hadn't voted for me in the election or didn't support every decision I had made, acknowledged the fundamental truth of what was happening. One man stood up and said, "I didn't vote for him in the last election, and I don't agree with everything he's done. But I won't stand by and watch this kind of politics. This isn't about right and wrong. This is about power. And I'm not going to pretend otherwise just because I'm not his biggest supporter."

What the Grand Council Was—And Wasn't

The opponents of the Grand Council tried to dismiss it before, during, and after the gathering.

Opponents dismissed it as a political rally, a pep rally, an orchestrated show of support. Thirteen hundred Tribal members who showed up to exercise their constitutional right to speak might have disagreed with that characterization.

The Votes

When the time came to vote, ballots were distributed on blue paper, six measures put before the people, each one discussed and debated before the vote was taken.

The counting was public and transparent, witnessed by citizens who could see for themselves how their neighbors were voting and what the results revealed about the collective will of our Nation.

When the votes were counted, the message was overwhelming and unmistakable. The following percentages are based on the official count announced that day:

Approximately 84 percent of those present voted to halt the impeachment proceedings.

Approximately 82 percent voted to rescind the resolution that had authorized the investigation into my office.

Approximately 77 percent voted to reject the narrative the Council had constructed about my alleged misconduct.

Only three Council members even bothered to attend.

More than 1,300 citizens showed up to exercise their democratic voice, the largest political gathering in modern Cherokee history, and nine of the twelve Council members stayed away.

The Three Who Came

Teresa McCoy from Big Cove attended the Grand Council.

Richard French from Big Cove attended.

Tommye Saunooke from Painttown attended.

The same three who would later vote against my impeachment. The only three who showed up to face the people. Nine stayed away.

The Aftermath—Courts and Politics Collide

But power does not surrender easily, and the impeachment coalition had no intention of letting the voice of 1,300 citizens interfere with their plans.

Tribal Council sought and obtained a ruling from the lower Tribal Court that would give them the legal cover they needed to ignore what the people had said.

The court ruled that the Grand Council decisions did not have "force of law"—that the gathering was advisory rather than binding, that the Council was free to disregard the expressed will of the people because the constitutional language could be interpreted to permit such disregard.

Armed with that ruling, the Tribal Council proceeded with the impeachment exactly as if the Grand Council had never happened.

The result was a constitutional crisis that cut to the heart of what democracy means in our Tribe.

The Council held legal authority to proceed with the impeachment. But the people held moral legitimacy based on the overwhelming vote at the Grand Council. Which mattered more?

Could a government truly claim to be democratic if it ignored an 84 percent vote of the citizens it was supposed to represent? What was the point of a Grand Council if the people's voice could simply be dismissed as nonbinding?

These questions have never been fully resolved. But the Council members who proceeded with the impeachment did so knowing that 84 percent of the citizens who showed up opposed their actions. They proceeded anyway.

CHAPTER 24

THE DRIVE HOME

"The hardest thing in the world is to watch your children suffer for your choices."

— Patrick H. Lambert

I watched Nelson receive his LL.M. in Las Vegas while two thousand miles away, prosecutors built the case to remove me. No one else's words could carry that weight.

◆ ◆ ◆

ON MAY 12, 2017, my son, Nelson, walked across a stage in Las Vegas and received his master of laws degree, LL.M., in gaming law and regulation from the University of Nevada, Las Vegas.

I sat in the audience with Cyndi, our daughter Gina, and Nelson's wife, Kim, and our grandson, Rhett, watching Nelson accept his diploma, and I felt what any father feels watching his son achieve something remarkable: pride so deep it almost hurt, joy that brought tears, gratitude for everything that had brought us to this moment.

For a few precious hours in that auditorium, I was just a father at his son's graduation. Not the Principal Chief of the Eastern Band of Cherokee Indians. Not the target of an impeachment proceeding that had consumed Cherokee politics for months. Not the man whose career and reputation were about to be put on trial before a hostile Council.

Just a father, celebrating his son, surrounded by family, experiencing the simple happiness that comes from watching your children succeed.

But back home in Cherokee, North Carolina, in a conference room inside the Tribal Council House more than two thousand miles away, another kind of ceremony was taking place.

The attorney the Council had hired to prosecute me, their handpicked lawyer, sat with Council members, preparing their case, planning their strategy, building the machinery that would grind into motion the moment I returned. Yes, the prosecutor working directly with the jury members/judges to plan the hearing.

They had tried to schedule the impeachment hearing for the very week I would be driving home, forcing me to choose between my son's graduation and defending myself against their charges. At the last minute, they moved it to May 22—the Monday after I was scheduled to arrive back home. They could wait a few more days. They were confident about the outcome.

The Drive Begins—Leaving Las Vegas

After the graduation ceremony and the celebrations that followed, we helped Nelson pack up his apartment and load his belongings into his Jeep Grand Cherokee. His lease was up, and he and his wife and son were moving back home to North Carolina.

Someone had to drive the Jeep and the U-Haul trailer hitched to the back across the country, and while everyone else made arrangements to fly, I volunteered for the job.

I told myself it was practical—someone had to get the vehicle and trailer home, and I was available. But the truth was both simpler and more complicated than logistics.

I needed the time alone. I needed the silence of the road, the empty miles between Las Vegas and Cherokee, the space to think and pray and prepare myself for what was waiting. I needed to make that journey by myself, processing everything that had happened and everything ahead, arriving home not in the compressed hours of a flight but in the slow, deliberate passage of days on the highway.

I left Vegas on the morning of May 15, pulling out of the city as the desert sun climbed higher and the casinos faded in my rearview mirror. The first day I made it to Albuquerque. The next morning I was back on the road before dawn, pushing through New Mexico and into the Texas Panhandle, watching the landscape change from desert to plains as the miles accumulated behind me.

I did not turn on the radio. I did not play music or listen to podcasts or audiobooks. I just drove in silence, hour after hour, the hum of the tires on pavement the only constant sound, my thoughts the only conversation.

I prayed, not formal prayers with structured words, but an ongoing conversation with God that had sustained me through every difficult passage of my life. I thought about my family, about the Tribe, about what I had tried to accomplish and what forces had aligned against me. I thought about justice and injustice, about truth and the lies that were being told about me, about whether the system I had devoted my life to serving would ultimately vindicate or destroy me.

The miles passed slowly, each one bringing me closer to home and closer to the reckoning that awaited.

The Calls—Updates from Cherokee

My phone rang throughout the day, calls from my staff back in Cherokee, updates on Tribal business that still needed my attention even though I was a thousand miles away in a Jeep on Interstate 40.

Purchase orders awaiting approval. Travel authorizations that needed my signature. Contract questions that required decisions. Personnel matters that couldn't wait.

The daily work of running a government continued regardless of the political crisis consuming the Council, and I was still the Principal Chief until the moment they removed me.

But there were other calls too. Calls from allies with whispered updates about the Council's preparations, about the mood in the Tribal Council House, about the confidence my opponents weren't bothering to hide. Calls about the giddiness some Council members displayed when they thought no one from my administration was watching, the anticipation, the certainty that they were finally going to succeed in taking me out.

Calls from staff members who were scared, for themselves as much as for me. What would happen to their jobs if I was removed? What would happen to the reforms we had fought so hard to implement? Would the new administration protect them or purge them?

And there was one more piece of news that my staff shared during one of those calls: The audit had been released to the press. One of the primary forensic audits, the one documenting improper credit card expenditures, had gone public. The *Asheville Citizen-Times* was publishing the findings, laying out in black and white the evidence of misuse, of personal expenses charged to the Tribe, of what I believed to be the corruption I had promised to root out when the voters elected me.

I thought maybe that would change things. I thought maybe the weight of evidence would be too heavy to ignore, maybe the transparency I had promised and delivered would finally work in my favor.

But as history shows, it didn't slow them down at all. They just barreled forward, appearing confident that they had the votes they needed regardless of what the evidence showed.

Meteor Crater—The Call with Cyndi

Around noon on that first day, somewhere in Arizona, I pulled off Interstate 40 at the exit for Meteor Crater.

It's a rest stop as much as a tourist destination, a place to stretch your legs, use the bathroom, buy a bottle of water from the vending machine. But it's also one of those places that puts things in perspective, that reminds you how small human concerns really are when measured against geological time.

A hole in the earth nearly a mile wide, punched into the desert fifty thousand years ago by a rock from space, still there after all those millennia, indifferent to the empires that have risen and fallen in the time since it was formed.

I stood at the overlook for a few minutes, looking out at the vastness of the crater, and I called Cyndi.

The sound of her voice told me everything I needed to know before she said a word.

She had been hearing things from her friends, from people in my administration, from the whispers circulating through Cherokee as the impeachment hearing approached. She knew what the Council was planning, knew the confidence they displayed, knew that the outcome most people expected was my removal from office.

She was scared. Not angry. Not defiant. Not ready for battle the way she had been during earlier stages of this fight. Just scared. Scared for me, scared for our family, scared about what our lives would look like on the other side.

I could hear the weight in her voice, the heaviness that came from carrying fear for both of us while I was two thousand miles away and unable to help.

I tried to be strong for her. I tried to sound calm and confident, like I believed everything was going to be okay, like the truth would prevail and justice would be done. But I could hear my own voice cracking, and I knew she could hear it too. We had been together long enough that we couldn't hide much from each other, even over the phone, even across all those miles.

We didn't talk long. What was there to say that we hadn't already said a hundred times in the months leading up to this moment? I told her I loved her. She told me she loved me. We said we would get through this together, the way we had gotten through every other hard thing in our thirty-plus years of marriage.

Then I got back in the Jeep and kept driving.

Sleeping in Rest Stops

That night, I pulled into a rest stop somewhere near Albuquerque and parked under a streetlight at the edge of the lot. I reclined the driver's seat as far as it would go, pulled a jacket over myself for warmth, and tried to sleep while eighteen-wheelers idled nearby and headlights swept across the windshield as travelers came and went throughout the night.

I did the same thing the next night, the days blurred together after a while, one rest stop looking much like another, one stretch of highway indistinguishable from the next.

I wasn't trying to save money on hotel rooms. I just didn't want to stop moving. As long as I was on the road, the hearing hadn't started. As long as I was somewhere between Las Vegas and Cherokee, I was still just a man driving his son's belongings home. As long as I kept the wheels turning, the moment of reckoning stayed somewhere in the future rather than arriving in the present.

When I did eat, it was at gas stations, a sandwich from the cooler, a bag of chips, a bottle of water. Nothing that required sitting down at a table. Nothing that required stopping the forward motion, even for an hour. I ate in the Jeep, one hand on the wheel, chewing mechanically while my mind raced through everything that was coming.

The Thoughts That Wouldn't Stop

I went over every detail of the past year and a half as I drove. Every decision I had made. Every authorization I had signed. Every meeting I had held. Every policy I had enforced.

I searched my memory for anything that might legitimately be called misconduct, anything that crossed a line, anything that gave my opponents a genuine basis for the charges they were bringing.

I had done nothing wrong. The charges were manufactured—procedural disputes and policy disagreements dressed up as impeachable offenses. The truth about my administration and the reforms we had implemented, the accountability we had restored—none of it mattered to people who had already decided the outcome.

But I also knew something else, something that sat heavy in my chest during those long hours on the road: Fear is stronger than truth when people feel cornered.

The audits had exposed problems they couldn't explain away. The FBI was asking questions about Qualla Housing and credit card expenditures and contracts that, at the time, did not appear to add up. The comfortable system that had protected them for years was collapsing under the weight of the transparency I had delivered.

And they blamed me—for allowing the truth to surface. I had kept the promise I made on inauguration day, to follow the truth wherever it leads.

Crossing Back onto the Boundary

On Thursday or Friday, I lost track of the exact day somewhere in Oklahoma, I crossed back onto the Qualla Boundary.

The familiar mountains rose around me, the roads I had traveled my entire life, the landscape that was home in the deepest sense of the word.

I had been gone for maybe a week, attending my son's graduation, packing his apartment, driving two thousand miles across the country, while the machinery of my destruction was being assembled in my absence. And now I was home.

But I didn't feel the relief that usually accompanied returning to Cherokee after time away. I felt dread. The weight that had been building with every mile of the journey settled fully on my shoulders as I passed the signs welcoming me to Tribal land. Whatever was going to happen was going to happen here, in the place I loved most, among the people I had devoted my life to serving.

The Homecoming

When I walked into the house, Cyndi was waiting.

There was no celebration, no excited conversation about the trip or Nelson's graduation or the long drive. Just a somber, quiet embrace that lasted longer than usual, both of us holding on because we knew what was coming and wanted one more moment of peace before we had to face it.

Then she pulled back, looked at me with those steady eyes that have seen me through every crisis of my adult life, and I said: "Okay. Catch me up. Tell me what's on your mind. What's happening? What have you heard?"

We sat down at the kitchen table—the same table where we had shared so many conversations over the years, the same table where we would process everything that happened in the days and weeks and years to come—and she told me everything she had been hearing while I was gone.

The rumors. The preparations. The confidence the Council had that this was finally going to work. The names of people who were supporting the impeachment and the names of people who were wavering. The mood in the community, divided between those who supported me and those who had been convinced by the accusations.

It felt less like a homecoming and more like a military briefing before a battle. Which, in a sense, is exactly what it was.

Working Through the Weekend

That weekend, the last weekend before the hearing was scheduled to begin, I went into my office at the Tribal Council House. Sage Dunston met me there.

Through everything, the attacks, the accusations, the mounting pressure, he had stayed loyal.

That weekend, Sage and I sat in my office and worked through the mound of paperwork that had piled up during the week I was gone. Purchase orders. Travel authorizations. 638 contracts. Personnel matters. Hiring approvals. All the routine, daily work of running a tribal government, work that doesn't stop just because the Chief is under attack.

I could have let it wait. I could have said the paperwork would have to sit until after the hearing, that I had bigger things to worry about than purchase orders and travel authorizations.

But that's not how I was raised, and that's not how I had conducted myself throughout my career. The work needed to be done. The programs needed those approvals. The people depending on those authorizations shouldn't have to wait because the Council was playing politics with my administration.

So I signed every document. I reviewed every contract. I responded to every request that required my attention.

By the time I walked out of that office Sunday night, there was no mound of paperwork left behind. Everything that needed my signature had it. Everything that needed a decision had one.

I had done my job.

Because even though I knew what was coming—even though I knew that in less than eighteen hours I would be sitting in a hearing where people would accuse me of crimes I didn't commit and misconduct I hadn't engaged in—I was still the Principal Chief. And I was going to act like it until the very last moment.

The Thought in the Desert

During those long hours in the Jeep, somewhere between the meteor crater and the Oklahoma border, I had a thought that I've returned to many times in the years since.

Maybe this was supposed to happen.

I had done nothing to deserve it.

But because maybe fate works in ways we don't understand in the moment, ways that only become clear much later when we can see the full picture.

Maybe I needed to fall so others could rise. Maybe I needed to be removed so the right people could be in the right places for what came next. Maybe the strength I had built over a lifetime of overcoming obstacles was needed precisely so I could survive what others couldn't, could endure what others would be destroyed by.

I don't know if that's true. I don't know if there's a grand design working through the chaos of human events, or if bad things just happen to good people sometimes, or if it's all just politics and fear and human weakness playing out the way it always does.

I've never been certain about questions like that, and the experience of the impeachment didn't make me more certain.

What I Should Have Seen

Somewhere between the meteor crater and the Oklahoma border, the silence of the road gave me space I hadn't allowed myself in months.

And in that space, I started hearing the warnings I had ignored.

Political allies had told me, more than once, "Slow down, Chief. You're making enemies you don't need to make. Give people time to adjust. Let them catch up."

I hadn't listened. I had twenty-one years of knowing what needed to be fixed, and I had four years to fix it. The math felt simple: Move fast, get it done, let the results speak for themselves.

But politics doesn't work that way. Results don't speak for themselves—people speak for results, or against them, depending on whether they feel included or excluded from the process.

I also failed to share the spotlight. In regulatory work, credit doesn't matter, results matter. But in politics, recognition is currency. The Council members needed to feel ownership of the reforms, even the ones they hadn't initiated. They needed to stand at press conferences, cut ribbons, take credit. That's how political capital gets built.

I didn't give them that. Not out of arrogance or disrespect—I just wasn't paying attention to it. My focus was on the work, not the politics of the work. And that blindness cost me.

Looking back now, with two thousand miles of empty highway behind me and an impeachment hearing waiting ahead, I could see it clearly: My ouster was as much my fault for moving too fast as it was wrong on their part to do what they did. The charges, fabricated. The process, corrupt. The outcome, unjust.

Monday Morning—May 22, 2017

On Monday morning, May 22, 2017, I woke up early, put on a suit, and drove to the Tribal Council House.

The hearing would begin in hours. I was as ready as I could be.

I had counted the votes. The numbers were against me regardless of what the evidence showed.

I had seen too much of how the process had been corrupted to believe

justice would prevail that day.
    But because I had done everything I could.
    The circus was about to begin.
    And I was ready to face it.

CHAPTER 25

THE PROCEEDING

"Injustice anywhere is a threat to justice everywhere."

— Martin Luther King Jr.

The four-day impeachment hearing was a political performance dressed as justice. The verdict was decided before the first witness spoke.

◆ ◆ ◆

THEY SCHEDULED THE IMPEACHMENT hearing to last three days.

What follows is my understanding of how these events fit together, based on what I witnessed, the record available to me, and what unfolded afterward.

It lasted four days, long enough for every mask to drop, every whispered agenda to surface, and every ounce of dignity in the process to be stripped away.

From the moment I walked into the Council House that first morning, I knew we were not entering a court of law.

We were walking onto a stage, a set, a performance.

And everyone there, the prosecutor, the Council members, the Vice Chief, understood their roles perfectly.

Monday Morning, May 22, 2017

I wore what I always wore to work: a suit and tie. Jacket, pressed white shirt, dark tie. If they were going to try to take my office, I was going to walk in looking like the Principal Chief I had been elected to be.

I arrived at my office at seven thirty that morning, same as always. The office of the Principal Chief was in the Council House—down the hall, around the corner from the very chamber where they would hold the hearing.

Scott Jones, my attorney, met me there. We spent an hour going over the plan for the day—what to expect, how to respond, when to object, when to stay silent. Scott was steady, experienced, methodical. A well-known attorney from Asheville with a reputation for precision and integrity. But even he couldn't hide the concern in his eyes.

"They've already made up their minds," he said quietly.

"I know."

"But we make them say it on the record anyway."

"That's all we can do."

Just before 9:00 a.m., I walked down the hallway, around the corner, toward the chamber.

The same building I had worked in every day for nearly two years.

The same hallways I had walked a thousand times.

But today, everything felt different.

The parking lot was already full when I had arrived earlier.

They had beaten us there.

The opposition—the people supporting the Council members who wanted me gone—had arrived early, packed the chamber, filled every bench, claimed every seat. It was strategic, calculated. If they controlled the room, they controlled the optics. If the cameras showed a chamber full of people jeering at me, it would look as if the whole Tribe had turned against me.

But that wasn't the truth.

The truth was that most of my supporters couldn't get in. The Council Chamber is small—bench seating like church pews, no individual chairs, maybe fifty people maximum if everyone squeezes in tight. First come, first seated. And the opposition had come first.

So the hallways were packed. People standing shoulder to shoulder outside the doors, trying to hear, trying to see, unable to get in.

As I walked toward the entrance, I saw a small group of women standing near the doorway. Tribal employees. They had been subpoenaed as witnesses. Their faces were tight with fear.

I stopped.

Made eye contact with each of them.

"I appreciate y'all being here," I said quietly. "And all I ask, all I expect, is that you speak the truth. That's all you can do. That's all any of us can do."

One of them nodded, eyes glistening.

"I'm sorry you and everybody else is having to go through this," I continued. "But just be truthful. That's all."

I didn't say the rest of what I was thinking: I know you're scared. I know they've been to your homes. I know they've told you your jobs are at risk. I know how this place works—fear has always been the currency of control here. But I won't be part of that. Tell the truth, and there will be no repercussions from me.

They understood.

The hallways were a gauntlet.

People everywhere—some supportive, some silent, some smirking.

A few voices rose above the murmur:

"Good morning, Chief."

"Keep your head up, Chief."

"It's gonna be okay, Chief."

I nodded. Kept walking. Kept my face steady.

But my chest felt tight.

Entering the Chamber

The room was already full when I walked in.

Every seat taken. Standing room only along the back wall. The air thick with body heat and tension.

The opposition had claimed the left side of the gallery—bench after bench of people who had shown up early to fill the space, to create the illusion of popular support. Some of them looked at me with open hostility. Others smirked. A few leaned over and whispered to each other, eyes never leaving me.

My seat was reserved on the front row bench—right side, closest to the Council table. My attorney sat beside me. Scott Jones, calm and composed, legal pad already out, pen ready.

Cyndi sat directly behind me on the second bench. I could feel her presence without turning around—steady, quiet, terrified but refusing to show it. My mother sat beside her, face unreadable, hands folded in her lap. My son, Nelson, was there, too, just home from Las Vegas, sitting with them.

Gina was out of state. She and her husband had moved away. Part of me was glad she didn't have to see this.

The Council members sat at their curved wooden table at the front of the room, nameplates in front of each seat. Some of them wouldn't look at me. Others stared with barely concealed satisfaction.

Travis Smith sat near the center on the right side. Smirking.

Teresa McCoy from Big Cove caught my eye and gave a small, almost imperceptible nod. Solid. Steady. One of the three who would vote against this madness.

Richard French sat beside her. Same quiet dignity.

Tommye Saunooke from Painttown, directly across the horseshoe. The third supporter.

The rest avoided my eyes.

The walls of the chamber were paneled in wood. Above the Council table hung seven ceremonial clan masks in wooden frames—Deer Clan, Wolf Clan, Long Hair Clan, Blue Clan, Wild Potato Clan, Paint Clan, and Bird Clan—watching over everything like silent witnesses. In another context, it might have felt like home. But today it felt like a cage.

The prosecutor stood near the podium at the center of the room.

Rob Saunooke was a big man—tall, broad-shouldered, imposing. Gray goatee, booming voice, the kind of presence that fills a room and demands attention. He carried himself like a man who believed he was the most important person in the building.

And the Council let him believe it.

He wasn't just acting like the prosecutor.

He was acting like the judge, the jury, and the executioner.

The Hearing Begins—9:00 a.m.

At exactly 9:00 a.m., the hearing began.

No formal introduction. No statement of rules. No acknowledgment of the 84 percent of Cherokee people who had voted at the Grand Council to stop this.

Just the prosecutor's voice, loud and confident, filling the room.

Scott Jones stood first. His opening statement was measured, careful, and devastatingly honest:

"I've been coming to Cherokee as an attorney for twenty-five years. Today is the saddest of the trips I've made here. Long before I was a lawyer, I was raised by my parents to believe in fairness. When I went to law school, I learned that lawyers call that due process. But fairness was something that I had with me long before that."

He paused, looked at each Council member.

"The reason I say today is the saddest day is because I came here believing that you have already made up your minds before you've heard any evidence. That's not fairness."

Someone in the opposition section shifted uncomfortably.

Scott continued: "The evidence will show that Principal Chief Patrick Lambert has acted within his authority, has governed with integrity, and has done nothing that rises to the level of impeachable conduct. But I fear that won't matter. Because this isn't about evidence. This is about politics."

He sat down.

Then Rob Saunooke stood.

"We are here today," he began, voice booming, "because Principal Chief Patrick Lambert has violated his oath of office, abused his authority, and endangered the Tribe. The evidence will show a pattern of misconduct that cannot be ignored."

Someone in the opposition section clapped.

Someone else whistled.

The prosecutor didn't stop them.

He kept talking, pacing in front of the Council table, gesturing broadly, building his case not on facts but on performance.

I sat perfectly still.

Hands folded on the table in front of me.

Breathing steady.

But inside, I was thinking: *This is surreal. This isn't even happening. This can't be happening.*

I had spent my entire life trying to do the right thing. I had negotiated gaming compacts with six governors. I had built the systems that brought stability and revenue to this Tribe. I had implemented transparency, ordered audits, enforced accountability.

And now those same strengths, those same principles, were being turned into weapons against me. The very principles and strengths I had based my entire career—my entire life—on were being disregarded as if I had none of them. They knew what my strengths were, and they took direct aim at them.

The Witnesses Begin—10:00 a.m.

At 10:00 a.m., the prosecutor called his first witness.

"The prosecution calls Erik Sneed, secretary of budget and finance."

Erik walked to the podium in the center of the room. No witness stand. No separation. Just a podium, a microphone, and fifty people watching from inches away, almost breathing down your neck.

The prosecutor began his questions.

I don't remember the specifics of Erik's testimony. I don't remember most of the witnesses' testimony, honestly.

The whole week felt as if I were in a tunnel—sounds muffled, faces blurred, time moving both too fast and too slow.

What I remember is the tone.

Witness after witness, called to the podium. Some of them Tribal employees, scared and reluctant. Others eager to perform, to say whatever the prosecutor wanted them to say.

Sage Dunston, my chief of staff—loyal, brilliant, caught in an impossible position.

Megan Yates, purchasing manager.

Sharon Blankenship.

Rebecca Claxton from the Office of Internal Audit.

Each one questioned. Each one cross-examined. Each one trying to navigate the minefield of telling the truth while not angering the people who held power over their jobs.

None of it amounted to anything impeachable.

HR complaints. Procedural disputes. Grievances about decisions I had made in the course of running a government.

But nothing criminal.

Nothing corrupt.

Nothing that met the constitutional standard for removal.

And yet the prosecutor treated every minor complaint as if it were evidence of a crime.

Vice Chief Richie Sneed Testifies

Then they called Vice Chief Richie Sneed.

He walked to the podium with the confidence of a man who knew exactly what was coming.

Under our governing structure, my removal would make him Principal Chief, immediately, automatically, without having to earn it from the people.

He testified for the prosecution—painting a picture of a Chief who was out of control, who didn't listen, who acted unilaterally.

I sat there, listening to my own Vice Chief, the man I had worked beside for nearly two years, testify against me in front of the entire Tribe.

Scott took notes. Whispered to me occasionally. Prepared for cross-examination.

But we both knew: Richie Sneed had the most to gain from my removal. He should have recused himself entirely. Instead, he testified as a witness, knowing full well that hours later he would be sworn in as Principal Chief.

Council Members Testify Against Me

Then something even more absurd happened.

The prosecutor called Council member Albert Rose.

Albert stood up from his seat at the Council table—the rectangular wooden bench where he sat as a judge and jury member—and walked to the podium to testify as a witness against me.

He wasn't recusing himself.

He wasn't stepping down from the case.

He was literally playing three roles at once: judge, jury, and witness for the prosecution.

When he finished testifying, he walked back to his seat at the Council table and sat down—ready to deliberate and vote on my guilt based in part on his own testimony.

Then they called Council member Bo Crowe.

Same thing.

Stood up from the Council bench. Walked to the podium. Testified against me. Walked back. Sat down. Ready to vote.

Scott leaned over and whispered, "This just went beyond a kangaroo court. Council members are acting simultaneously as witnesses, judges, and jurors."

I nodded.

I already knew.

Monday Ends—5:00 p.m.

By 5:00 p.m., the prosecution had called all their witnesses for the day.

Tosh Welch, the Cherokee recreation life manager, had been the last to testify.

The hearing recessed.

I stood, turned around, made eye contact with Cyndi.

She didn't say anything.

She didn't need to.

I could see it in her face: This is really happening.

I walked out of the chamber, down the hallway, past the crowd still gathered outside.

Someone said, "We're with you, Chief."

I nodded. Kept walking.

Went back to my office.

Sat down at my desk.

Stared at the wall.

And thought: *One day down. How many more to go?*

Tuesday, May 23, 2017

The Defense Begins—9:00 a.m.

I arrived at my office early again Tuesday morning. Same routine. Similar suit and tie. Same walk down the hallway to the chamber.

But today felt different.

Monday had been their day—the prosecution's parade of witnesses, their carefully constructed narrative, their performance for the crowd.

Today was ours.

Today, Scott Jones would begin calling witnesses for the defense. Today, we would show that every decision I made was legal, authorized, and in the best interest of the Tribe.

Today was ours.

The chamber was packed again. Same faces in the opposition section. More supporters squeezed into the hallway, unable to get in. Same Council members at their rectangular table, watching, waiting.

At 9:00 a.m., the hearing resumed.

The prosecutor called one more witness—Curtis Wildcatt, interim manager for the Tribal Employment Rights Office. More testimony about HR complaints, procedural grievances, nothing rising to the level of impeachable conduct.

Then, finally, it was our turn.

Scott Jones Calls the Defense Witnesses—10:00 a.m.

Scott stood and called our first witness.

"The defense calls Melanie Foreman, Harrah's Cherokee Casino revenue manager."

Melanie walked to the podium. Composed. Professional. Someone who had worked with me for years and knew the truth about how decisions were made, how contracts were authorized, how the business of running a billion-dollar gaming operation actually worked.

Scott asked her questions about the hotel contract—one of the charges against me. The prosecution had tried to paint it as some sort of corrupt deal, an abuse of authority.

Melanie calmly explained the process. The approvals. The revenue projections. The partnership structure. The benefits to the Tribe.

It was legal.

It was proper.

It was good governance.

But I could see the faces of the Council members. They weren't listening. They were waiting for this to be over so they could vote the way they had already decided to vote.

Scott called more witnesses throughout the morning.

Erik Sneed—called back by the defense to clarify his earlier testimony, to explain the budget processes that the prosecution had twisted into something sinister.

Marsha Jackson, secretary of human resources—testifying about the HR complaints that had been inflated into impeachable offenses.

Angie Votaw, Tribal planning and analysis manager—providing context, data, evidence that every decision I made was informed, deliberate, and within my authority.

Adele Madden from Harrah's—more testimony about the casino operations, the partnership, the contracts.

Each witness provided documentation.

Each witness dismantled the prosecution's narrative piece by piece.

And each time, the opposition section sat silent. No applause. No jeers. Just the uncomfortable silence of people watching their case fall apart but knowing the outcome was already decided.

I Take the Stand—2:00 p.m.

At 2:00 p.m., Scott called me as a witness.

"The defense calls Principal Chief Patrick Lambert."

I stood.

Walked to the podium, about five paces.

Placed my hands on the wooden surface.

Looked out at the chamber—at Cyndi in the second row, at my mother beside her, at Nelson watching quietly. At the Council members who would decide my fate. At the crowd packed into every available inch of space.

And I began to tell my story.

Scott asked me about each charge.

The hotel contract. The legal services contract. The office renovations. The HR complaints. The authorization disputes.

One by one, I explained every decision.

I explained how the hotel contract had been negotiated, written, and approved prior to the election and signed prior to me even taking office by the appropriate departments, how it followed established procedures, how it benefited the Tribe financially and economically.

I explained how the legal services I had authorized were for Tribal business, for defending the Tribe's interests, for ensuring we had proper counsel on complex gaming and sovereignty issues.

I explained how the office renovations had been necessary—how the building had needed repairs, how the work had been properly bid and contracted, how every expenditure had been documented.

I explained how the HR complaints were either fabricated, exaggerated, or routine employment disputes that had nothing to do with my conduct as Chief.

I explained every single thing they had accused me of.

I answered every charge.

But it wasn't what they wanted to hear—because the truth never was. Everyone in the room knew it.

I testified for hours.

Scott asked questions. I answered.

At one point, Scott asked me directly: "Chief Lambert, did you at any time act with corrupt intent? Did you at any time use your office for personal gain? Did you at any time violate your oath?"

"No," I said. "I did not."

"Did you order audits because you believed there was corruption that needed to be exposed?"

"Yes."

"And did those audits reveal improper expenditures?"

"Yes."

"And is that why we're here today?"

Scott had made his point.

And everyone in the room knew the answer.

By 5:00 p.m., Scott finished his direct examination.

The hearing recessed for the day.

I walked back to my seat. Sat down beside my attorneys.

Cyndi leaned forward from the row behind me and whispered, "You did good."

I nodded.

But I felt as if I were in a tunnel.

Surreal. Detached. Watching my own life from a distance.

Tomorrow, the prosecutor would cross-examine me.

Tomorrow, they would try to break me.

Tuesday Night

That night, I went home.

Cyndi and I sat at the kitchen table.

She didn't ask how I thought it went. She didn't ask if I thought we were winning.

She just asked, "How are you holding up?"

"I'm okay," I said.

But I wasn't sure if that was true.

I kept thinking about Council members stepping down from the Council table to testify against me, then sitting back down to judge me.

I kept thinking about Richie Sneed testifying as a witness while knowing he would become Chief within days.

I kept thinking about the prosecutor controlling the room like a dictator, inventing rules, silencing objections, playing to the crowd.

I kept thinking about the people in the hallway who couldn't get into the chamber because the opposition had packed it with supporters.

This wasn't justice.

This was a performance.

And the ending had already been written.

But I also thought about the witnesses who stood up.

I thought about Melanie Foreman calmly explaining the hotel contract.

I thought about Erik Sneed providing documentation.

I thought about Marsha Jackson and Angie Votaw standing up under pressure and refusing to lie.

I thought about Teresa McCoy, Richard French, and Tommye Saunooke—the three Council members who had voted against this from the beginning and would vote against it to the end.

It was on the record now.

Even if they voted to remove me, even if they ignored the evidence, even if they went through with this sham—everything was on the record.

And someday, that would matter.

I went to bed that night knowing what was coming.

Tomorrow, they would attack.

And Thursday, they would vote.

But I had done what I came to do.

I had done what I was elected to do. Wednesday, May 24, 2017

Cross-Examination—9:00 a.m.

Wednesday morning began with Rob Saunooke standing to cross-examine me.

I returned to the podium. Placed my hands on the wooden surface. Looked out at the chamber—same packed room, same faces, same tension.

Saunooke approached with the confidence of a man who had already won.

He asked his questions. I answered them.

But something about the entire exchange felt surreal.

Every answer I gave dismantled his case. Every explanation I provided showed that the charges were fabricated, exaggerated, or twisted beyond recognition. Every piece of documentation I referenced proved that I had acted within my authority, followed proper procedures, and governed with integrity.

And he knew it.

I could see it in his face.

He knew my answers were destroying his narrative.

But he just kept going anyway.

Because it didn't matter.

The decision had been made months ago—long before this hearing began, long before any evidence was presented, long before I ever took the stand.

This was about theater.

And Saunooke was playing his part, knowing that no matter how weak his case was, no matter how thoroughly I refuted each charge, the Council would vote to remove me. And he would still get paid.

After Saunooke finished, Scott Jones stood for redirect examination.

He asked a few clarifying questions, tightened up a few points, reinforced the key facts.

Then he thanked me.

But I didn't return to my seat.

The hearing wasn't over.

Council Members Ask Questions

Then something even stranger happened.

Council members—the same people who had been sitting as judges throughout the entire proceeding, the same people who would deliberate and vote as jurors in a few hours—now put on the hat of prosecutors and began asking me questions directly.

Judge. Jury. Prosecutor.

All three roles. Same people.

I stood at the podium, waiting.

One by one, Council members had the opportunity to ask their questions.

Some were hostile. Some were confused. Some seemed genuinely curious. Others were clearly performing for the crowd.

I answered each one.

Calmly. Factually. Truthfully.

But the absurdity of it kept running through my mind: *When do the hot tar and feathers come out?*

This wasn't a trial.

This wasn't even a hearing.

This felt less like a hearing and more like a public execution dressed up as due process.

Final Arguments—2:00 p.m.

After the questioning ended, the hearing moved to final arguments.

Rob Saunooke stood first.

He paced in front of the Council table, voice booming, gesturing dramatically. He recounted the charges. He painted a picture of a Chief who had acted recklessly, who had abused his authority, who had violated the trust of the people.

It was a performance—polished, rehearsed, designed to give the Council the cover they needed to do what they had already planned to do.

When he finished, he sat down.

Then Scott Jones stood.

Scott didn't pace. He didn't shout. He didn't perform.

He simply spoke.

"You have heard the evidence," he said. "You have seen the documentation. You have heard from witnesses on both sides. And the evidence is clear: Principal Chief Patrick Lambert has committed no impeachable offense. He has acted within his authority. He has governed with integrity. He has done exactly what the people elected him to do—bring transparency and accountability to this government."

He paused.

"But I fear that won't matter. Because this was never about the evidence. This was about stopping the audits. This was about protecting people who didn't want the truth to come out. This was about punishing a Chief who refused to look the other way."

Scott looked at each Council member.

"You have the power to remove him. But history will remember why you did it."

He sat down.

My Final Statement

Then Scott turned to me.

"Chief Lambert, do you have anything you'd like to say?"

I remained standing at the podium.

Looked out at the chamber.

At Cyndi. At my mother. At Nelson.

At Teresa McCoy, Richard French, and Tommye Saunooke—the three who had stood with me from the beginning.

At Travis Smith and the others who had worked so hard to get to this moment.

At the opposition section—people who had filled the room early, who had jeered and clapped on cue, who believed this was justice.

And I said what was in my heart.

"This has been hard on everyone," I began. "Hard on my family. Hard on my supporters. Hard on this Tribe."

I paused.

"To my family and my supporters, thank you. Thank you for standing with me. Thank you for believing in what we were trying to do. Thank you for not giving up."

Then I turned toward the opposition section.

"And to my opponents—I want you to know that I hold no ill will. I love you."

The words hung in the air for a moment.

Then I heard it.

Hissing. Blowing. Mocking sounds from the opposition benches.

Someone whispered something I couldn't hear.

I stood there, letting the moment settle.

Then I asked, "Is it okay for me to say that?"

Several voices from my supporters: "Yes, Chief."

"It's fine," someone said.

And then Council member Tommye Saunooke, one of the three who would vote against my removal, spoke up clearly:

"Yes. It's fine."

I nodded.

Because I meant it. And I meant more than the words themselves.

I was acknowledging something I had come to understand during those long months of investigation and accusation: We were all part of this community. We would all still be here when the hearing ended—living on the same Boundary, shopping at the same stores, attending the same funerals and graduations and ballgames. Our children would grow up together. Our grandchildren would inherit whatever we built or destroyed.

I had pushed hard. Maybe too hard. I had backed people into corners—people who felt they had no choice but to push back. Some of them were corrupt and deserved to be exposed. But others were just scared, or proud, or protective of a system they had learned to navigate. I hadn't given them room to adjust, to save face, to find a way forward that didn't require my destruction.

That didn't excuse what they were doing. The charges were still fabricated. The process was still corrupt. The outcome would still be unjust.

But standing there in that chamber, facing people who had worked for months to destroy me, I understood that hatred would only chain me to this moment forever. And I refused to be chained.

So I said I loved them. Not because they deserved it. But because I needed to mean it—for my own sake, for my family's sake, for the sake of the person I wanted to be when this was over.

And I did mean it. Even then. Even there.

I returned to my seat.

Scott leaned over. "That took courage."

I nodded.

But I didn't feel courageous.

I just felt tired.

Closed Deliberation Begins—3:45 p.m.

At 3:45 p.m., the Council announced they would begin closed-door deliberations.

The chamber was cleared.

Everyone filed out—supporters, opposition, media, staff, witnesses.

Everyone except the twelve Council members who would decide my fate.

I walked into the hallway with Cyndi, my mother, and Nelson.

My mother looked exhausted. She was seventy-eight years old, and she had sat through three days of watching her son dragged through a political circus. The worry was etched on her face.

"Mom," I said gently, "I don't expect them to decide tonight. This is going to take time. You should go on home and rest."

She looked at me for a long moment.

"Are you sure?"

"I'm sure. Nelson can take you. Get some rest. I'll call you when I know something."

She nodded, reached out, and touched my face.

Then she and Nelson walked down the hallway toward the exit.

Cyndi stayed with me.

At 5:00 p.m., word came that the Council had ended deliberations for the day.

They would resume tomorrow.

Thursday.

The final day.

I drove home that night in silence.

Cyndi sat beside me, looking out the window.

When we got home, we didn't talk much.

We just sat together.

Waiting for tomorrow.

Waiting for the end.

Thursday, May 25, 2017—The Vote

The Final Morning

I woke up Thursday knowing what was coming.

The deliberation. The vote. The end.

I put on my suit and tie. Same as every other day. Same routine.

If this was going to be my last day as Principal Chief, I was going to walk in looking like one.

Cyndi didn't say much that morning. She just looked at me across the kitchen table with the same quiet strength she'd carried through this entire ordeal.

"Whatever happens," she said, "we'll be okay."

I nodded.

But I wasn't sure I believed it.

I arrived at the Council House around midmorning. My office, still mine for now, was quiet. A few staff members were there, waiting, watching, unsure what to say.

I went through the motions. Checked emails. Signed a few last documents. Tried to focus on something, anything, other than what was happening down the hall.

At noon, word came that the Council had resumed deliberations.

Waiting—Noon to 3:00 p.m.

Those three hours felt like days.

I stayed in my office. Scott Jones was there. Cyndi sat with me. A few supporters stopped by—people who had stood with me from the beginning, people who knew this was the end but couldn't stay away.

We didn't talk much.

What was there to say?

The evidence had been presented. The theatrics had played out.

Now twelve people sat in a room deciding whether to overturn the will of the voters.

At one point, Scott said, "You know they're going to vote to remove you."

"I know."

"And you know it has nothing to do with the charges."

"I know."

"Then why does it still feel like this?"

I looked at him.

"Because I thought, even after everything, I thought maybe right would stand up. I thought maybe someone would remember their oath. I thought maybe the truth would matter."

Scott nodded slowly.

"It should," he said. "But it doesn't. Not today."

The Decision—3:00 p.m.

At 3:00 p.m., someone knocked on my office door.

"They've reached a decision. They're calling everyone back to the chamber."

I stood.

Looked at Scott. Looked at Cyndi.

And I made a decision.

"I'm not going back in there."

Scott looked surprised. "You're not?"

"No. I'm not going to give them, or that hateful bunch, the satisfaction of watching me while they vote."

I turned to Cyndi.

"We'll watch it on TV. From here."

She nodded.

Scott understood.

So while the chamber filled with supporters and opposition and media and staff—while everyone gathered to watch the final act of this political theater—Cyndi and I sat in my office.

Safe. Quiet. Together.

I turned on the television.

And we watched.

The Vote

The Council members filed in and took their seats at the rectangular table.

The chairman called the session to order.

"The Tribal Council has concluded its deliberations on the articles of impeachment against Principal Chief Patrick Lambert. We will now vote on each article."

One by one, they called the roll.

One by one, they read the charges.

And one by one, they voted.

I don't remember the exact order of the votes.

I don't remember which articles they found me "guilty" of and which they dismissed.

What I remember is sitting beside Cyndi, holding her hand, watching the screen.

Hearing the voices.

"Guilty."

"Guilty."

"Not guilty." (Teresa McCoy, clear, strong, defiant.)

"Guilty."

"Guilty."

"Not guilty." (Richard French, steady, principled.)

"Guilty."

"Guilty."

"Not guilty." (Tommye Saunooke—the third who refused.)

"Guilty."

"Guilty."

"Guilty."

Nine guilty votes.

Three not guilty.

Then came the final vote—the one that mattered most.

"Resolution 596, to approve the immediate removal of Chief Lambert as Principal Chief and the installation of Vice Chief Richard G. Sneed into the top position."

The roll was called again.

Nine voices said yes.

Three said no.

The gavel fell.

"Chief Patrick Lambert is hereby impeached and removed from office, effective immediately. Vice Chief Richard G. Sneed is now Principal Chief of the Eastern Band of Cherokee Indians."

Cyndi and I sat together in silence.

The room erupted on the television screen, shouting, anger, chaos.

But in my office, it was quiet.

We just sat there.

Holding hands.

Watching.

Then Cyndi turned to me and we hugged.

No words.

Just a long, quiet embrace.

It was done.

The Chaos Outside

Within minutes, people were at my office door.

Knocking. Opening it. Flooding in.

"Chief, what do you want us to do?"

"Should we raise hell?"

"We're ready to fight this!"

The anger in the chamber had spilled into the hallways. My supporters were furious, ready to explode.

I looked at them.

"It's up to you," I said. "But be peaceful."

They nodded and rushed back toward the chamber.

A few minutes later, someone from the Council came to my door.

"You have one hour to pack your personal items and leave."

One hour.

To clear out an office I had worked in for nearly two years.

To gather my things and walk away from a job the people had elected me to do.

One hour.

I didn't argue.

I just started packing.

Personal photos. A few files. Some books. Small items from my desk.

But I left everything else in place.

A fully functioning office.

All the furniture. All the supplies. All the working files.

Everything organized, documented, ready for whoever came next.

Because that's what you do when you're a professional.

When I had walked into this office in October 2015, it had been a mess—disorganized, neglected, chaotic.

Now, as I walked out, I left behind an office that worked.

Day and night difference.

And I made sure they knew it.

Richie Sneed Flees

While I packed, word came from the chamber:

Richie Sneed had tried to be sworn in.

But the crowd erupted in anger.

"Let the people speak!"

"This is our government!"

"You can't do this!"

The shouting grew so loud, so intense, that police officers surrounded Richie and rushed him out the back door of the chambers.

He was taken to the Cherokee Tribal Courthouse, the EBCI Justice Center, where he was sworn in privately, away from the people, away from the anger.

The new Principal Chief was too afraid to face the people he was supposed to lead.

I Walk Outside—5:00 p.m.

When my hour was up, I carried my box of personal items down the hallway.

Scott walked with me. So did a few close supporters.

And when I stepped outside, I saw them.

Hundreds of people.

My supporters—the ones who couldn't get into the chamber, the ones who had been waiting in the parking lot, the ones who had stood with me from the beginning.

They erupted in applause when they saw me.

"Chief! Chief! Chief!"

I set down my box.

Stood on the steps of the Council House.

And I told them the truth.

The Speech

"What we just saw today was nine people. How many people are in this crowd that support me?"

The crowd roared.

"I think those nine just overruled seventy-one percent of this Tribe!"

More cheers. More anger.

"What we saw in there, as well, was those nine trying to swear in a new Chief. However, that new Chief would not allow the people to speak. He was surrounded by the police then got carted off down to the courthouse to hide from the people."

Boos filled the air.

"So, I think that's a bad way to start a new administration. I think the people should have had a chance to speak."

I paused.

"I've always stood on that side, and I remember an elder coming to the podium one time, and being shut down that quick. They wouldn't even let an elder of our Tribe up there to talk."

My voice tightened.

"So I'm a little angry about that piece still. But I'm not angry about the impeachment. Understand that?"

The crowd quieted.

"Because, you know what? We haven't stopped fighting."

Cheers erupted again.

"What this boils down to, the reason that just happened, pure and simple."

I pointed back toward the Council House.

"You remember a few weeks ago, a few months ago, the FBI rolled up right over there to that office, and loaded up a whole truckload of boxes out of the TOP office. All right. And a little while later, a few weeks later, they went over to the housing office and loaded out some boxes and file cabinets over there."

I paused.

"But guess what? They've never rolled in here and took any boxes out of my office!"

The crowd erupted.

"Taken together, the timing of these events raises questions about what this was really about.

"You know, I appreciate everyone coming out today and all the support over this whole time that we've had together. Because it truly boils down to the FBI investigating, and that's what I ran on, right? Clean up corruption and the mess within this Tribe."

Applause.

"But from where I stood, the forces driving this were greed, fear, and money."

Then I looked out at the crowd and said the words that would define what came next.

"Let's organize and show them the real power of the people.

Elections are just a few weeks away! Beat them out at the polls! Give them a taste of their own medicine. Let's go!"

The crowd erupted one final time.

After the Speech

I picked up my box.

A group of supporters gathered around me.

"Chief, let's go get some food. We need to talk. We need to plan."

I looked at them—good people, loyal people, people who wanted to keep fighting.

But I was exhausted.

Completely, utterly exhausted.

"Y'all go ahead," I said. "Cyndi, you should go with them."

Cyndi looked at me, concerned.

"You sure?"

"I'm sure. I just need a little time. I'll wait for you at home."

She hesitated, then nodded.

I got in my car.

And I drove home alone.

Alone

When I walked into the house, the silence hit me like a wave.

No crowds. No voices. No cameras. No chaos.

Just stillness.

I set the box down on the kitchen table.

Stood there for a moment.

And then everything I had been holding inside for four days, for weeks, for months, came flooding out.

I sat down.

Put my head in my hands.

And I let myself feel it.

The sadness.

Not for me.

But for the Tribe.

For my family, Cyndi, my mother, Nelson, Gina, who had watched me dragged through this.

For my staff—good people who had worked so hard to bring

transparency and accountability, who now faced an uncertain future.

For my supporters—thousands of people who had believed in change, who had voted overwhelmingly for a new direction, only to watch nine politicians erase their voices.

For the elders—who had lived through so much, who deserved better leadership than what they were about to get.

For the future—for the children and grandchildren who would inherit whatever came next.

I don't know how long I sat there.

But by the time Cyndi came home, I had pulled myself together.

When she walked in, I was standing at the kitchen counter.

Calm. Steady. Okay.

"How was it?" I asked.

"Good. Everyone's fired up. They're ready to fight in September."

"Good."

She looked at me closely.

"You okay?"

"I'm okay."

She didn't press.

We just stood there together in the quiet house.

And we began the process of figuring out what came next.

They Voted—Now We Vote

Four months later, September 2017, the Cherokee people went to the polls.

And they delivered their judgment.

The majority of the Council members who had voted to impeach me were removed from office by the voters in the next election cycle—who all got beat—by my count, at least seven of the nine.

Travis Smith—the man who had led the charge against me, the man who had smirked his way through the entire hearing—was resoundingly defeated in Birdtown, finishing at the bottom of the field.

The people had spoken.

Not with nine votes in a closed chamber.

But with thousands of votes at the ballot box.

And they said: We remember.

CHAPTER 26

WHAT THEY FOUND

"You may encounter many defeats, but you must not be defeated."

— Maya Angelou

The morning after the vote, I stayed in bed for the first time in decades—no office, no staff, just silence. They removed me from office. They did not defeat me.

◆ ◆ ◆

I WOKE UP THE MORNING after the vote and did something I hadn't done in years, maybe decades. I stayed in bed.

For the first time in as long as I could remember, I had nowhere to go. No office to report to. No staff waiting for instructions. No purchase orders to sign. No meetings to attend. No government to run.

I lay there in my sleeping clothes, staring at the ceiling, trying to process what had happened. For twenty-one years as executive director of the Gaming Commission, I had bounced out of bed every morning with purpose and energy—quick workout, shower, suit and tie, out the door before most people were finishing breakfast. For nearly two years as Principal Chief, the routine had been even more demanding, the responsibilities even heavier, the sense of obligation to the Cherokee people even more acute.

But that morning, there was nothing to bounce toward. Just silence. Just the slow, creeping realization that it was really over, that the vote had actually happened, that I was no longer Principal Chief of the Eastern Band of Cherokee Indians.

Cyndi brought me coffee. She set it on the nightstand, sat on the edge of the bed, and put her hand on my arm.

"You need anything?" she asked.

"No. I just need to sit here a minute."

She nodded. She didn't try to fill the silence with reassurances. She just let me be.

The Calls and Messages

My phone started ringing before I got out of bed and didn't stop for days.

The message was almost always the same: "Keep your head up, Chief. Don't let them get away with this. Keep fighting. We're with you."

One call stood out. An old friend, a man I had worked with for years in gaming regulation, said something that cut through the noise: "Patrick, they didn't remove you because you did something wrong. They removed you because you were about to prove they did. That's the only thing that makes sense."

He was right. And I appreciated every call, every message, every voice reaching out to remind me that I wasn't alone. In those first dark hours, those calls were lifelines. They reminded me that the nine politicians who had voted to remove me didn't speak for the Cherokee people.

But I also knew something my supporters didn't fully grasp yet: The fight had fundamentally changed. I was no longer Principal Chief. I no longer had the office, the staff, the authority, the platform. The battle would continue, I was certain of that, but it would be fought on different terrain. In courtrooms rather than Council Chambers. Through elections rather than executive actions. By the people themselves rather than by the government that was supposed to represent them.

The Investigation That Found Nothing

Richie went after me, determined to find evidence of what they had charged and removed me with.

For months after I left office, they went through everything. Every authorization I had signed. Every purchase order I had approved. Every travel voucher I had submitted. Every decision I had made as Principal Chief, examined and reexamined in search of something, anything, that could retroactively justify my removal.

They found nothing. Not one violation of law or policy. The investigation that was supposed to produce the smoking gun came up completely empty. After months of effort to find something to charge me with, they quietly moved on and hoped everyone would forget.

Instead, they turned their attention to what the real goal had always been—the Tribal reserves. What followed was a spending spree of a scale the Eastern Band had never seen, dressed up as "diversification." They returned us to a heavy debt burden after I had delivered us 100% debt free for the first time in modern history. They stood up LLC after LLC and committed hundreds of millions of dollars to investments that were half-considered at best and outright failures at worst. In doing so, they discarded the sound fiscal policies and long-range fiscal planning I had been instituting—work designed precisely to prepare the Tribe for a future that might not include a gaming monopoly. I had seen that day coming. They acted as if it never would. It did. The people who impeached me for imaginary financial misconduct then presided over what will likely be remembered as the most reckless period of financial stewardship in Tribal history.

The New Impeachment Law

After they removed me, after the dust settled, after they had achieved everything they wanted—they passed a new law. A new code section establishing formal impeachment procedures.

They had impeached me without any such procedures in place. They conducted an entire proceeding, investigation, charges, hearing, vote, removal, without any established rules governing how it should work. They made it up as they went along.

And then, after I was gone, they wrote the rules that should have existed before any of it started.

That law still stands. Every time a future Council opens the impeachment procedures code, they can check the date it was enacted and do the math for themselves.

Indian Country Responds

News of the Cherokee impeachment traveled fast through Indian Country. A Cherokee Nation official observed: "This will be remembered not for what you were accused of, but for how they treated the office of Chief. They degraded the position itself."

The people who had orchestrated the impeachment probably thought they would be celebrated as reformers. Instead, they became cautionary tales, examples of how *not* to conduct tribal governance, subjects of discussion at legal conferences where the Cherokee impeachment of 2017 was held up as everything that can go wrong when political self-interest overrides democratic principles.

Inside the Boundary—Unity Rises

Inside Cherokee communities, the political fallout began almost immediately. Council members who had voted for impeachment were confronted at community events, at grocery stores, at family gatherings. People started asking questions, not just about me, but about the people who had voted to remove me.

The anger spread—not the hot, destructive anger that leads to violence, but the cold, determined anger that expresses itself through organization and voting and long memories. Tribal members filled social media with questions and outrage. Employees whispered the truth in hallways. Former leaders who had stayed quiet during the proceedings started speaking out.

The Twelve Articles of Impeachment—A Factual Record

The twelve articles accused me of misuse of tribal resources, abuse of authority, and violations of tribal law. Scott Jones, my attorney, analyzed every one of them in a formal legal memorandum written shortly after the proceedings concluded. His findings were unambiguous.

Four articles were acquitted by the Council's own vote—and they impeached me anyway. Three articles involved standard tribal policy that my administration had followed exactly as prior administrations had—routine actions reframed as misconduct when it became politically convenient. Three more involved lawful decisions that no law, ordinance, or policy prohibited. One article was a duplicate charge repackaged to pad the count. One named me for an action taken by another official entirely.

Zero charges showed any wrongdoing.

The complete legal analysis, the vote tallies, and the full text of all twelve articles are preserved in the Evidence Vault at PatrickLambert.com. I encourage everyone who wants the detailed truth to visit the Evidence Vault and decide for themselves. The charges didn't survive the evidence.

PART IV

REBUILDING AND VINDICATION

CHAPTER 27

AFTER THE FALL

"The wound is the place where the Light enters you."

— Rumi

I went into the mountains and wept on a ridge above Fontana
Lake. The healing didn't come from philosophy—it came
through the wound itself.

◆ ◆ ◆

WHEN YOU FALL FROM a great height, the impact doesn't come all
at once. There's the initial shock—the vote, the faces, the finality.
But the real damage reveals itself slowly, over days and weeks and
months.

That was my world in May 2017. One day, I was carrying the
responsibilities of Principal Chief. The next, I was standing outside the
walls of the same government I had devoted my life to building.

The phone started ringing early. Some calls were from people
offering support. Those calls helped, but they also hurt because each one
required me to relive it. I didn't take most of the reporter calls. I needed
space to process what had happened in private.

The Mountains Were the Only Place That Made Sense

I needed air. I needed distance. I needed the land. So I went into the
mountains. I threw a small pack over my shoulder and disappeared onto
the trails I had known since boyhood—trails where my father once
walked beside me, where we fished cold streams, where we camped
beneath the sweep of the Milky Way.

I wasn't running from anything. I was returning to myself.

The trails I walked were memory paths—places where my childhood
still lived in the roots and rocks. The creek where my father taught me to
fish. The ridge where we hunted squirrel and rabbit. The clearing where
we camped and he told stories about his father. These weren't just hiking

trails. They were anchors.

Some days I hiked alone. Other days my sisters joined me. And Cyndi, steady, quiet, unwavering, walked beside me when the weight felt especially heavy.

The Moment the Weight Broke Open

There was one hike I will never forget.

I was hiking alone on a strenuous trail close to Fontana Lake, and about halfway up the ridge, I stopped. The wind moved through the trees, and the ache inside me felt louder than the forest. I lowered myself into the grass and the fallen leaves, right there on the side of the mountain. And I wept.

Not for the office. Not for the title. I wept because I was exhausted—not physically but spiritually and emotionally drained. I wept for my family—for Cyndi, who had carried this weight beside me. For my mother, who had watched her son dragged through a political circus. For my children, who had to defend their father to friends and strangers. I wept for the betrayal—by Council members and by the system I had helped build. I wept because I had done it all right—and it hadn't mattered.

I'm not sure how long I was like that, but after I composed myself, I didn't get up. I just lay there, staring up through the canopy, listening. The slight wind moved through the branches above me. Somewhere nearby, a small animal rustled through the leaves—maybe a squirrel trying to find that last acorn to store away for winter, or maybe a fox positioning itself for the evening hunt. I didn't move. I made no sound. And I wondered: How loud had I been? Had the forest heard me? Had the wind paused while I wept? Had the squirrel stopped its work to listen?

I lay there for nearly an hour, just breathing, just listening, just being still on the side of that mountain. And then the light began to shift, the shadows growing longer, and I realized it would be dark soon. That's when I sat up. Because the wind hadn't stopped. The squirrel hadn't stopped. Life hadn't stopped. Neither the forest nor the world would pause and wait for me to be ready.

I rose, brushed the leaves from my clothes, and started back up the mountain. Not because the pain was gone. But because the mountains had reminded me of something I had forgotten: Endurance is older than politics. Strength is deeper than any storm. And life does not wait—just like the river, it simply continues. And so must I.

The Appalachian Trail—A Solitary Healing

As the days went on, I pushed higher and farther. Eventually, I hiked the entire seventy-mile stretch of the Appalachian Trail through the Great Smoky Mountains—ridge after ridge, mile after mile, until the wind itself felt like medicine. Up there, I wasn't a former Chief. I wasn't a political target. I wasn't a headline. I was simply Patrick—a man walking ancient ground, matching my breath to the pulse of the mountains.

Some days I walked until my legs burned and my lungs ached. I climbed steep grades until sweat soaked my shirt. I pushed through exhaustion until my body had no choice but to quiet my mind. Physical pain has a way of drowning out emotional pain. Not permanently. But long enough to catch your breath. And on those trails, with every step, every breath, every mile—I was slowly catching my breath again.

The First Flicker of Light

Something happened on those trails—slowly, like dawn creeping through dark trees. The grief didn't vanish, but it lost its claws. The anger cooled into clarity. And the sense of betrayal settled into something else entirely: resolve.

I remembered what my mother always told me: "Son . . . you must choose that for yourself."

I couldn't change what had happened. I couldn't rewrite the past. But I could choose my response. And I decided—there on a ridge with the wind sweeping through the firs—that the end of my time as Principal Chief would not be the end of me. Not my purpose. Not my voice. Not my service to my people. It would be a beginning. A hard one. A painful one. But a beginning.

Hiking with Family—The Silent Support

My sisters sometimes walked with me during those months. They didn't ask probing questions. They didn't force conversation. They just showed up—boots laced, water bottles filled, ready to walk. One afternoon, after a particularly steep climb, we stopped at an overlook.

The valley stretched out below us, the Boundary unfolding like a quilt of green and shadow. My oldest sister, Pat, turned to me and said simply: "You're still here, Patrick. That's what matters."

I nodded. Because she was right. I was still here. Broken, maybe. Wounded, certainly. But still here. And that counted for something.

The hikes with Cyndi were different. We walked side by side, sometimes we talked about the kids, the grandchildren, the businesses. Sometimes we talked about nothing at all. But one evening, as the sun dropped low and the light turned gold through the trees, she stopped on the trail and turned to me. "Patrick," she said, "I know you're hurting. But I also know you. And you're going to be okay."

The Mountains as Witness

There's an old Cherokee teaching that the mountains are witnesses. They watched our ancestors walk these ridges. They watched the Removal survivors return. They watched generations rebuild. And now they were watching me. Not judging. Just witnessing.

There was something deeply comforting in that. Knowing that whatever happened in the Council Chambers, whatever lies were told, whatever politics unfolded—the mountains knew the truth. They had seen me walk these trails as a boy. They had seen my father walk them before me. They would see my grandchildren walk them after me.

What Came Next

Cyndi and I sat at the kitchen table one morning after I'd returned from a particularly long hike, coffee going cold in my cup, not saying much.

"What do you want to do?" she finally asked.

I didn't have an answer. For the first time in my adult life, I genuinely didn't know what came next. Every major decision I'd made for the past two decades had been oriented toward Tribal service—becoming Tribal attorney, building the Gaming Commission, running for Chief. Now that path was closed, blocked not by my choice but by political forces I couldn't control. I felt unmoored in a way I hadn't felt since I was a young man trying to figure out who I was and what I was supposed to do with my life.

"I don't know," I told her honestly. "I need to think."

She nodded.

People ask me sometimes if I'm angry at the Council members who voted against me. The answer is no. I'm disappointed in them. I believe they made the wrong choice for the wrong reasons and that history has proven them wrong. But anger? That's a fire that burns the one who holds it far more than it burns anyone else. I could spend years nursing resentment, rehearsing grievances, imagining confrontations that will never happen—and at the end of all that time and emotional energy, the only person worse off would be me.

So I chose to let it go—not because those who orchestrated the impeachment deserved forgiveness, but because I deserved peace. Because Cyndi deserved a husband who wasn't consumed by bitterness. Because my children and grandchildren deserved a father and grandfather who was present rather than lost in old grievances. Letting go of anger is not the same as forgetting. I remember everything that happened. I remember who did what and why. I remember it all as history, as lessons learned, as experiences that shaped me—not as wounds that still bleed, not as injustices that still demand response.

What I carry forward from this experience is far more valuable than any anger or resentment could ever be.

I carry the lessons—about leadership, about courage, about the difference between allies and friends, about what institutions can and cannot be trusted to do. I carry clear eyes—about what really happened, about why, about who was responsible and what motivated them. I carry gratitude for the people who stood when it mattered, who spoke when silence would have been safer, who voted their conscience when the political pressure said otherwise.

And I carry forward the same commitments I made on Inauguration Day, the promises that made me a target in the first place. I kept those promises. I did my job right. Whatever they took from me, they couldn't take that.

Years later, people ask me: "Was it worth it? Would you do it again, knowing what it would cost?"

The pain wasn't worth it. The damage to my family, the stress on my marriage, the worry on my mother's face—none of that was worth it. The years consumed by legal battles and political warfare could have been spent building rather than defending.

But here's what was worth it: The audits that uncovered millions in misuse. The systems we built that still protect the Tribe today. The precedent we established that Chiefs can enforce accountability without fear. The example we set for future leaders that transparency is possible, that corruption can be confronted, that the people will ultimately support those who fight for them.

If I had looked the other way—if I had ignored the corruption, kept quiet about the problems, preserved the comfortable arrangements that had protected the wrong people for too long—the Tribe would have been worse off. The misuse would have continued. The weak oversight would have persisted. The culture of unaccountability would have deepened. And I would have spent the rest of my life knowing that I had the power to make things right and chose not to use it.

I didn't look the other way. I used the power the people gave me to do exactly what I promised to do. And even though it cost me the office, even though it cost me years of my life, even though it cost my family pain they didn't deserve—I would make the same choice again.

CHAPTER 28

THE WORLD OPENS

"Not all those who wander are lost."

— J.R.R. Tolkien

Cyndi and I circled the globe after the impeachment—not running from anything, but expanding into everything. Tolkien wrote that line about a king in exile. It fits a chief in exile just as well.

◆ ◆ ◆

WHEN THE POLITICAL STORM ended, the silence felt too loud. For months, every corner of my life had been filled with noise—accusations, arguments, procedures, headlines, whispers. And then suddenly, as if someone had flipped a switch, it all went quiet. The impeachment was over. The office was gone. The daily machinery of Tribal governance that had consumed my waking hours for years simply stopped, leaving behind a vacuum I didn't know how to fill.

I didn't want quiet. I needed movement. I needed distance. I needed perspective—something big enough to remind me that life was not measured in the Council Chambers or political victories or the opinions of nine people who'd decided my fate on a May afternoon. So Cyndi and I did something we had never done before: We set out to see the world.

Not as Principal Chief. Not as a Tribal attorney. Not as a public figure whose every move might be scrutinized or judged. But as a man healing, and as a couple reclaiming the joy that politics had slowly, steadily drained from our lives.

The Decision to Go

Cyndi found me in the car wash equipment room around ten one night, wiping my hands on a rag that was already too dirty to be useful. I'd been throwing myself into the businesses since the impeachment, the car wash, the laundromat, the hotel, because physical work gave me something concrete to solve. A broken pump either worked or it didn't. There was no spin, no interpretation, no political calculation.

She leaned against the doorframe watching me the way she does when she's waiting for me to arrive at a conclusion she's already reached.

"What?" I finally asked.

"When's the last time we did something just because we wanted to?" she said. "Not because we had to. Not because it served some purpose or advanced some goal. Just because it sounded good."

I thought about that. Couldn't remember.

"Not sure," I admitted.

"Me neither," she said. "And I think that's a problem."

She was right. We'd spent decades in service mode. Service to the Tribe, service to our businesses, service to our family. All worthy things. But somewhere along the way, we'd forgotten how to simply enjoy being alive.

"What do you have in mind?" I asked.

"I don't know yet," she said, and smiled. "But I think we should find out."

Building the Itinerary

Over the next few weeks, we researched destinations we'd only seen in magazines. We talked about places that had always intrigued us but seemed impossibly far away when we were younger and money was tight, or later when time was the scarce commodity.

Asia kept calling to us. Maybe because it was about as far from Cherokee as you could get, geographically and culturally. Maybe because neither of us had ever been there and it felt like genuinely new territory.

We booked tickets. Hong Kong, Taiwan, Japan, South Korea, China, then west to Dubai and Abu Dhabi, a stop in Amsterdam, and finally home. A monthlong journey heading west the entire way—a complete circumnavigation of the earth. It felt extravagant in a way that made me slightly uncomfortable—I'd grown up poor enough that spending money on anything that wasn't strictly necessary still triggered guilt decades later. But Cyndi was right. We needed this.

Hong Kong—The Vertical City

We landed in Hong Kong in late afternoon, the plane descending through layers of humidity into a city that rose from the harbor like steel and glass mountains. I'd seen plenty of American cities, but nothing prepared me for the sheer vertical intensity of Hong Kong. Buildings climbed toward the sky with an ambition that felt almost defiant.

Our hotel was in Kowloon, and that first evening we rode the Star Ferry across the harbor just to see the skyline from sea level. The ferry was packed with commuters heading home from work, and we stood at the railing watching the city lights begin to flicker on as the sun dropped behind the buildings. Around us, people spoke Cantonese in rapid bursts that sounded almost musical. Nobody paid us any attention. We were just two more tourists among millions, anonymous and unburdened.

"This is so far from home," Cyndi said, not sadly but with a kind of wonder.

"Yeah," I said. "So glad to be here."

We spent three days in Hong Kong, eating dim sum in restaurants where we pointed at pictures because we couldn't read the menu, riding the tram up Victoria Peak to look down on the entire glittering sprawl. What struck me most wasn't the famous stuff but the ordinary moments. Watching an elderly woman practice tai chi in a tiny park at dawn. Sitting in a corner noodle shop at lunch, slurping soup alongside construction workers. Riding the escalators that climb the hillside neighborhoods, passing apartments where entire families lived in spaces smaller than our garage back home.

Taiwan—Night Markets and Generosity

From Hong Kong we flew to Taipei, and if Hong Kong was a vertical ambition, Taiwan was a horizontal welcome. The first night, we ventured into the Shilin Night Market—a maze of stalls and vendors producing smells that ranged from intoxicating to alarming. We tried foods we had never heard of like oyster omelets and stinky tofu (which earned its name) and bubble tea and grilled squid on sticks. We didn't know what half of it was. We just pointed and smiled and trusted, much of it didn't get eaten but just lightly sampled.

What I remember most about Taiwan wasn't the food, though the food was incredible. It was the people. We got lost trying to find our way back to the hotel one evening, wandering down increasingly narrow streets. I pulled out the hotel card to show a passerby, hoping for directions.

The young woman—maybe in her twenties, dressed like she'd just left work—looked at the card, spoke briefly with her companion, then turned to us and said in careful English, "Very far. We take you."

"No, no," I protested. "Just directions—"

But she was already walking, gesturing for us to follow. For twenty minutes we walked through Taipei while this stranger led us back toward our hotel, asking us questions about where we were from and what we thought of Taiwan. When we finally reached the hotel, I tried to offer her money for her trouble. She looked genuinely offended.

"No, no," she said. "Welcome to Taiwan. Enjoy."

And then she was gone, disappeared into the evening crowds. That moment stayed with me. The casual generosity of it. It reminded me of Cherokee, actually—of the old ways, the teaching that hospitality isn't optional, that you care for people because that's what people do for each other.

Japan—Precision and Beauty

Japan was different again. Where Hong Kong was chaos and energy, and Taiwan was warmth and generosity, Japan was precision and beauty existing in perfect balance. We spent a week there, moving from Tokyo to Kyoto to Osaka, and everywhere we went I was struck by the attention to detail. The way a shopkeeper wrapped a simple purchase as if it were a gift. The way gardens were maintained with such care that every rock seemed deliberately placed.

In Kyoto we visited temples that were hundreds of years old, wooden structures that had survived wars and earthquakes through meticulous care. We walked through a bamboo grove on a misty morning, the tall stalks swaying above us, light filtering through in shafts that turned the whole grove green and gold and otherworldly.

One afternoon in a small tea house, with several customers, an elderly woman performed a traditional tea ceremony. Every movement was deliberate, practiced, almost ritual. It took nearly an hour, and I'd be lying if I said I understood all the symbolism. But I understood the larger point: that you honor simple acts by doing them well, that beauty can be found in everyday gestures if you're paying attention, that rushing through life means missing most of what makes life worth living.

The impeachment had forced me to rush through so much. Reacting, defending, surviving. I'd forgotten how to slow down. Japan reminded me.

South Korea—Resilience Made Visible

South Korea felt like a country in conversation with itself—ultramodern and traditional, forward-looking and historically rooted, loud and quiet all at once. In Seoul we wandered through neighborhoods where centuries-old palaces sat surrounded by glass office towers. We visited the DMZ, that strange heavily fortified border, and stood looking across the divide at a country that might as well be on another planet despite being just a few miles away.

What struck me about South Korea was the resilience. This was a country that had been devastated by war within living memory, divided from itself, occupied and fought over and nearly destroyed. And it had rebuilt. Thrived. It refused to let trauma define its future.

I thought about Cherokee history. About the Removal. About the decades of grinding hardship my parents' and grandparents' generations had endured. About how we'd survived and rebuilt and created something strong from nothing. If my ancestors could resist the Trail of Tears and rebuild a Nation after being destroyed, I could survive an impeachment and build a life on the other side.

The Great Wall—The Moment Everything Shifted

From Seoul we flew to Beijing, and from Beijing we took a bus out to the Great Wall. I'd seen pictures, of course, everyone has. But pictures don't prepare you for the reality of it. The sheer audacity of building a wall that runs for thousands of miles across mountains and deserts. The age of it. The fact that you can stand on stones that were laid down centuries before Columbus sailed and they're still solid under your feet.

We climbed to one of the high overlooks in the late morning, the stones warmed by the sun, red flags snapping in the wind. It was crowded with tourists, everyone taking pictures, guides explaining history in a dozen languages. I was hot and tired from the climb and thinking about finding some shade when I turned and saw Cyndi standing a few feet away.

The Chinese national flag waved behind her, bright red against the impossibly blue sky. She wasn't posing or trying to capture a particular image. She was just standing there, looking out over the wall as it snaked away across the ridges, and she was smiling. Not for the camera, not for me, but just . . . smiling. The kind of genuine, unselfconscious smile that only comes when you're completely present in a moment.

And something broke through in me.

Because in that moment, high above the world, standing on one of humanity's most ambitious creations, watching my wife of nearly four decades simply exist in a moment of pure joy, the truth hit me with a force that took my breath away:

She was still here.

After everything we'd been through—the poverty of our early years, the struggles of building a life together, the intensity of my career in Tribal service, the brutality of the impeachment, the humiliation and hurt and uncertainty—she was still here. Still beside me. Still my best friend, my partner, my anchor. Still choosing us, choosing me, choosing this life we'd built together despite all the reasons she could have chosen differently.

The world opened that day. Around me—though standing on the Great Wall with Asia stretching out in all directions certainly provided physical evidence of the world's vastness. But within me. Some tightness I'd been carrying since the impeachment, some fear I hadn't fully acknowledged, suddenly loosened its grip.

I walked over to where she stood and took her hand. She looked at me and saw something in my face because her expression changed from simple contentment to something deeper, more knowing.

"You okay?" she asked.

"Yeah," I said. And meant it. "I really am."

We stood there together for a long time, holding hands on the Great Wall of China, and I realized something that should have been obvious all along: The impeachment had tried to take everything from me, but it couldn't touch this. Couldn't touch us. The politicians who'd voted to remove me had no power here, no voice, no relevance. They existed in a world thousands of miles away that suddenly felt very small and very distant.

Dubai and Abu Dhabi—Standing Taller

From China we flew west to the United Arab Emirates. We rode camels across desert sands that looked like they belonged in a storybook. We floated in a hot air balloon at sunrise over landscapes so stark and beautiful they didn't seem real. And we stood atop the Burj Khalifa in Dubai, the tallest building in the world, looking down at the city glittering beneath us like a map of light and ambition.

The observation deck was on the 148th floor, so high that clouds passed below us. I stood at the window with my hand pressed against the glass, looking down at the city that had risen from the desert in barely a generation.

Cyndi stepped beside me and looked down at the lights far below.

"Patrick," she said quietly, "look how far we've come."

She meant the trip. But she also meant everything else.

What the Journey Taught Me

We came home from that trip changed. Not healed—healing isn't that simple or that fast. But opened. Reminded that we were more than what had happened to us in Cherokee, more than a political scandal or a removed office.

I brought that expansion back to the businesses and worked differently. Less frantically. Less like I was trying to prove something. More like I was building something worth building because the work itself had value.

I started reading again—not just legal briefs but actual books. History. Biography. Philosophy. I read about other leaders who'd been knocked down and rebuilt themselves.

CHAPTER 29

MY OWN HANDS

"A man is not idle because he is absorbed in thought. There is visible labor and there is invisible labor."

— Victor Hugo

I rebuilt my businesses with my own hands—crawling under equipment, replacing pumps, scrubbing tile. The visible labor of rebuilding a car wash was also the invisible labor of rebuilding a man.

◆ ◆ ◆

WHEN TITLES FALL AWAY, the work of your own hands becomes your anchor.

After the impeachment, people often asked me, "How did you keep going?" They expected something dramatic—a speech about iron discipline or unshakable resolve. Some kind of philosophical framework I'd constructed to make sense of the senseless. The truth was simpler and more ordinary than anyone wanted to hear: I went back to work.

Not political work. Not legal work. Not public work. Real work—the kind you can touch, fix, build, and steady yourself with. The kind of work that doesn't care about your title or your reputation or what people are saying about you. Work that only cares whether you show up and whether you know what you're doing.

Because when life knocks you down hard, sometimes the way back isn't philosophical at all. Sometimes it begins with a toolbox, a problem that needs solving, and the simple dignity of making something work that was broken.

Returning to What I Built Long Before Politics

Long before I was Principal Chief, long before the compact negotiations, or the years spent building the Cherokee Gaming Commission, I was an entrepreneur. I built businesses the same way I built a life: with sweat, with stubbornness, with long hours, and with a belief that honest work never lies. You can spin politics, manipulate narratives, create favorable optics. But you can't spin a water pump that doesn't work. You can't manipulate a washing machine into running when the motor's shot.

So when the political world grew dark and chaotic, I returned to the businesses that had shaped me long before anyone knew my name: the car wash, the laundromat, and the Cherokee Grand Hotel. They didn't ask for explanations. They didn't care about rumors or accusations. They weren't swayed by opinion or influenced by whoever held power in the Tribal Council. They just needed work. And I needed purpose.

During my years in office, I'd necessarily stepped back from the day-to-day operations of these businesses. I had managers, employees, systems in place. They ran without me, which was good—it meant I'd built them right. But it also meant they'd aged without my attention. Equipment had worn out. Maintenance had been deferred. Small problems had compounded into larger ones. Walking back into these businesses in the months after the impeachment was like visiting old friends who'd fallen on hard times. They needed help. And I needed to help them.

The Car Wash—Crafting Order Out of Ruin

The car wash had aged the most during my years in office. Equipment was failing, pumps were tired, hoses were cracked. The first day I really took stock, my list grew longer the more carefully I looked.

Most people in my position would have hired it out. But I didn't, I wanted my hands dirty. I wanted to rebuild something, even if that something was just a car wash.

So I got under it. Literally.

I remember the first night I stayed late. I was lying on the concrete floor of the equipment room with a flashlight clamped between my teeth, tracing wires through old control boxes. My back was complaining. My hands were covered in old grease.

And I felt more clearheaded than I had in months.

There was a purity to this work that politics had never offered. The pump either worked or it didn't. No committee to convince. Just me and the problem and the solution waiting to be found.

Piece by piece, bay by bay, the place came back to life. The work took months, and I did most of it myself. When I finally stood in the parking lot and watched all four bays running perfectly, I felt something I hadn't felt since before the impeachment.

Pride. Simple pride. The pride of building something with your own hands and building it right.

The Laundromat—Order, Rhythm, and the Return of Control

The laundromat was next. For months, it became my second home. I installed new commercial washers and dryers. I rebuilt the electrical system, added cameras, better lighting. I upgraded the water lines, which meant jackhammering through sections of concrete floor—brutal, exhausting work that left my shoulders aching for days.

The physical work became emotional release.

I repainted everything. Modernized the payment systems. Made the place bright and clean and welcoming.

The first evening after the renovation, I sat in my truck watching through the big front windows. The new machines ran in perfect rhythm. A young mother came in with a couple of kids, and I watched her face when she walked in—a little surprise, a small smile, the look of someone who'd expected one thing and found something better.

That look meant more to me than any political poll ever had.

The sound of those machines—the mechanical rhythm of washers filling and agitating and spinning, dryers tumbling in their steady rotations—was more than just the sound of working equipment. It was the sound of order restored. Of chaos tamed. Of something broken made whole again.

It was healing.

The Cherokee Grand Hotel—A Full Resurrection

The hotel was the biggest project of all—a top-to-bottom overhaul that demanded physical work, vision, patience, and a willingness to commit resources when I wasn't entirely sure how they'd be recouped. The Cherokee Grand Hotel had good bones, a solid structure, but the rest needed work. The rooms were dated. The furniture was worn. The fixtures were from another era. The technology was practically nonexistent. The lobby felt tired.

It wasn't just renovation the building needed. It was resurrection.

So that's what we gave it.

We gutted the rooms down to the studs and concrete, then rebuilt them into something people would actually want to stay in. New beds, new furniture, new fixtures, new TVs, new everything. We redid the bathrooms completely—new tile, new showers, fixtures that actually worked and looked good doing it. We upgraded all the technology: high-speed internet, smart TVs, modern climate control, electronic locks. We replaced the HVAC systems. We rewired significant portions of the building.

The lobby got the most dramatic transformation. We tore out the old wallpaper and outdated furniture and created something that felt modern. Local art on the walls. Better lighting. Comfortable seating. A check-in desk that felt professional rather than makeshift. We wanted people to walk in and immediately understand that this wasn't just any hotel—this was a Cherokee hotel, run with pride and attention to detail.

The work took over a year and we stayed open for business while the work was going on. There were moments when I wondered if we'd bitten off more than we could chew, times when the budget got tight and the timeline stretched and problems popped up that nobody had anticipated. But we pushed through, and I was there for almost all of it. Not just writing checks and making decisions, but getting my hands dirty when it mattered. Moving furniture. Inspecting rooms. Testing systems. Making sure every detail met the standard I'd set.

The day we finished, I stood in the lobby early in the morning and looked around at what we'd built. A building worn down by time stood tall again. The transformation was complete. And in a quiet, unexpected way, so was mine.

Working Beside Cyndi—Building as Partners

Through every late-night repair, every design decision, every setback and small victory, Cyndi was there. Not always physically present, she had her own work, her own life, but present in the ways that matter. Encouraging when I was discouraged. Grounding when I got too ambitious. Celebrating small wins when I was too focused on the next problem to notice we'd accomplished something.

Real marriage isn't built on the big moments—the wedding day, the anniversary trips, the public celebrations. The businesses we rebuilt together are better than they would have been if I'd done it alone. Not just better managed or better designed, but better in spirit. They reflect both of us—my work ethic and her wisdom, my determination and her grace.

The Dignity of Quiet Victories

Political victories are loud. They come with headlines and applause and the immediate validation of vote counts and public approval. Political wins feel big in the moment, important, historic sometimes.

Business victories are quiet. A construction win gets dust in your hair and nobody writes about it. When you fix a water pump that was broken, there's no press release. When you renovate a hotel room, there's no ceremony. The work is done in private, judged in private, rewarded in private—if it's rewarded at all.

But the quiet wins last longer.

These were the victories I needed in those years after the impeachment. Small, quiet, undeniable.

CHAPTER 30

GRANDCHILDREN & THE RETURN OF JOY

"A grandchild fills a space in your heart that you never knew was empty."

— Unknown

After the noise of impeachment, it was the smallest people who brought me back to myself. A grandson's weight against my chest. A granddaughter's laugh.

◆　◆　◆

WHEN THE STORM OF impeachment finally quieted, I didn't need politics. I didn't need titles. I didn't need to fight anymore.

I needed life.

And life returned to me in the smallest, purest form possible—grandchildren whose laughter softened places inside me that politics had nearly hardened for good.

Cyndi and I have been blessed with nine grandchildren. Five of them, Haley, Tawny, Trinity, John, and Bear, live in Oklahoma with their mother, our oldest daughter Tiffany. Distance makes those relationships different, measured in phone calls and holiday visits and the ache of missing milestones. But the other four, Rhett, Henrik, Lilou, and Ava, live close enough to be woven into the fabric of our daily lives. And in the years after the impeachment, when I needed healing most, those four became my teachers.

In the months after the impeachment, well-meaning friends would ask how I was doing, and I'd give them the standard answer: "I'm fine. Moving forward." But the truth was more complicated. I wasn't broken, but I wasn't whole either. I was functioning, rebuilding, working—but there was a heaviness that settled in my chest some mornings that no amount of productivity could lift.

Then I remembered I had a grandson who needed his PopPop, and that was enough to get me out of the chair.

The First Light After the Storm—Rhett

Rhett had arrived in June 2016, almost a year before my political world collapsed. I remember the day my son, Nelson, called to tell us Kim was in labor, the rush to the hospital, the hours of waiting. When they finally let us into the room, Nelson looked exhausted and proud in that way new fathers do, and Kim was radiant despite everything she'd just been through. And there was Rhett—impossibly small, wrapped in one of those standard-issue hospital blankets, his tiny fists curled near his face.

When they placed him in my arms, he made a small sound—not quite a cry, more like a question—and then settled against my chest as if he'd found exactly what he was looking for. I felt the warmth of him through the blanket, felt the rise and fall of his breathing, and I remember thinking: *This is what matters. This is what lasts.*

I didn't know then how much I would need that memory.

When the impeachment came almost a year later, when the world was buzzing with noise—rumors, opinions, commentary swirling around what had happened—I found myself reaching for Rhett. He was walking by then, babbling in that language only toddlers speak, completely oblivious to the storm swirling around his grandfather. He didn't know who I had been or what had happened. He didn't know what was taken from me. He didn't know the cost of integrity or the scars of leadership. He only knew he was safe in his PopPop's arms.

That small weight against my chest reminded me of something I had forgotten: I was still needed. I was still capable of love. I was still alive.

In the weeks that followed, I'd hold him while he napped, watching his face twitch with whatever dreams toddlers have, and I'd think about the future in a way I hadn't been able to since the impeachment. Not my future in politics, that felt distant and uncertain, but his future. The world he would grow up in. The kind of man I hoped he might become. The lessons I might still have time to teach him.

One afternoon when Rhett was about eighteen months old, I was holding him while he fought sleep the way children do—eyes drooping, then popping open as if he might miss something important. Cyndi walked past and smiled that knowing smile she has. Later she told me, "You looked more peaceful holding that boy than you've looked in a year."

She was right. Happiness had begun returning in small footsteps.

Henrik—The Bold Explorer

Henrik came next—curious, fearless, full of motion from the moment he could crawl. A boy who reminds me so much of myself that I sometimes laugh out loud just watching him. He touches everything. He wants to understand the world with his hands, his feet, his whole little body before his mind even catches up.

I remember one Sunday afternoon at our house when Henrik was maybe eighteen months old. We were in the garage—I was organizing some tools, and he had toddled out behind me before anyone noticed. Most grandparents would have scooped him up and carried him back inside to safety. Instead, I watched him for a moment. He was completely absorbed in a cardboard box, trying to figure out how to climb into it, his little legs pumping with determination every time he slipped back down.

"You want in that box?" I asked him.

He looked up at me with those bright eyes and nodded, completely serious about his mission.

So I helped him. Held the box steady while he climbed in, then watched as he stood up inside it, triumphant, grinning like he'd just conquered Everest. He stayed in that box for twenty minutes, sitting down, standing up, moving it around the garage floor like a vehicle. Completely content in his own little world of discovery.

When I see him run across a room now, head full of wonder, launching himself at furniture or people or life itself with complete confidence that someone will catch him, I see the boy I was before responsibility settled on my shoulders. Before I learned that the world doesn't always catch you. Before I understood that sometimes you fall and you fall hard and you have to catch yourself.

Henrik brought that memory back—not with sadness, but with something closer to gratitude. He reminded me that fearlessness isn't foolishness. It's trust. And watching him trust the world so completely was renewing to me.

Lilou—The Soft Light of the Family

Then came Lilou. From the moment she was born, she had this way of looking at people, direct, open, trusting, as if she could see straight into your heart and liked what she found there.

I'll never forget the first time she wrapped her arms around my neck. She was maybe two years old, and I'd been down on the floor playing with her and Henrik. When it was time for me to get up and leave, she just walked over, put her little arms around my neck, and held on. Didn't say anything. Just held on. Her hair smelled like baby shampoo and something sweeter—maybe just the particular sweetness that belongs to children. I stayed crouched there on the floor longer than I needed to, feeling that small embrace, and thought about my mother.

Lilou carries echoes of my mother in ways that sometimes catch me off guard. Not in appearance, though there's something in the eyes, but in spirit. That softness that is not weakness, but quiet strength. My mother never raised her voice, never demanded attention, but when she spoke, people listened. When she loved you, you felt it in your bones. Lilou has that same quality already, even at her age.

Ava—Wise Eyes and a Calm Spirit

Ava arrived with the calmest eyes I've ever seen on a baby—as if she came into the world already understanding things most of us spend a lifetime trying to learn. She doesn't rush. She watches. She absorbs. Even as a newborn, she brought a peace into the room that you could feel settle over everyone.

I remember the first time I held her, just hours after she was born. The hospital room was full of people—nurses, family, the controlled chaos that surrounds a new arrival. But when they placed her in my arms, she just looked at me. Didn't cry, didn't fuss. Just looked at me with these steady eyes, and I had the strangest feeling that she was taking my measure. Deciding whether I was trustworthy. And apparently I passed the test, because she let out a small sigh and closed her eyes, content.

The Myrtle Beach Sanctuary

In 2020, when the wounds from the impeachment had scarred over but still ached in certain weather, Cyndi and I bought a small place at

Myrtle Beach. Nothing extravagant. Just a refuge. A place where no one knew Principal Chief Patrick Lambert or the impeachment or any of it. A place where I could just be PopPop.

That little beach house quickly became the heart of our family life in a way I never anticipated. Some of the happiest days I've ever lived happened there: kids splashing in the surf, sandcastles collapsing under the tide, tiny footprints drying on warm planks of wood, evening walks with Cyndi's hand in mine while the sky turned pink and gold.

Watching my grandchildren play at the water's edge made everything else feel small too. The impeachment, the accusations, the politics—all of it shrank down to its proper size when measured against a child's laughter or the perfect spiral of a seashell or the way Henrik would shriek with delight every time a wave chased him up the beach.

We established rhythms there. Morning walks to collect shells. Afternoons in the pool. Evening meals on the deck while the sun set over the water. Bedtime stories. These became the bookmarks of healing, the small, repeated moments that slowly, imperceptibly, built something new inside me. Not a replacement for what was lost, but something different. Something that belonged only to us and couldn't be voted away or taken by political enemies.

The Day It Broke Through

One evening near sunset, I was sitting in a beach chair watching the kids play. Cyndi had taken the girls inside to rinse off, and I was alone with the boys. Rhett was maybe six by then, and Henrik was about three—both of them at that perfect age where everything is an adventure and fear hasn't learned to creep in yet.

I was tired. Not the good tired that comes from physical work, but the deeper tiredness that settles into your bones when you've been carrying weight for too long. I'd been working hard on the businesses, trying to rebuild what the impeachment had damaged, and even here, even in this place of refuge, I sometimes felt the shadow of it all. The what-ifs. The if-onlys. The replaying of moments I couldn't change.

Rhett and Henrik were running back and forth in the shallow surf, laughing at nothing and everything all at once. The water was calm, the waves gentle, and the evening light turned everything gold. I watched them, grateful they existed, grateful for this moment, but still carrying that heavy thing inside my chest that wouldn't quite let go.

Then Henrik came running toward me full speed—which for a three-year-old means more stumbling than running—his legs pumping with absolute commitment. He was maybe ten feet away when he hit a patch of soft sand, and his feet went out from under him. He went down face-first with a thud that made me start to get up, that old instinct to protect and rescue kicking in immediately.

For half a second, I tensed, waiting for the cry that usually follows a fall like that. But instead, he jumped up, sand coating his cheeks and forehead, hair wild from the wind and water, and yelled: "PopPop, look! I fell!"

And he laughed. Full, loud, unbothered, completely delighted by his own tumble.

I felt something inside me crack open. Not a wound, a shell. Something that had been sealed tight to protect what was inside, but in protecting had also been preventing growth, preventing light, preventing gladness from getting back in.

I put my head in my hands and laughed and teared up all at once, the way men do later in life when emotions touch places that remain raw from everything they've endured. Not tears from stress or grief, but from release. From the sudden, overwhelming realization that delight was still possible. That my grandchildren didn't need me to be the Principal Chief or the lawyer or the fighter. They just needed me to be present. To be PopPop. To watch them fall and get back up and laugh about it.

Rhett ran over, concerned in that sweet way children are when they see adults cry. "PopPop, are you sad?"

I pulled him close, one arm around him and the other reaching for Henrik, who had finally made it to my chair. "No, buddy. I'm happy."

"Then why are you crying?"

"Because sometimes when you're really, really happy, it comes out in tears."

He considered this seriously, then nodded as if it made perfect sense. "Okay. Can we get ice cream?"

I laughed again, wiped my face, and stood up. "Yeah. Let's get ice cream."

And as we walked back toward the house, both boys holding my hands, sand between all of our toes, I realized the heaviness had finally let go.. The heaviness had finally lifted. Not tentatively, not partially—but fully, completely, with the force of a wave that had been building offshore for years and finally crashed over me and washed something clean.

Watching My Children Become Parents

There is no moment in life quite like watching your own children raise children. You see reflections of yourself, your strengths, your flaws, your lessons, your hopes, and you realize the sacrifices you made were not lost. They were inherited.

Seeing Gina and Nelson become parents deepened my understanding of my own parents in ways I couldn't have anticipated. I watched them comfort crying babies at 3:00 a.m. and thought of my mother doing the same for me. I watched them work long hours to provide for their families and thought of my father's hands, scarred from decades of labor. The circle wasn't just continuing—it was revealing itself, showing me patterns I'd been part of without fully understanding.

And I saw things in my children I didn't know I'd taught them. The patience. The quiet strength. The way they handled frustration, celebrated small victories, protected fiercely while encouraging independence. These weren't things we'd sat down and discussed. They were things they'd absorbed by watching Cyndi and me navigate our own lives, our own challenges.

It humbled me. Made me realize that everything we do in front of our children—how we handle loss, how we treat each other, how we get back up after falling—all of it becomes part of their instruction manual for life.

CHAPTER 31

THE SCHOLAR RETURNS

"It is never too late to be what you might have been."

— George Eliot (pen name of Mary Ann Evans)

At fifty-eight, the high school dropout enrolled in the same LL.M. program his son had completed. George Eliot reinvented her own life against all expectations—she wrote the only line that fits.

◆ ◆ ◆

BUT AFTER EVERYTHING THAT happened in 2017, the storm, the loss, the grief, the rebuilding, I felt something very different. I wasn't done. Not even close. There was a fire in me that no political vote, no manufactured charge, and no smear campaign could extinguish. And that fire was pushing me toward one more mountain to climb—not for a title, not for a career, not for recognition, but for myself. For my own mind. For my own dignity. For my own future.

So at fifty-eight years old, I went back to school. Not just any school. The William S. Boyd School of Law at the University of Nevada, Las Vegas—home to the nation's premier program in Gaming Law and Regulation. The place where the experts, regulators, scholars, and legal architects of the gaming world go to sharpen their craft.

And I walked in not as the young high school dropout who once struggled to find his footing, but as a man who had lived an entire lifetime since then—and still had something left to prove.

Following in My Son's Footsteps

The decision to pursue an LL.M. didn't come out of nowhere. It came from watching my son, Nelson, walk across a stage a few years earlier with the same degree from the same program. Nelson had earned his master of laws in gaming law and regulation from UNLV, and I'd been there to watch him do it, proud in that deep way fathers are when they see their children surpass them.

There's something humbling about watching your children achieve things you never did. Nelson had gone straight through his education without the detours and false starts that marked my path. He'd been focused, disciplined, strategic. And when he graduated with his LL.M., I remember thinking that's the kind of specialized knowledge that will shape the future of Indian gaming.

But I also remember thinking something else, something I didn't say out loud at the time: *I wonder if I could do that.*

The idea sat with me for a while. Through the impeachment. Through the rebuilding. Through the quiet years of fixing car washes and renovating hotels and trying to figure out who I was without a title. And eventually, that wondering turned into a decision. Not to compete with Nelson—that was never the point. But to prove to myself that I wasn't finished learning, wasn't finished growing, wasn't finished becoming.

So I applied. And when I was accepted, I felt something I hadn't felt in years: excitement about the future. Not anxiety, not dread, not the heavy weight of political calculation. Just pure, simple excitement about learning something new.

Gina had also earned her law degree, graduating from the University of North Dakota with a concentration in Indian law. Watching both of my children pursue advanced legal education in Indian law and gaming regulation felt like vindication of a different kind. The work I'd done, the battles I'd fought, the systems I'd helped build—they mattered enough that my own children wanted to understand them deeply, to carry that work forward in their own ways.

And now I was joining them. Not leading them, but following. Learning from the same professors, studying the same materials, earning the same credential. There was something beautifully circular about it.

Why an LL.M.? Why Then? Why There?

Some people wondered why I did it. Why would someone who had negotiated a historic gaming compact, helped draft the per capita system, built the Tribe's first regulatory structures, chaired tribes nationally, served as Principal Chief, and earned more real-world experience than most professors ever see—why would that person go back to sit in a classroom again?

The LL.M., master of laws, is the highest law degree available, specialization at the doctoral level. You can't just walk in off the street and pursue an LL.M. You have to already be a lawyer, already have your JD, already have proven yourself in the field. Then you choose an area of deep specialization and you go deeper than you've ever gone before.

For me, that specialization was gaming law and regulation. And UNLV's Boyd School of Law wasn't just good at it—they were the best. The program had been built by some of the most respected minds in gaming law. The faculty included former regulators, former gaming commissioners, attorneys who had shaped the industry from its earliest days. If you wanted to truly master the legal and regulatory framework of gaming—not just in Indian Country, but nationally and internationally—this was where you came.

The Pandemic Challenge

I started the program in 2020, which meant I walked into one of the strangest academic years in modern history. Just as we were getting oriented, just as I was settling into the rhythm of graduate-level work, the world shut down. COVID-19 turned everything upside down. Campuses closed. Classrooms emptied. And suddenly, we were all staring at computer screens, trying to learn complex legal concepts through Zoom.

For a fifty-eight-year-old man who had grown up in an era when "remote learning" meant correspondence courses through the mail, this was jarring. But we adapted. We had to. And in some ways, the pandemic forced a kind of intimacy that in-person classes might not have created. When you're all stuck in your homes, all struggling with the same technological glitches, all trying to maintain focus while the world falls apart outside your window, you bond differently. You see each other more honestly.

Our class was not only diverse nationwide but international. We had students attending from time zones as far away as sixteen hours ahead of Las Vegas. I'll never forget learning that some of our international classmates were attending our 11:00 a.m. classes at 3:30 or 4:00 a.m. their time. They'd set alarms, wake up in the dark, make coffee, and log into Zoom while the rest of their city slept.

That kind of commitment humbled me. Here I was, thinking about the inconvenience of online learning from my comfortable home office, while classmates on other continents were sacrificing sleep just to participate. It reminded me that education is a privilege, that access to knowledge is worth almost any sacrifice, and that I had no right to take any of this for granted.

Professors Who Cared

The faculty at Boyd made the pandemic bearable, and sometimes even joyful, in ways I didn't expect. These were serious scholars, people at the top of their fields, and they could have treated the shift to online learning as a burden. Instead, they threw themselves into making it work, into keeping us engaged, into making sure we weren't just surviving the pandemic but still actually learning.

I'll never forget Professor Rolnick's approach to combating the isolation and depression that Zoom learning created. She understood that we weren't just students anymore—we were human beings stuck in our homes, cut off from normal social interaction, dealing with fear and uncertainty and the grinding monotony of lockdown. So she made it her mission to bring lightness into our virtual classroom.

One day, she showed up to class wearing a bright pink wig. Just completely out of nowhere, this serious legal scholar teaching complex regulatory theory, wearing a pink wig and acting like it was the most natural thing in the world. The chat box exploded with laughter and comments and emojis. For that brief moment, we forgot about the pandemic. We forgot about our isolation. We were just a class again, laughing together at something absurd and wonderful.

Professor Anthony Cabot brought decades of gaming law expertise to every lecture, but he also brought patience and understanding. When the technology failed he'd wait calmly while we all reconnected, sometimes using the downtime to tell stories from his years in the industry. Those stories became some of the most valuable parts of our education.

Professor Jennifer Roberts pushed us hard on regulatory theory, but she also recognized when we were drowning and threw us lifelines. She extended office hours, created study groups, made herself available in ways that went far beyond the job description.

My Remarkable Classmates

The class of 2021 wasn't just diverse—it was impressive in ways that humbled and inspired me. These weren't students fresh out of law school. These were accomplished professionals at the top of their fields.

Antonio Lobo Vilela came from Portugal, already a renowned author and expert on gaming law. Pedro Cortés was a managing partner at his law firm while also teaching and preparing for a new baby. Katie Kaufman pulled off a cross-country move and passed two bar exams while completing her LL.M. Rhianna had been instrumental in launching Nevada's cannabis industry while raising children. Scott Frederick had been a litigator, judge, business owner, and real estate broker. Matthew McCorkle came down with severe COVID during the program but never complained, never asked for special treatment, just quietly persevered.

These were the people I was learning alongside and being inspired by every week.

The Discipline Returns

Going to law school at fifty-eight feels different than at thirty. You're wiser. You're calmer. You're not trying to impress anyone. You're there to learn, period.

One morning, after a dense lecture on federal oversight structures, a younger student asked me, "Patrick . . . how do you already know all of this?"

I smiled and said, "I lived it before I studied it."

Cyndi—My Constant Through Every Chapter

Through all of this—the reading, the late-night writing, the immersion in complex regulatory theory—Cyndi was there. Steady. Proud. Encouraging without saying much. She sat with me at the kitchen table while I highlighted cases. She quizzed me before exams. She reminded me, simply by being who she is, that I was still capable of more than circumstance had tried to suggest.

I often say she is the quiet strength behind every chapter of my life. This one was no different. We'd celebrated our thirty-fifth wedding anniversary just two weeks before graduation, a milestone that felt even more meaningful given everything we'd weathered together. Thirty-five years of marriage isn't just time—it's choosing each other, day after day, through triumph and disaster, through political storms and quiet rebuilding, through youth and middle age and the beginning of whatever comes next.

Age—And What It Really Means

Sitting beside classmates young enough to be my children, I realized something about age I had suspected for years: I didn't feel old. Some parts of me have slowed, the legs, the eyes, but my mind felt sharper than ever. Age, I've learned, is not decline. It's accumulation. Experience. Judgment. Pattern recognition. The ability to see consequences before they arrive. If youth is energy, age is accuracy. And in law, accuracy wins.

The Keynote Speaker

Close to graduation, I was informed that the faculty and my classmates had selected me to be the keynote speaker at commencement, representing all the LL.M. graduates.

I was stunned. Not because I didn't think I could do it—I'd given plenty of speeches in my life, stood before plenty of audiences. But because of what it meant. At fifty-eight years old, after the worst political attack of my life, after the deepest wounds, after rebuilding from the ashes—I was being chosen to speak to the next generation of attorneys. The faculty, these brilliant scholars who had just spent a year teaching me, thought I had something worth saying to the graduates and their families.

That recognition meant more to me than almost any political honor I'd ever received. Because it came from people who valued knowledge, who respected intellectual achievement, who judged you based on your mind and your character rather than your political connections or your ability to win elections.

May 14, 2021—Standing before the Stadium

Graduation day arrived warm and bright, held indoors in the UNLV stadium because of the spring heat in Vegas. Thousands of people filled the stadium—graduates, families, faculty, friends. The energy was different from normal graduations because we'd all been through something together, this shared pandemic experience that made gathering in person feel almost miraculous.

When it came time for me to speak, representing the LL.M. program, I walked to the podium and looked out at that sea of faces. I saw my classmates in their robes. I saw Cyndi in the stands, beaming with that proud smile she gets when she thinks I'm not looking. I saw Nelson, who had walked this same path before me and made it possible for me to imagine following, and I saw Gina, always beaming with pride at any accomplishment by a family member.

And I spoke from the heart.

"Thank you, Dean Hamilton," I began. "My name is Patrick Lambert, and it is my honor to deliver remarks on behalf of the LL.M. graduates. Let me give you a quick, brief bio of myself. Before you today is an atypical law school student: I never graduated high school. I quit high school at age fifteen, somehow managed getting enrolled into a community college and then into university. I later joined the US Army, and then in 1993 I graduated law school at the University of North Carolina in Chapel Hill. I've spent twenty-five years working in the field of Indian law and Tribal gaming law, and I served two years as Principal Chief of the Eastern Band of Cherokee Indians."

I told them about Nelson getting his LL.M. from this same program, about following in my son's footsteps. I told them about Gina earning her law degree from the University of North Dakota with her concentration in Indian law. I told them about Cyndi, about celebrating our thirty-fifth anniversary just two weeks before, about how we had three children together and were expecting our ninth grandchild that summer—a baby girl who would arrive on June 29 and be named Ava.

I acknowledged the remarkable faculty—and their dedication during the pandemic. Then I told them about our class. About students attending from sixteen time zones away, waking at three thirty in the morning to participate.

"Our class membership is not only very diverse geographically and culturally, but also very impressive in accomplishments," I said. And then I gave them what I'd learned: "We have all been given a great gift by being able to be a part of this great university, and I'm honored and so appreciative of being allowed to be a part of the class of 2021 and now forever being an alumni of UNLV Boyd School of Law."

I told them to be mindful of how they treat people. That honor, respect, and friendships can last forever and should be practiced, nurtured, protected. I told them it's never too late to keep learning—even from the humble start with a GED, and now in my late fifties standing here, education is key to success.

And I finished with words I hoped would stay with them: "Remember, there is no script. Just be outrageous, courageous, and be your best honorable, respectful, and professional selves. Congratulations, graduates. It's a great honor and a great experience in education. May God bless and keep every one of you. Best of luck. Live a good life!"

The stadium erupted in cheers and applause, but what I remember most clearly is the feeling that washed over me as I walked back to my seat. Not pride, exactly, though there was some of that. Not vindication, though there was that too. What I felt was completeness. Like a story that had started in poverty and doubt and failure had finally curved back around to something that made sense. The high school dropout had become not just a lawyer, but a scholar. The impeached Chief had become the keynote speaker. The wounded man had become whole again.

When I walked across that stage and accepted my LL.M. diploma, I didn't feel older. I felt younger. More alive. More certain of who I was.

CHAPTER 32

PRO SE: SUPREME COURT

"The arc of the moral universe is long, but it bends toward justice."

— Martin Luther King Jr.

Eight and a half years after the impeachment, I stood before the Cherokee Supreme Court alone—no attorney, no allies.

◆ ◆ ◆

THERE ARE MOMENTS IN life when the world tries to close a door on you forever. And there are moments when you decide you will not let it.

The impeachment took my office. Politics tried to take my future. But I refused to let anyone, Council, critics, or circumstance, write the last chapter of my life. In 2025, eight and a half years after the storm, I chose to open the door myself. Not out of anger. Not out of resentment. But out of principle. Out of the simple truth that no law born of fear and retaliation should ever decide the future of a Cherokee man—especially when that man is willing to stand before his people again without flinching.

And so began the quiet legal battle that restored my rights, my voice, and my place in the future of the Eastern Band of Cherokee Indians.

The Law That Tried to Erase Me

After the impeachment, the Tribal Council passed a law that barred anyone who had ever been impeached—at any time, under any circumstances, regardless of the reason—from ever holding office again. The ordinance was Code § 161-3(d)(3), and they didn't say my name when they enacted it. They didn't have to.

It was political exile written into legislation. A door slammed shut. The message was clear: You will not return. You will not compete. You will not be chosen again. You will not threaten the system that tried to destroy you.

For years, I lived with that law hanging over my future like a permanent shadow. I rebuilt my businesses. I earned my LL.M. I watched my grandchildren grow. I circled the globe. I found peace in ways I didn't expect. But I never forgot about Code § 161-3(d)(3). I never accepted it as legitimate. And I never stopped believing that someday, somehow, it would have to be challenged.

That day came in early 2025, when I decided to file for the Birdtown Tribal Council seat.

Filing to Run—Forcing the Question

The only way to challenge the law was simple and bold: file to run. Not because I was necessarily committed to serving on the Council—that was a separate question I was still wrestling with. But because filing forced the system to answer a constitutional question that had been hanging unresolved for nearly a decade: Does the Tribal Council have the authority to override the Cherokee Charter and permanently bar a Tribal member from serving their people?

I met every qualification in Charter Section 9, the supreme law of our Tribe: I was enrolled. I was over twenty-one years old. I had lived on the Qualla Boundary for more than six months. These were the only qualifications the Charter imposed, the only criteria the Cherokee people themselves had established when they ratified our governing document. But, Cherokee Code § 161-3(d)(3) added a fourth qualification—never having been impeached—that appeared nowhere in the Charter.

When I submitted my paperwork to the Board of Elections in early 2025, I knew exactly what would happen. They would have to make a choice: follow the Charter or follow the ordinance. Follow the people's law or follow the Council's law.

The Board went quiet. No immediate questions. No dialogue. No acknowledgment of the constitutional tension they were facing. Just long silence—a familiar kind of silence that reminded me of 2017, when the institutions that should have protected me chose instead to protect themselves.

They waited until the final possible day allowed by law. Then they ruled against me, citing Code § 161-3(d)(3) as the sole basis for denying my candidacy.

Their written decision acknowledged that I met every Charter qualification. Enrollment, yes. Age, yes. Residency, yes. Everything the Cherokee people had said mattered, I satisfied. But the ordinance said no, and the Board chose the ordinance over the Charter.

That ruling wasn't an end. It was the key that opened the next door: the Cherokee Supreme Court.

The Decision to Represent Myself

When I decided to appeal to the Supreme Court, I faced a choice about representation. I could have hired an attorney—there were plenty of good lawyers who would have taken the case. But something in me resisted that path. This was personal. It was about my rights, my future, my relationship with my Tribe. Having someone else argue it felt wrong, like asking someone else to tell my own story.

So I made the decision to appear pro se—to represent myself before the highest court in our Tribal Nation. It was a risk. The old saying exists for a reason: A lawyer who represents himself has a fool for a client. But I wasn't a typical pro se litigant. I'd been practicing law for over thirty years. I'd argued before Tribal Courts, state courts, federal courts. I understood procedure and precedent. I knew how to build a legal argument.

More importantly, I understood what was at stake in a way no hired attorney ever could. This wasn't just about whether Patrick Lambert could run for office. It was about whether the Cherokee Charter, the document that embodies our people's sovereignty, still meant what it said. It was about whether the Tribal Council could rewrite the qualifications for office without asking the voters. It was about whether the voice of the people could be permanently silenced by nine politicians with an agenda.

I needed to make that argument myself. In my own words. With my own voice.

Preparing the Case

The weeks leading up to oral argument were intense in a way I hadn't experienced since law school.

I read and reread the Cherokee Charter until I could recite the relevant sections from memory. I studied every Supreme Court decision that touched on electoral qualifications, separation of powers, or the relationship between the Charter and tribal ordinances. I looked at federal cases like *Powell v. McCormack*, where the US Supreme Court held that when a constitutional document sets qualifications for office, those qualifications are exclusive—Congress can't add new ones, and neither can anyone else.

I examined the history of our own Charter, tracking how it had been amended over the decades. In 1986, the Cherokee people voted in a referendum to add the enrollment requirement to Section 9. That referendum proved something important: When the qualifications for office need to change, it requires a vote of the people. The Council can't just pass an ordinance and rewrite the Charter. If they could, that 1986 referendum would have been unnecessary.

I built my argument around several pillars: Charter Section 9 exclusively lists the qualifications for the Tribal Council, enrollment, age, and residency, and the Council lacks authority to add new ones. The Board of Elections, as a quasi-judicial body, had a duty to resolve the conflict between the Charter and the ordinance by prioritizing the supreme law. Allowing the Council to impose additional qualifications without a referendum violated democratic principles and usurped the voters' right to choose their leaders. Charter Section 22, governing impeachment, is silent on barring future candidacy, confirming no such disqualification exists.

The deeper I got into the research, the more confident I became. This wasn't a close case. The law was clear. The precedent supported my position. The only question was whether the Court would have the courage to enforce the Charter against the Council's political will.

July 10, 2025—Standing before the Court

The day of oral argument arrived hot and clear—a Thursday morning in the mountains, the kind of summer day when the humidity sits heavy on everything and the air itself seems to be waiting for something to break.

Cyndi, Nelson, and Kim came with me to the courthouse. I needed them there. This wasn't just my fight—it was our family's fight, the culmination of all those years of standing together through the storm. As we walked in, Cyndi squeezed my hand. No words necessary. She knew what this moment meant.

The courtroom was familiar—I'd been there before, both as an attorney and as Principal Chief. The Cherokee syllabary ran across the top of the wall in large bronze letters, a reminder that this was Cherokee justice, Cherokee law, Cherokee sovereignty. The EBCI seal hung behind the bench between the American flag and the Tribal flag. But walking in as a pro se appellant, about to argue my own constitutional rights, felt entirely different. The weight of it settled on my shoulders as I took my place at the counsel table on the left side of the courtroom.

Cyndi sat in the gallery directly behind me. I glanced back at her as I arranged my notes and checked my citations one last time. The wooden pews were mostly empty when we arrived—just a few observers scattered through the rows. I turned back to face the bench and tried to steady my breathing.

The three Supreme Court justices entered and took their seats: Chief Justice Bradley B. Letts in the center, Associate Justices Sharon Tracey Barrett and Robert C. Hunter on either side. I stood as they settled in, my heart pounding but my mind clear.

When Chief Justice Letts called the case—"Cherokee Supreme Court, Case Number CSC 25-02, Patrick Henry Lambert versus the Cherokee Board of Elections"—I felt the room contract around me. Nearly a decade of waiting. All those years of carrying the weight of that impeachment. All those years of watching politicians pretend I didn't exist, couldn't exist, would never exist again in Cherokee public life.

All of it came down to the next hour.

The following account of my oral argument is reconstructed from my notes and recollection. The specific legal citations referenced were contained in my written brief filed with the Court.

I stepped to the podium in the center of the courtroom and began: "May it please the Court, I am Patrick Henry Lambert, appearing pro se, to challenge the Board of Elections' unlawful denial of my candidacy for the Birdtown Tribal Council seat. This case is not about the 2017 impeachment—it's about one question: Will this Court uphold the Charter as the supreme law of the EBCI, or allow the Tribal Council to impose unauthorized qualifications that silence the voters' right to choose their leaders?"

I laid out the constitutional framework, walking the justices through each element of my argument. I addressed the Appellee's contentions point by point, my voice steady, my citations precise.

"First, the longevity of Code § 161-3(d)(3) does not shield it from review. The Appellee claims that this section, enacted in 1997, is valid because it's existed for twenty-eight years. This argument is legally baseless. A law's age does not immunize it from scrutiny. Code § 7-5(b) empowers this Court to strike down any law violating the Charter, as it did in *Crowe v. EBCI* in 2003, where it invalidated an ordinance despite prior use. For a hundred and twenty-nine years, from 1868 to 1997, no such disqualification existed, proving it's not part of our foundational law."

Halfway through my argument, I glanced back toward Cyndi. What I saw stopped me for just a moment. The courtroom that had been nearly empty when we arrived was now filling up. Word must have filtered out that the hearing was happening. People were slipping quietly into the pews—Tribal members, friends, supporters who'd been afraid to speak up for years. They'd come to watch. They'd come to bear witness.

I turned back to face the justices and felt the full weight of why I was there.. This wasn't just about me anymore. It never had been.

I emphasized the Board's failure: "Second, the Board's failure to exercise its quasi-judicial duty is a clear error of law. The Board admitted in its Final Written Decision that I meet all of Charter § 9's qualifications, enrollment, age, and residency, yet they robotically applied § 161-3(d)(3) without questioning its conflict with the Charter. As a quasi-judicial body, the Board is not a mere administrator but a guardian of our electoral process."

I cited their own precedent against them: "Code § 161-22(c) mandates the Board to review provisions inconsistent with the Charter. In *Crowe*, the Board refused to enforce an ordinance adding voter restrictions beyond the Charter. In In re: Primary Election, they declined to follow an ordinance that violated Charter election timing, a decision this Court upheld. The Board knows it has this authority. They simply chose not to exercise it."

I attacked the "supplement" argument directly: "Third, Code § 161-3(d)(3) violates the Charter and exceeds 'conduct' in § 6. The Appellee asserts this section is a permissible 'supplement' to Charter § 9, authorized by the Council's powers. This argument is flawed and dangerous. Charter § 6 authorizes the Tribal Council to 'enact rules and regulations for the conduct of Tribal elections.' The key word is 'conduct'—referring to procedural and administrative matters, not substantive qualifications. In legal usage, 'conduct' means managing or directing operations: filing fees, voter registration, polling hours, ballot design. Extending 'conduct' to include substantive disqualifications stretches the term beyond its textual and historical meaning."

I pointed out a critical contradiction: "The Appellee's reliance on Section 6 is in complete disagreement with the Board's own position in the *Crowe* hearing, where they wrote: 'Section 6 allows the Tribal Council and the Board of Elections to set rules and regulations. However, it does not allow those rules and regulations to take precedence over the eligibility standards provided in the Charter.' In *Crowe*, the issue was voter qualifications. Here, it's candidate qualifications. The same principle applies."

I addressed the bad-faith tactics: "The Appellee's brief insinuates fraud in the 2017 impeachment, referencing legitimate payments to a respected Asheville attorney. These aspersions are irrelevant distractions. The Board's decision rests solely on § 161-3(d)(3). If the Appellee believes I defrauded the Tribe, they must prove it in a proper forum, not attempt to prejudice this Court with unfounded claims. This conduct demands judicial correction."

And then I made my final argument, connecting our law to broader democratic principles: "Our current president was impeached twice, and some state bodies attempted to keep him off the ballot. The US Supreme Court in *Trump v. Anderson* ruled those attempts invalid and a violation of the Constitution, leaving the decision ultimately to the voters. Just as the fate of his candidacy was left to the voters, so should mine be—not to unlawfully added disqualifications attempting to usurp the power and authority of the voters."

I concluded: "The Board's decision rests on an ordinance that violates our Charter, the supreme law of our Tribe. Code § 161-3(d)(3) is ultra vires, imposing a qualification not found in Charter § 9, exceeding the scope of 'conduct' in § 6, and usurping the voters' sacred right to choose. The Board's failure to exercise its quasi-judicial duty compounds this error. Upholding § 161-3(d)(3) would allow the Tribal Council to rewrite the Charter without voter consent, eroding the democratic foundation of our Tribe. For over a hundred and fifty years, our people have guarded the right to choose our leaders. This Court must protect that legacy."

I looked directly at the three justices, Letts, Barrett, Hunter, and made my final plea: "I therefore respectfully urge this Court to reverse the Board's error, declare Code § 161-3(d)(3) void, and remand with instructions to certify me as a candidate for elected Tribal office. The voters—not the Tribal Council or the Board—should be allowed to decide my candidacy. As guardians of our Tribe's democracy, you hold the power to ensure the voters' voice prevails."

When I finished and stepped back from the podium, I felt drained but certain. I'd said everything that needed to be said. I'd made the best argument I knew how to make. Thirty years of legal practice, distilled into one hour before the highest court of my people.

Now it was in their hands.

Walking Out into the Unknown

I gathered my papers and walked back to the counsel table. Cyndi's eyes met mine from the gallery, and she nodded once—that small gesture that carried forty years of partnership in it. Nelson and Kim were there beside her, my son who'd watched his father get torn down by politics and had never stopped believing in him.

We walked out of the courthouse together into the July heat. The sun was brutal, the kind of high-summer glare that makes you squint even in the shade. People who'd been in the gallery stopped us on the courthouse steps—handshakes, quiet words of support, the kind of encouragement that had been whispered for years but was now being spoken aloud.

"You did good, Dad," Nelson said.

"Thank you, I said what I needed to say," I told him. "The rest is up to them."

Cyndi and I had been talking about getting away for a few days—a trip to Myrtle Beach while we waited for the ruling. Could be weeks before they decided, maybe longer. Might as well not sit around staring at the phone.

We said goodbye, went home, and packed. By early afternoon, Cyndi and I were on the road, heading east toward the coast. The mountains fell away behind us as we descended through the foothills, trading the familiar curves of Cherokee for the flat coastal plains of South Carolina.

I tried not to think about the case. Tried to focus on the road, on Cyndi beside me, on the simple pleasure of a few days at the beach with nothing to do but rest. The Court would take its time. These things always took time. Weeks, probably. Maybe longer. I'd done my part. Now I had to let go and trust the process.

We were somewhere on I-26, the South Carolina low country stretching flat and green on either side of us, when my phone rang.

It had been less than four hours since I'd walked out of that courtroom.

EPILOGUE

VINDICATION AND RENEWAL

*"When you were born, you cried and the world rejoiced.
Live your life so that when you die, the world cries and
you rejoice."*

— Cherokee Proverb

This book opens with Cherokee wisdom and closes with it. It is a
Cherokee truth for a Cherokee story.

◆ ◆ ◆

T HE CALLER ID SHOWED the Cherokee Supreme Court.

I looked at Cyndi. She looked at me. Less than four hours. We'd
barely made it out of the mountains.

I pulled off on the side of I-26, the car coming to rest on the gravel
shoulder as eighteen-wheelers thundered past. My hands were steady as I
answered, but my heart was not.

It was the Court clerk. "Mr. Lambert, the Court has issued its
decision in your case. I'm emailing you a copy now."

"Already?" I said. "It's been—"

"Less than four hours, yes, sir. The Court was unanimous."

I thanked her, hung up, and opened my email with Cyndi leaning
over from the passenger seat, both of us staring at my phone screen as
cars roared past inches from our windows. The email was there. The
attachment was there. I opened it.

And then I read the words aloud to Cyndi, right there on the shoulder
of Interstate 26, somewhere between the mountains that made me and the
ocean we'd reach before the end of the day:

"The decision of the Cherokee Board of Elections is REVERSED,
and the Court orders PATRICK HENRY LAMBERT be immediately
certified by the Cherokee Board of Elections as a candidate in the 2025
Birdtown Township Tribal Council election."

Reversed.

Immediately certified.

Unanimous.

Cyndi grabbed my arm. Her eyes were wet. So were mine.

Nearly a decade. Two thousand, nine hundred and seventy-three days of carrying the weight of that impeachment, of watching politicians pretend I didn't exist, of being told in a hundred different ways that my public life was over.

And now, in less time than it takes to drive from Cherokee to the coast, three Supreme Court justices had restored what nine Tribal Council members had tried to take away forever.

The math of it still staggers me. In 2015, 71 percent of Cherokee voters elected me Principal Chief—the highest margin in modern Tribal history. In 2017, nine politicians voted to end my career, ignoring the will of thousands. In 2025, three justices—Chief Justice Bradley B. Letts, Associate Justices Sharon Tracey Barrett and Robert C. Hunter—unanimously ruled that the Charter means what it says, that the people's voice cannot be silenced by political vendetta.

Seventy-one percent. Nine. Three.

Numbers tell a story. But that afternoon on I-26, I wasn't thinking about numbers. I was thinking about the woman beside me who had never stopped believing, even when I struggled to believe myself. I was thinking about the Charter and what it means when courts have the courage to enforce it. I was thinking about every person who'd told me to give up, move on, accept my fate.

I was thinking: *not today*.

We made it to Myrtle Beach that evening, though I barely remember the drive. The phone started ringing almost immediately—family, friends, supporters who'd heard the news. The ruling was already spreading through Cherokee. People who'd been afraid to speak up for years were suddenly calling to say they'd always believed in me.

That night, Cyndi and I sat on the balcony, listening to the Atlantic roll in and out in the darkness. The wooden railing was still warm from the day's sun. The salt air was cool, the stars were bright, and for the first time in nearly a decade, the weight was gone.

"So what now?" she asked.

I thought about the question. It was bigger than she meant it to be. The Court had restored my rights—I could run for office again, serve my people again, step back into the arena. But should I? After everything they'd put us through? After nearly a decade of rebuilding a life outside politics, finding peace in family and work and the quiet satisfaction of a good day's labor?

"Now we have to decide," Cyndi said, "if we're gonna try to help again . . . or just lead our own private lives."

I looked out at the ocean, black and endless under the stars.

"I don't know yet," I said. "But for the first time in eight years, the choice is ours to make."

That's what vindication really means. Not revenge. Not bitterness satisfied. Just the restoration of something that should never have been taken: the right to choose your own future.

I'm not announcing anything today. The 2027 elections are still ahead, and I haven't decided what role, if any, I'll play in Cherokee's political future. But I know this: The door is open again. The door that nine politicians tried to nail shut forever now swings free, opened by three justices who understood that in a democracy, it's the people who decide.

Cyndi and I have built something good in these years of exile. We've watched grandchildren grow. We've traveled the world together—almost every continent, a full circumnavigation of the earth, seeing things we never dreamed we'd see when we were young and poor and just starting out. We've learned that there's more to life than politics, more to legacy than office.

But we've also learned that some fights are worth having. That integrity matters. That when you've been given gifts, education, experience, the ability to serve, you have a responsibility to use them. Some legacies don't require a title.

I started this book with the mountains—the ancient, patient mountains that have watched over the Cherokee people since before memory. They were here when our ancestors walked these ridges. They were here when the Trail of Tears tried to erase us. They were here when I was born in poverty, when I worked underground after the army, when I came home to build a life on the Boundary.

They were here through the storm of impeachment, the long years of exile, and now the dawn of vindication.

I sit on my porch some mornings, coffee in hand, watching the mist rise from the creeks. The same view my father saw, and his father before him. The land doesn't care about politics. It doesn't care about vindication or exile or the petty maneuvers of powerful men. It just endures, season after season, holding the bones of everyone who came before and making room for everyone yet to come.

That's the Cherokee way, I think. We endure. We adapt. We survive. And when the time is right, we rise.

The Cherokee have always known the river—*Yun'wi Gunahita*, the Long Man. He stretches his full length across the land, his head in the mountains, his feet in the lowland waters, speaking in a voice that never stops. Our ancestors went to him for cleansing, for guidance, for strength. They understood what the river teaches: You don't defeat water by blocking it. The river doesn't fight the rock. It flows around. It finds another way. And given enough time, it wears the rock to sand.

For years, I have walked the River Trail from Cherokee to the Park Homestead and Job Corps. Along the way, there's a sign describing the Long Man. I'd pause there sometimes, thinking about what it meant—what the river could teach me about patience, about persistence, about finding a way forward when every path seemed blocked.

They built dams and walls against me. But they didn't understand the ancient truth.

When they blocked me from office, I flowed into business. When they tried to dam my future with legislation written in anger, I found the cracks in their construction and pushed through. When they blocked my candidacy, I flowed into the courts. I didn't rage against them. I just kept moving.

The truth is like that too—like water, like the Long Man. It doesn't stop because someone builds a wall. It pools, it rises, it finds the weakness in the structure. And one day it breaks through, and everything they built to hold it back washes away.

That's what happened in that courtroom on July 10, 2025. Not magic. Not luck. Not political winds shifting in my favor. Just plain, stubborn, undeniable fact—flowing around every obstacle until it reached three justices willing to let it pass.

The Charter says what it says. The law means what it means. And no dam of political maneuvering could hold those words back forever.

My story isn't over. None of our stories are over until we draw our last breath. But if this book has an ending, it is this: You cannot silence the truth forever. You cannot erase a man who refuses to be erased. And you cannot close a door that the Charter—and the will of the people—demands to stay open.

Three justices understood that.

And the vindication didn't stop with me. For nearly a decade, my children carried a stigma they never earned—walking through Cherokee under a shadow that had nothing to do with who they were and everything to do with what Council did to their father. In February 2026, the same Tribal Council that voted to impeach me confirmed my son Nelson as the newest member of the Cherokee Tribal Gaming Commission—the same commission I built from the ground up and led for twenty-one years, the same seats where J.L. Burgess, Tom Haigler, and Birdie Saunooke once sat as the original commissioners when Cherokee gaming was nothing but a bingo hall and a dream. The Chief Justice of the Cherokee Supreme Court swore him into office on February 17, 2026. The shadow was gone. Not just from me. From all of us.

As I finish writing these words, the mountains outside my window are golden with autumn. Another season turning. Another year of life granted. My rights restored. My future open. My story—our story, the Cherokee story—continuing.

The Long Man keeps moving. So do I.

ACKNOWLEDGMENTS

No one survives what I survived alone.

To my wife Cyndi: You carried weight during those years that no spouse should have to carry, and you did it with a grace that still humbles me. Every page of this book exists because you were beside me when I wrote the story—and when I lived it. Forty years of marriage, and I'd choose you again tomorrow.

To our children, Tiffany, Gina, and Nelson, and to our nine grandchildren: You are the living proof that the best things in my life had nothing to do with politics. Watching you grow, succeed, and build your own families has been the greatest privilege of my life. Thank you for your patience during the years when Daddy or PopPop was consumed by battles that weren't yours to fight.

To my mother, who raised six children in a three-bedroom house and taught us that poverty was a circumstance, not an identity. Everything I became started with what you gave me.

To my father, who didn't live to see me get elected as Principal Chief, or the subsequent impeachment and vindication, but whose voice I still hear when I need steadiness. I hope I made you proud.

To my sisters—who shared the dirt bikes, the struggles, and the laughter. The Boundary raised us together.

To Tonya "Sunshine" Toinetta: Two decades as my right hand at the Gaming Commission. You kept the office running, kept me honest, and made sure nothing fell through the cracks. The Commission worked because you made it work. Thank you, Sunshine.

To Rick Saunooke, Wyatt Chiltoskie, and Pam Sneed—and to every inspector and office staff member who served with the Tribal Gaming Commission: Wanda, Melissa, Heather, and Libby. You stuck together and made the Commission strong, respected, and successful in protecting and safeguarding the entire Tribe. You were the infrastructure of integrity. You showed up, you did the work, and you protected the people. Gaming in Cherokee worked because you made it work every single day.

To Scott Jones and my legal team: You saw what others refused to see, and you fought for the record when the politics made that dangerous. The vindication belongs to you as much as it does to me.

To the Cherokee Supreme Court, for having the courage to examine the evidence and follow the law wherever it led. Justice delayed was still, in the end, justice.

To the Tribal members who spoke the truth at the Grand Council, who refused to whisper, who stood with me when standing was costly: I remember every one of you. Your courage sustained me through the darkest moments.

To those who opposed me: You taught me what I was made of. I hold no bitterness.

To the Eastern Band of Cherokee Indians—the Nation that shaped me, the people I served, the community I will always call home: This story is yours as much as it is mine. May it serve as a record and a vision for what we can become.

And finally, to everyone who told me I should write this down: You were right. Here it is.

A Letter to My Grandchildren and the Youth of Our Tribe

To my grandchildren. And to the great-grandchildren I may never meet, the ones who will carry our name into years I cannot imagine:

I'm writing this to you because someday you're going to have questions about me that I might not be around to answer. You'll hear stories. Some of them will be true. Some of them won't. And I want you to have something in my own words—not a politician's words, not a lawyer's words, but your PopPop's words—that tells you what I believed and what I hoped for you.

First, know this: you were the best part of my life. Not the titles. Not the accomplishments. Not the battles won or lost. You. The weight of you in my arms when you were small. The sound of your laughter filling up a quiet house that had seen too much silence. The way you looked at me like I had all the answers, even when I didn't have a single one.

I want to be honest with you, because you deserve honesty more than you deserve a hero.

I was not a perfect man. I pushed too hard sometimes. I backed people into corners when I should have left them room to find their own way out. I spent years so focused on fighting for what was right that I sometimes forgot to be gentle with the people around me. I missed things—moments, conversations, quiet evenings—because I was working or worrying or preparing for the next battle. Your parents and your grandmother could tell you about the times I got it wrong. There were more of those times than I'd like to admit.

But here's what I learned from getting it wrong, and this is what I most want you to carry with you:

Integrity is not something you're born with. It's something you build, one decision at a time, in the moments when nobody's watching and it would be easier to cut the corner. You will be tempted—by shortcuts, by easy money, by people who tell you that everybody does it, by the voice in your own head that says just this once. Don't listen. Not because I said so. Because the person you become when you take shortcuts is someone you won't recognize in the mirror ten years later, and the cost of getting yourself back is higher than you can imagine.

Be kind. I know that sounds simple, and I know the world will sometimes reward people who aren't. But kindness is not weakness. The strongest thing I ever did in my life was stand in front of a room full of people who had just destroyed my career and tell them I loved them. I meant it. Not because they deserved it—but because the hate would have eaten me alive if I'd let it stay. You will meet people who hurt you. Some of them will be people you trusted. Forgive them, not for their sake, but for yours. Bitterness is a poison you drink yourself.

Work with your hands. I don't care what degrees you earn or what titles you hold—and I hope you earn many—never lose the ability to fix something that's broken, to build something from nothing, to get your hands dirty and feel the dignity of labor that doesn't need an audience. Some of the clearest thinking I ever did was lying on a concrete floor under a car wash pump with a flashlight between my teeth. The world will try to convince you that important people don't do that kind of work. Don't believe it.

Protect your money. I know that sounds unromantic, and I know you'd rather hear PopPop talk about courage and honor than about savings accounts. But listen to me: money is time, and time is the one thing you can never get back. Learn what compounding interest means—really learn it, until you feel it in your bones. A dollar saved at eighteen is worth more than ten dollars saved at forty, not because of magic but because of math. The Tribe has given you resources that most young people in this country will never have. That is not a gift to be spent. It is a seed to be planted. Plant it early. Water it with patience. And let time do what time does.

Know where you come from. You are Cherokee. That is not a line on a form or a card in your wallet. It is a fire that has burned in these mountains for longer than anyone can count. Your ancestors chose to stay when the government tried to force them out. They hid in these hills, they bled for this land, they endured things I pray you will never have to endure—so that you could be here. You owe them your life. Honor that debt by knowing your history, by learning your language, by understanding that being Cherokee is not something you inherit passively. It is something you carry forward actively, every single day, in how you live and what you stand for.

Don't let anyone else write your story. People wrote mine for me for nearly a decade—people who didn't know me, people who had reasons to tear me down, people who found it easier to repeat a lie than to look for the truth. I built this website and wrote this book so you would have the real record, by my own hand, in my own voice. If someone tells you something about your PopPop that doesn't sound right, come here. Read the documents. Look at the evidence. Draw your own conclusions. I trust you to be fair because I raised your parents to be fair, and they're raising you the same way.

Love fiercely. I have loved your grandmother since I was barely older than some of you are now. Forty years and she is still the first person I want to talk to in the morning and the last voice I want to hear at night. That kind of love is not luck. It is a choice you make every single day—to stay, to listen, to forgive, to show up even when it's hard, especially when it's hard. Find someone who makes you want to be better than you are. Then spend your life trying to deserve them.

And when the world gets loud—and it will—find the river. Walk along it. Listen to it. Remember that water doesn't fight the rock. It flows around. It finds another way. And given enough time, it wears the rock to sand.

I may not be there for every graduation, every wedding, every first child placed in your arms. I wish I could promise you I will be, but life doesn't work that way, and I've learned not to make promises I can't keep. But know this: whether I'm sitting beside you or watching from somewhere you can't see, I am proud of you. Not for what you've accomplished. For who you are. That was always enough.

The hardest path is usually the right one. The truth always surfaces. And the people who love you—really love you—will still be standing there when the storm passes.

Stand tall in your truth. Take care of each other. And never forget where you come from.

All my love,

Patrick H. Lambert

P.S. — I originally wrote this letter as part of my legacy and estate planning—a private note to my grandchildren. It was Cyndi who encouraged me to open the door wider and also include the youth in our Tribe. She was right. I have always believed that with the right guidance, love, and support, the children of our Tribe can excel at anything they put their minds to. I see it in my own grandchildren every time I'm with them—the intelligence, the curiosity, the fire. And I see it in the young people of the Eastern Band all around me. We have a bright future because of you, not in spite of what you'll face, but because of how you'll face it. So take these words however they find you—whether you're one of mine or simply one of ours. Stay strong. Stay true. Live a good life. Be fearless, and do right. God bless you all.

THE EVIDENCE VAULT & PHOTO ARCHIVES

PatrickLambert.com contains the Evidence Vault—a permanent repository of documentary files from Patrick Lambert's life and career, including the forensic audit findings, federal correspondence, legal filings, and Cherokee Supreme Court records discussed in this book. The Vault currently holds the primary documents from the impeachment and vindication years and will continue to grow as new files are added from decades of work in Cherokee gaming governance and tribal leadership.

The site also contains the Photo Archives, a Searchable Index, the Timeline, and additional resources for readers.

PatrickLambert.com

Access Code: THERIVER2026

ABOUT THE AUTHOR

Patrick Lambert is an enrolled member of the Eastern Band of Cherokee Indians and a lifelong resident of the Qualla Boundary in Western North Carolina. He served as executive director of the Cherokee Tribal Gaming Commission for twenty-one years, helping transform Cherokee gaming from a modest bingo hall into one of the most successful tribal gaming operations in the United States. In 2015, he was elected Principal Chief of the Eastern Band with 71 percent of the vote.

Lambert holds a juris doctor from the University of North Carolina at Chapel Hill and a master of laws in gaming law from the University of Nevada, Las Vegas, which he earned at age fifty-eight. In July 2025, the Cherokee Supreme Court unanimously restored his civil rights following his 2017 impeachment, fully vindicating his record.

He and his wife, Cyndi, have been married since 1986. They have three children and nine grandchildren, and continue to live on the Qualla Boundary.